"*C'est l'homme qui fait l'homme*":
Cul-de-Sac *Ubuntu-ism* in Côte d'Ivoire

Francis B. Nyamnjoh

Langaa Research & Publishing CIG
Mankon, Bamenda

Publisher
Langaa RPCIG
Langaa Research & Publishing Common Initiative Group
P.O. Box 902 Mankon
Bamenda
North West Region
Cameroon
Langaagrp@gmail.com
www.langaa-rpcig.net

Distributed in and outside N. America by African Books Collective
orders@africanbookscollective.com
www.africanbookscollective.com

ISBN: 9956-762-52-0

Praise for this Book

The idea that human beings are inextricably bound to one another is at the heart of this book about African agency, especially drawing on the African philosophy Ubuntu, with its roots in human sociality and inclusivity. Ubuntu's precepts and workings are severely tested in these times of rapid change and multiple responsibilities. Africans negotiate their social existence between urban and rural life, their continental and transcontinental distances, and all the market forces that now impinge, with relationships and loyalties placed in question. Between ideal and reality, dreams and schemes, how is Ubuntu actualized, misappropriated and endangered? The book unearths the intrigues and contradictions that go with inclusivity in Africa. Basing his argument on the ideals of trust, conviviality and support embodied in the concept of Ubuntu, Francis Nyamnjoh demonstrates how the pursuit of personal success and even self-aggrandizement challenges these ideals, thus leading to discord in social relationships. Nyamnjoh uses a popular Ivorian drama with the same title to substantiate life-world realities and more importantly to demonstrate that new forms of expression, from popular drama to fiction, thicken and enrich the ethnographic component in current anthropology.

"In several respects, the book is a treasure-trove, as it poses problems encountered by ordinary people in their daily lives, such as the problem of relations between social elders and juniors, the big and the small. In the background are themes such as the migration of young Africans to Europe, the garden of Eden, in search of self-fulfilment and a better life for themselves and their families, even amid all the attendant frustrations, including relations with those left behind."

Aghi Bahi
Professor at the Université Félix Houphouët-Boigny
Abidjan – Côte d'Ivoire

"This book's readers will recognize how acutely it projects the very contemporary experience of "being African" and its predicaments. Predation and altruism, monopolization and circulation of resources, unequal exchanges and Ubuntu-like generosity, who "belongs" and who doesn't to shifting constellations of wealth, power and community, market and gift economies: the worlds of Milton Friedman (with not at all subtle touches of Ayn Rand) and Desmond Tutu, converge and mingle. So, also, the text is informed by the fluid, transactional character of human lives not defined by such binary constraints."

Milton Krieger
Emeritus Professor, Western Washington University
USA

"An absorbing narrative. In this sociological tour de force, Nyamnjoh explores the hardships, challenges, and dilemmas that confront Africans in the Diaspora, as well as those who seek to undertake adventures in different parts of the world. Mobile Africans seeking "greener pastures" overseas are affected by social and cultural expectations and norms, as well as social obligations to cater for their kith and kin in villages and cities. The adventures are fraught with risks. Yet the dangers are not enough to discourage the adventurers from undertaking their journeys. Beyond all these is the challenge that modern lifestyle and market forces pose to the welfare, security and wellbeing of families, individuals, and friends across Africa. Anyone who is interested in understanding the social, political, cultural, and structural factors that underpin the lives of Africans will find this absorbing narrative by Nyamnjoh riveting. In it, there is something for everyone."

Levi Obijiofor (PhD)
Senior Lecturer in Journalism, School of Communication
and Arts
The University of Queensland Brisbane
Australia

Acknowledgements

C'est l'homme qui fait l'homme has materialised largely thanks to relationships and interactions I and others have mutually cultivated and maintained with one another. I have leaned on far more shoulders in my journey of the making of this book than is possible to do justice to in a brief acknowledgement.

I would like to express my most sincere gratitude to all those who in one way or another have contributed with humbling generosity their ideas, time, suggestions, discussions, intellectual and related energy to inspire my efforts.

In particular, I am grateful to Les Guignols d'Abidjan, a theatre troupe of which Gohou and Nastou are founding members. Les Guignols d'Abidjan are most famous in francophone Africa, and their plays and TV drama series seek to bring to the stage and television the ups and downs of the everyday lives of Africans. Their popularity extends beyond francophone Africa into Europe, especially to African immigrants.

My gratitude goes as well to Teena Dewoo who assisted with the transcription and translation into English of the original dialogue in French; to Polycarp Ambe-Niba, who translated the preface by Aghi Bahi into English from the French original; to Achille Kouhon, a doctoral student in Social Anthropology at Félix Houphouët Boigny University in Côte d'Ivoire, for his detailed comment elaborating on the origin and popularity of *C'est l'homme qui fait l'homme* in Côte d'Ivoire; to Crystal Powell, Divine Fuh and Mohammed Umar who readily pointed me in the direction of relevant literature; to Simon Bekker, Dominic Boyer, Ingrid Brudvig, Oscar Hemer, Mary Kinyanjui, Ute Klingemann, Bernard Lategan, Lindiswa Jan, Jimu Malizani, Ayanda Manqoyi, Motoji Matsuda, Munyaradzi Mawere, Robert Morrell, Patience Mususa, Noxolo Nozuko, Xolela Ntsebeza, Henrietta Nyamnjoh, Walter Nkwi,

Levi Obijiofor, Itaru Ohta, Sophie Oldfield, Sanya Osha, Cecilia Rosengren, Mats Rosengren, Mike Rowlands, Primus Tazanu, Jean-Pierre Warnier, Joanna Woods and participants at the writing workshop of May 16-18, 2014 at Mont Fleur Conference Venue in Stellenbosch, South Africa for reading and commenting various drafts of the book.

I am most grateful for two fellowships, one from the Stellenbosch Institute for Advanced Study (April – June 2015) and one from the Graduate School of Asian and African Area Studies of Kyoto University (June – July 2015), which enabled me to complete the book. I benefitted enormously from the generosity, both intellectual and social, of fellows and staff of the two institutions. I am in their debt.

Special thanks go to both Aghi Bahi and Milton Krieger for generously agreeing to write a Preface and an Epilogue respectively, despite their busy schedules.

I acknowledge with profound gratitude the editorial contributions of Rosemary Ekosso, Mieka Ritsema and Kathryn Toure.

Last but not least, I am grateful to Dr Julien Adhepeau of the Département des Sciences de la Communication, UFR Information Communication et Arts, Université Félix Houphouët-Boigny d'Abidjan, for permission to use his lovely photo of the towering and welcoming *Monument Akwaba* of Abidjan, on the way from the Félix Houphouët-Boigny International Airport. Created by the Ivorian sculptor Koffi Donkor in the 1990s, the monument is an appropriate symbol for the generous hospitality, conviviality and open-ended humanity that the ideal of Ubuntu evokes.

Table of Contents

Préface

Enfant d'*Abakwa*, fils de Bamenda, de cette région des *Grassfields* camerounais d'une grande richesse culturelle, enfant d'Afrique et surtout véritable citoyen du monde, Francis Nyamnjoh est aujourd'hui bien plus qu'un simple enseignant chercheur universitaire ou, dans les termes de Jean-Paul Sartre, beaucoup plus qu'un « technicien du savoir pratique » (Sartre 1972 : 29). En effet, ce travailleur infatigable et prolifique est un intellectuel véritable, solide dans ses positions, ouvert dans ses dispositions et courageux dans ses prises de position sur les grands sujets qui agitent ces « temps qui tanguent » pour reprendre l'expression de Bernard Zadi Zaourou[1]. Cet amoureux et défenseur de l'Afrique n'en demeure pas moins un de ses observateurs attentifs et lucides. Grand esprit de notre temps, ce penseur hors du commun se démarque toujours et naturellement des produits intellectuels en vogue dans le (super)marché mondial des idées à la mode sur la culture populaire. C'est, je crois, avec cela à l'esprit qu'il faut entrer dans l'univers de ce livre *C'est l'homme qui fait l'homme. Cul de sac Ubuntu-ism in Côte d'Ivoire*. En effet, l'homme peut-il advenir et devenir seul ? Peut-il même être seul ? Peut-il être homme sans les autres hommes ? Lecteur de Francis Nyamnjoh depuis ses premiers écrits déjà critiques, dont *Mind Searching* (1991) ou *The disillusionned African* (1995), c'est en tant que liseur « indigène » que je prends la parole car l'*Ubuntu-isme* est étudié dans le contexte de la Côte d'Ivoire, d'Abidjan en particulier, lieu de mon vécu quotidien ordinaire et de mes propres recherches.

---

[1] Bernard Zadi Zaourou (1938-2012), professeur de littérature africaine à l'Université de Cocody, poète, dramaturge, écrivain, ministre de la culture (1993-1999). Sous le nom de Bottey Moum Koussa, il publiait de 2002 à 2006, dans Fraternité Matin, quotidien ivoirien de service public, la fameuse « Chronique des temps qui tanguent » (Zadi 2008 : 156) où, avec dérision et acuité, il passait au crible d'une analyse caustique les apories d'une société ivoirienne en proie à la guerre civile.

Ubuntu... terme à la mode, sur de nombreuses lèvres et dans de nombreux écrits. L'effet de mode ne change pas le fait qu'*Ubuntu* reste un terme difficile à traduire en français et probablement dans la plupart des langues dominantes. En outre, ce terme reste peu connu sous nos latitudes ouest-africaines francophones franco-centrées. *Ubuntu*, essence d'être humain, est proche des concepts d'humanité et de fraternité alors entendue en son sens le plus ancien c'est-à-dire le propre de l'espèce humaine. L'identité individuelle est supplantée par l'identité collective (sociétale) plus large. La vie humaine, sociale, dépourvue de fraternité ne serait-elle pas quelque chose de hideux ?

Les caractéristiques de l'*Ubuntu* (en tant qu'idéaltype) seraient en somme : hospitalité, altruisme, solidarité, entraide, partage, dévotion, convivialité, confiance... Les mots de l'Archevêque Desmond Tutu (Tutu 1999) habitent encore nos mémoires. Les déclinaisons locales de l'*Ubuntu* sont nombreuses comme le rapporte bien l'auteur du présent livre : « On est ensemble », « c'est l'homme qui fait l'homme », « si tu manges, je mange », « c'est un homme qui fait un autre homme[2] ," « je suis parce que tu es »... Une personne pleine d'*Ubuntu* est ouverte et disponible aux autres. La société confère aux êtres humains leur humanité dit l'*Ubuntu*... Mais, toutes les valeurs citées plus haut et qui fondent l'*Ubuntu* ne l'épuisent pas. Plus largement, le succès d'un membre de la communauté est le succès de la communauté elle-même, la richesse de l'un est en quelque sorte la richesse des autres. La confiance est un maître mot de cette fraternité essentielle. Sans elle, l'individu peut être aisément abusé.

Dans ce livre, Francis Nyamnjoh s'aventure hors du Cameroun, un terrain qu'il connaît bien pour lui avoir consacré de nombreuses recherches. Il tourne plutôt son regard vers la Côte d'Ivoire. C'est là qu'il va mettre à l'épreuve l'*Ubuntu* et son « inclusivité » en pointant les relations entre frères dans toute la

---

[2] Il s'agit d'une maxime *agni* (sud-est de la Côte d'Ivoire).

plasticité du terme. Nous sommes dans un contexte social où la notion de « frère » est étirable et où elle peut englober selon les situations le frère de sang – le frère biologique, le cousin, le ressortissant d'un même village, d'une même ville voire d'une même région, le compatriote… Le comportement de Gohou (qui n'est déjà pas très honnête) et de Nastou, en effet, abusant de la confiance de leurs frères, n'est pas sans rappeler l'ethos « couper-décaler » car il s'agit bien de « couper » le frère (la sœur) ou l'ami(e) qui vit en Europe. Cette situation que l'on peut retrouver dans bon nombre de régions d'Afrique est d'autant plus tragi-comique que l'argent « coupé » est utilisé en « travaillement », autant dire gaspillé. Ceux qui sont allés faire fortune en Europe – en Occident, « chez les Blancs » deviennent des sortes de nouveaux nababs, des nantis, voire comme des « Blancs » dans l'imaginaire populaire local et donc comme des gens que l'on peut « couper ». Où est donc la fraternité ? La prédation ne vient-elle pas mettre à mal l'idéal de communion fraternelle ? Mais, les vieux clichés sur ces valeurs prétendument africaines ont longue vie…

La fiction télévisuelle constitue alors une porte d'entrée dans la culture populaire sans pour autant exclure les autres formes/modes d'expression telle que la musique populaire (le *zouglou* notamment). L'auteur n'est évidemment pas dupe. Il sait bien que cette émission s'inscrit dans une logique commerciale dans laquelle l'*audiencemaking* (Ettema & Whitney 1994) est d'une importance capitale et est même une condition de programmation/diffusion. Les télévisions produisent et diffusent en effet ce qui « marche ». Les circuits parallèles d'économie souterraine par lesquels l'on peut se procurer des épisodes d'émissions telles que *Ma Famille* sont, en l'absence d'une quelconque doxométrie ou de mesure d'audience fiable, un indicateur non négligeable de popularité. Cette fiction humoristique, *C'est l'homme qui fait l'homme*, propose un contrat de vérisme au spectateur/public dans lequel la vérité diégétique compte davantage que la véridicité. Cette « pure » fiction repose sur notre vécu quotidien, sur des choses que nous avons vécues ou que nous sommes susceptibles de vivre, mais aussi sur ce qu'il y a de typiquement ivoirien bref sur cette « ivoirité ,» « ivoirienneté ,» « ivorianité » (Bahi 2013), ou « ivoiricité » qui épaissit la description et donne du piment au récit. Parce qu'elle est à même de porter à l'écran ce quotidien ordinaire en le traitant autrement, l'émission en arrive pratiquement à constituer un *alternative media* (qu'il a lui-même conceptualisé dans son ouvrage *Africa's media, democracy and the politics of belonging* (Nyamnjoh 2005). Ici, le fait est que cet *Ubuntu-isme* aisément dévoyé est plus une source d'embarras que de bonheur, semble être sans issue, conduit à une impasse… bref, ne mène à rien.

Ce n'est pas un hasard si le thème de la construction d'une maison sert de socle à la réflexion de l'anthropologue. La construction de la maison est un symbole de réussite. Toutefois, les lieux d'expressions de cette réussite sont quelque peu modifiés. Hier, c'était le citadin ordinaire construisait au village ; aujourd'hui, c'est le parigot[3] qui construit dans une zone résidentielle d'Abidjan. Cette action se fait dans un élan de solidarité, certes, mais s'opère aussi pour le capital symbolique du groupe. La réussite de cet individu est aussi la réussite symbolique de ses frères et de sa famille au sens le plus large. Mais cette réussite n'est complète que si les autres bénéficient de ses largesses[4]. C'est une situation où les valeurs de solidarité, d'organisation, d'honnêteté et d'être ensemble sont aisément mises à l'épreuve. Comment la disponibilité et l'esprit d'ouverture du frère sont abusés… Comment l'*Ubuntu* est instrumentalisée et se transforme finalement en quelque

---

[3] Ce mot d'argot français est utilisé en français populaire ivoirien où il perd de son caractère péjoratif et désigne ceux qui viennent de Paris et plus largement de France ou d'Europe.

[4] Je pense par exemple au *krogbognon* de la société « traditionnelle » bété – centre-ouest de la Côte d'Ivoire – qui se doit d'être généreux, de venir en aide voire de s'occuper non seulement de sa famille au sens le plus large mais aussi de son entourage. En effet, dans cette société, il est inconcevable d'être heureux tout seul…

chose d'autre, en quelque chose qui ressemble à s'y méprendre à de la filouterie.

A bien des égards, ce livre s'avère être d'une grande richesse, posant des problèmes que rencontrent les hommes ordinaires dans leur vécu quotidien. Dans le même temps, se trouvent singulièrement posés les rapports entre aînés et cadets sociaux, grands et petits. De même, en toile de fond, des thèmes tels que la migration des jeunes Africains partant ailleurs en Europe se chercher, chercher une vie meilleure, pour eux-mêmes et leurs proches, cet éden rêvé et toutes les déceptions qui l'accompagnent. L'auteur aborde aussi les relations entre ceux qui sont restés au pays et ceux qui sont partis en Europe chercher une vie meilleure. Ces « jeunes gens » semblent fascinés par l'Europe et, pour eux, avoir vécu ou vivre en Europe participe de la construction d'une identité positive. Mais le rôle prométhéen de ces Africains de la diaspora est d'ailleurs raillé par l'auteur : le spectateur doit se demander si Dahou pourra extirper Gohou de son oisiveté initiale ? Plus loin, cette interrogation se précise davantage : le travail des diasporas africaines peut-il vraiment « sauver » l'Afrique ?

De fil en aiguille, l'auteur nous fait entrer dans une situation d'une grande complexité et montre comment, sous les apparences légères de ces intrigues individuelles, se jouent des enjeux socioéconomiques plus importants. Par exemple, les flux monétaires de la diaspora africaine profitent autant à l'Afrique qu'aux compagnies occidentales de transfert de fonds. C'est dire à quel point Francis Nyamnjoh, dans cette étude, entre dans les logiques sociales qui travaillent actuellement, et en profondeur, la société ivoirienne. Une des grandes forces de son travail anthropologique provient du fait qu'il s'enracine dans le particulier apparemment banal. Comment, à travers ces situations sans aucun doute ordinaires, l'anthropologue parvient à mettre en évidence des logiques individuelles contradictoires au cœur de la dynamique sociale ? Comment encore, il les articule à des problématiques plus générales, c'est ce que la lecture de cet ouvrage permettra de découvrir. Car Francis Nyamnjoh nous livre là une étude vivante et passionnante qui transcende la particularité ivoirienne analysée pour atteindre un niveau de questionnement plus global.

Ainsi, la question de l'*Ubuntu-isme* se trouve posée dans une violence conceptuelle originale que Francis Nyamnjoh connait bien. Les valeurs de la fraternité (et ses valeurs connexes) sont mises à mal par la cupidité des hommes. L'*Ubuntu* est l'objet d'un détournement, d'une instrumentalisation. Aujourd'hui, *Ubuntu-isme* et opportunisme sont tous deux dans l'environnement des Africains. Francis Nyamnjoh se demande alors dans quelle mesure l'extension (la généralisation) de l'*Ubuntu-isme* aiderait-elle les Africains, ferait-elle bon ménage avec l'opportunisme et ce qu'elle leur offrirait d'important ? Certes occasion et opportunisme sont l'avers et le revers de la même médaille. Mais là encore l'auteur demande : « comment exploite-t-on les opportunités qui elles-mêmes sont inextricablement enchevêtrées et interconnectées à l'opportunisme » (p.129) ? En définitive, l'*Ubuntu-isme* voire l'*Ubuntu* serait-il dans une impasse ? « Violentes questions ![5] ». L'auteur de ce livre nous place dans un contexte où la parenté n'offre même plus d'appui « traditionnel[6] ». Les tableaux dépeints n'offrent ni sécurité ontologique ni gage de fraternité, mais conduisent plutôt à leur remise en question voire à leur vacillement… Face aux situations analysées dans ce livre, que deviennent les valeurs de l'humanisme africain ? Où est donc passé ce socialisme typiquement africain ? Qu'advient-il alors quand les relations humaines sont instrumentalisées, lorsque les fondements mêmes de l'*Ubuntu* sont détournés et ses valeurs dévoyées ? C'est aussi à cette réflexion que nous invite l'auteur de ce passionnant ouvrage.

---

[5] Expression propagée en Côte d'Ivoire par le chanteur populaire ivoirien N'Guess Bon Sens.

[6] Je pense ici à la sentence *bambara* selon laquelle « les premiers amis, les vrais, les amis sûrs de l'individu, sont ses parents, ses frères et ses sœurs ».

La question de l'écriture, du style propre, de la personnalité littéraire a été et est encore un sujet très important chez les anthropologues. Chez Francis Nyamnjoh, cette préoccupation est dépassée. Sur un ton vif, il nous fait entrer dans les méandres d'une intrigue dont le rebondissement, même s'il est prévisible, reste passionnant à suivre. Le style, à la fois pétillant et romancé allié à l'humour et au sarcasme qu'il manie à merveille, donne du dynamisme à ce texte attachant. C'est incontestablement la marque d'un grand conteur. En outre, ce texte, qui peut être approché avec l'aisance d'un roman, reste une importante étude anthropologique. C'est la signature d'un grand anthropologue, qui a trouvé un style d'écriture par lequel il traduit sa pensée scientifique. Il faut donc relever le foisonnement, la diversité, la fécondité et l'intensité du travail proposé par celui qui se dit ironiquement « *blinded by sight* » (Nyamnjoh 2012) mais qui est tout de même assez clairvoyant pour questionner le dogmatisme arrogant attaché à certaines valeurs galvaudées. Comment en arrive-t-on à un phénomène de mise à mort symbolique d'un concept aussi puissant que l'*Ubuntu* ? Francis Nyamnjoh investi l'espace épistémologique, nous confronte à des défis et enjeux essentiels et, par-là, inquiète les chercheurs autant que les politiciens. Dans le fond, le désenchantement n'est-il pas au mitan de sa pensée ? N'y-a-t-il pas toujours en lui-même un peu de cet Africain désillusionné qu'il a très tôt dépeint ?

AGHI BAHI
Professeur Titulaire
Université Félix Houphouët-Boigny
Abidjan – Côte d'Ivoire

Références

Bahi, A., (2013), *L'ivoirité mouvementée. Jeunes, médias et politique en Côte d'Ivoire*, Bamenda, Langaa Research & Publishing CIG

Ettema, J.S. & Whitney, D.C., (1994), "The Money Arrow: An Introduction to Audiencemaking," *Audiencemaking: How the Media Create the Audience*, James S. Ettema & D. Charles Whitney (eds), Sage Annual Review of Communication Research, 22: 1-18.

Nyamnjoh, F.B., (1991), *Mind Searching*, Awka, Kucena Damian Nigeria Ltd

Nyamnjoh, F.B., (1995), *The Disillusioned African*, Limbe, Nooremac

Nyamnjoh, F.B., (2005), *Africa's Media, Democracy and the Politics of Belonging*, London-New York-Pretoria, Zed Books – UNISA Press

Nyamnjoh, F.B., (2012), "Blinded by Sight: Divining the Future of Anthropology in Africa," *Afrika Spectrum, 47, 2-3*: 63-92

Sartre, J.P., (1972), *Plaidoyer pour les intellectuels*, Paris, Gallimard

Tutu, D., (1999), *No Future Without Forgiveness*, London, Rider

Zadi, B.Z., (2008), *Les quatrains du dégoût, Abidjan*, CEDA-NEI

Preface[1]

Francis Nyamnjoh, a child of *Abakwa* and son of Bamenda, a region of the Cameroonian *Grassfields* endowed with a very rich culture, is also a child of Africa and, in particular, a citizen of the world. Today, he is no ordinary teacher, researcher and scholar; to borrow Jean-Paul Sartre's words, he is much more than a "practical knowledge craftsman" (Sartre 1972: 29). In fact, this untiring prolific writer/researcher and genuine intellectual is steadfast in his stands, open-minded and courageous in his perspectives on the major issues of our "turbulent era," in the words of Bernard Zadi Zaourou.[2] A passionate lover and defender of Africa, he is also one of its most attentive and perceptive observers. He is one of the great thinkers of our generation and his work truly stands out among prized academic works on the global (super)market of topical ideas on popular culture. This should be borne in mind as we enter the universe of the book: *C'est l'homme qui fait l'homme. Cul de sac Ubuntu-ism in Côte d'Ivoire.* Indeed, can a human being be born and exist all by him/herself? Can a human being even live alone? Can a person be human without the others? Having read Francis Nyamnjoh from his early writings, including *Mind Searching* (1991) or *The disillusioned African* (1995), which were already critiques, I now speak as an "indigenous" reader, since *Ubuntuism* is studied in the context of Côte d'Ivoire, and, in particular, Abidjan, the setting for my everyday life and research.

---

[1] Translated from the French by Polycarp Ambe-Niba

[2] Bernard Zadi Zaourou (1938-2012), Professor of African Literature at the University of Cocody, poet, playwright, writer, Minister of Culture (1993-1999). From 2002 to 2006, under the pen name Bottey Moum Koussa, he published in the public-service daily *Fraternité Matin* the famous « Chronique des temps qui tanguent » (Zadi 2008 : 156) wherein he derisively and sharply scrutinized, through a caustic analysis, the weaknesses of Ivorian society in the throes of civil war.

Ubuntu…is a topical term on everyone's lips and it is used in numerous publications. Although it has become a buzz word, *Ubuntu* continues to defy translation into French and probably most of the dominant languages. Furthermore, the term is still little known in franco-centred francophone West Africa. *Ubuntu*, as the essence of being human, is closely related to concepts of humanity and fraternity in the oldest sense of the term, that is to say, the hallmark of the human race. Individual identity is supplanted by the broader collective (societal) identity. Is human social life void of fraternity not a hideous thing?

In a nutshell, *Ubuntu*, as an ideal, should be characterized by hospitality, altruism, solidarity, mutual supportiveness, sharing, dedication, conviviality and trust, *inter alia*. The words of Archbishop Desmond Tutu (Tutu 1999) are forever etched in our minds. There are manifold local manifestations of *Ubuntu*, as reported by the author: "we are together," "human beings make one another," "if you eat, I eat," "it takes a human being to make another,"[3] "I am because you are," etc. A person full of *Ubuntu* is open and available for others. Thanks to *Ubuntu*, society confers humanity on human beings… However, all these values in which *Ubuntu* is rooted do not wear it out. Broadly, the success of a member of the community is the success of the whole community; the wealth of one is, in a sense, the wealth of all. Trust is the kingpin of such all-important fraternity. Without it, the individual can easily be deceived.

In the book, Francis Nyamnjoh ventures out of Cameroon, a country he masters since he has carried out extensive research on it, and instead turns his gaze to Côte d'Ivoire. Here he tests *Ubuntu* and its "inclusiveness," focusing on fraternity in the most malleable sense of the word. In the given social context, the notion of "brother" is elastic and can encompass, depending on the setting, a blood-brother, a cousin, a native of

---

[3] This is a saying from *Agni* (south east of Côte d'Ivoire).

the same village, town or even region, a compatriot, etc. The behaviour of Gohou (who is already rather dishonest) and that of Nastou, which, in fact, abuses the trust of their brothers and sisters, reminds us of the *"couper-décaler"* [wheeling and dealing] ethos, since they are bent on "swindling" the brother (sister) or the friend living in Europe. This situation which is true of several African regions is all the more tragi-comic as the money is used for *"travaillement"* [shady work], in other words, squandered. Those who left to make a fortune in Europe, i.e. the West, in "the white man's country," become some kind of new fat cats, well-to-do, quasi "whites" in the eyes of the public and are therefore viewed as people who deserve to be swindled. Where then is the fraternity? Will such predation not erode the ideal of fraternal communion? Yet, the old stereotypes about these purportedly African values have a long lifespan…

Televisual fiction thus constitutes the gateway to popular culture albeit without excluding other forms and modes of expression such as popular music (in particular, *zouglou*). The author is obviously not a fool. He is well aware that the programme is consistent with a marketing strategy in which *audiencemaking* (Ettema & Whitney 1994) is crucial and even a programming and broadcasting requirement. In fact, TV stations produce and broadcast what "sells". In the absence of any dosimetry or reliable audience measuring tools, parallel channels of the underground economy through which episodes of programmes such as *Ma Famille* can be obtained are a non-negligible indicator of popularity. The comic fiction, "C'est l'homme qui fait l'homme" [It takes a human being to make another, proposes a verism contract to the viewer/public in which the diegetic truth matters more than truthfulness. This "pure" fiction is based on our daily life experiences, what we have experienced or are likely to experience, but also on what is typically Ivorian, in short, *"ivoirité"* [ivoirity], *"ivoiriennété"* [ivorianness], *"ivorianité"* [ivorianity] (Bahi 2013), or *"ivoiricité"* [ivoiricity] which renders the description more dense and adds pepper to the story. Since it is capable of projecting on the screen this ordinary daily experience by giving it an extraordinary spin, the programme virtually constitutes a media alternative (conceptualized in his book *Africa's media, democracy and the politics of belonging* (Nyamnjoh 2005)). Here, the fact remains that this easily diverted *Ubuntuism*, which is more of a source of embarrassment than of happiness, apparently leads to a dead end…in short, it leads nowhere.

It is no happenstance that the theme of house construction is used by the anthropologist as a basis for reflection. House construction is a symbol of success. However, the media for expressing such success are quite varied. Yesterday, it was the ordinary city dweller building in his village; today, it is the *parigot*[4] building in a residential area in Abidjan, admittedly, in an outburst of solidarity with a view to preserving the group's symbolic capital. The success of this individual also symbolizes the success of his brothers and sisters and his family in the broadest sense of the word. However, such success is incomplete unless the others benefit from his largesse.[5] Thus, the values of solidarity, organization, honesty and the community spirit are easily tested. We witness the abuse of a brother's or a sister's availability and open-mindedness…the manipulation and ultimate transformation of *Ubuntu* into something else, something that looks like a near perfect forgery.

In several respects, the book is a treasure-trove, as it poses problems encountered by ordinary people in their daily lives. At the same time, it also poses, in particular, the problem of

---

[4] This French slang word is used in colloquial Ivorian French wherein it loses its pejorative character and pertains to people from Paris and, more broadly, France or Europe.

[5] This brings to mind, for example, the *krogbognon* in "traditional" *Bété* society– centre-west of Côte d'Ivoire – who owe it to themselves to be generous and to assist and even take care not only of their family but of their entourage, in the broadest sense of the term. In fact, in that society, it is inconceivable to be happy alone…

relations between social elders and juniors, the big and the small. Similarly, in the background are themes such as the migration of young Africans to Europe, the garden of Eden, in search of self-fulfilment and a better life for themselves and their families, even amid all the attendant frustrations. The author also broaches the subject of relations between such migrants and those back home. These "youngsters" appear to be fascinated by Europe and equate life in Europe with the forging of a positive identity. Yet the promethean role played by these Africans of the diaspora is derided by the author: the spectator must wonder whether Dahou will be able to cure Gohou of his inherent idleness. Later on, this question is further clarified: Can the work of the African diaspora truly "rescue" Africa?

Gradually, the author ushers us into a highly complex situation and shows us how, beneath the benign appearances of individual intrigues, crucial socio-economic interests are played out. For example, the cash flows from the African diaspora benefit both Africa and the Western money transfer companies. This shows the extent and depth to which Francis Nyamnjoh delves into the social logics that drive present-day Ivorian society. One of the greatest strengths of his anthropological work stems from the fact that it is rooted in the seemingly commonplace individual. How does the anthropologist succeed, through unquestionably ordinary situations, in bringing to light contradictory individual rationales at the heart of the social dynamic? Reading this book will help the reader to discover how the author links such ordinary situations to more general problems. Francis Nyamnjoh presents us with a living and enthralling study that transcends the analysis of Ivorian distinctiveness and raises more global questions.

Accordingly, the question of *Ubuntuism* is posed in 'original conceptual violence' that is very familiar to Francis Nyamnjoh. The values of fraternity (together with its kindred attributes) are eroded by human greed. *Ubuntu* is hijacked and exploited.

Nowadays, *Ubuntuism* and opportunism co-exist in the African environment. Francis Nyamnjoh therefore wonders how the expansion (propagation) of *Ubuntuism* would help Africans; will *Ubuntuism* and opportunism make good bedfellows and will it offer Africans anything significant? Admittedly, opportunity and opportunism are the obverse and the reverse of the same coin. Yet here again the author asks: "how does one harness opportunities that are inextricably entangled and interconnected with opportunism" (p. 129)? In the final analysis, are *Ubuntuism* and *Ubuntu* at a dead end? "Violent questions!"[6] We are placed in a context in which kinship ties no longer offer even "traditional"[7] support. The scenarios depicted offer neither ontological security nor any guarantee of fraternity, but instead call them into question and make them uncertain and shaky… Faced with the situations analysed in the book, where do the values of African humanism stand? What has become of the distinctively African socialism? How strong can it be when human relations are exploited, when the very foundations of *Ubuntu* are hijacked and its values diverted? The author of this thrilling book also invites us to reflect on these questions.

The question of personal writing style and literary character has been and still is a matter of cardinal importance to anthropologists. On this score, Francis Nyamnjoh has exceeded expectations. With his lively tone, he leads us into the meanders of a plot whose development, though predictable, is no less captivating. The spicy and romanticized style enhanced by the humour and sarcasm, which are his stock-in-trade, bring this endearing book alive. These are, undoubtedly, the hallmarks of a great story teller. Furthermore, the book, which can be easily read like a novel, remains an important

---

[6] An expression propagated in Côte d'Ivoire by the popular Ivorian singer N'Guess Bon Sens.

[7] This conjures up the *Bambara* saying that "a person's first, truest and most sincere friends are his parents, brothers and sisters."

anthropological study. It is the work of a great anthropologist who has developed a writing style for conveying his scientific thought. We should therefore highlight and commend the prolific, diverse, fruitful and intense work done by a writer who ironically describes himself as "blinded by sight" (Nyamnjoh 2012), whereas he is far-sighted enough to question the arrogant dogmatism associated with certain debased values. How come such a powerful concept as *Ubuntu* is being symbolically killed? Francis Nyamnjoh ventures into the realm of epistemology and confronts us with key challenges and issues and, in so doing, jolts both researchers and politicians out of their complacency. Essentially, is disenchantment not at the heart of his thought? Isn't there still lingering in him a remnant of *The disillusioned African* he portrayed very early on?

AGHI BAHI
Professor at the Université Félix Houphouët-Boigny
Abidjan – Côte d'Ivoire

References

Bahi, A., (2013), *L'ivoirité mouvementée. Jeunes, médias et politique en Côte d'Ivoire*, Bamenda, Langaa Research & Publishing CIG

Ettema, J.S. & Whitney, D.C., (1994), "The Money Arrow: an Introduction to Audiencemaking," *Audiencemaking: How the Media Create the Audience*, James S. Ettema & D. Charles Whitney (eds), Sage Annual Review of Communication Research, 22: 1-18.

Nyamnjoh, F.B., (1991), *Mind Searching*, Awka, Kucena Damian Nigeria Ltd

Nyamnjoh, F.B., (1995), *The Disillusioned African*, Limbe, Nooremac

Nyamnjoh, F.B., (2005), *Africa's Media, Democracy and the Politics of Belonging*, London-New York-Pretoria, Zed Books – UNISA Press

Nyamnjoh, F.B., (2012), "Blinded by Sight: Divining the Future of Anthropology in Africa," *Afrika Spectrum, 47, 2-3*: 63-92

Sartre, J.P., (1972), *Plaidoyer pour les intellectuels*, Paris, Gallimard

Tutu, D., (1999), *No Future Without Forgiveness*, London, Rider

Zadi, B.Z., (2008), *Les quatrains du dégoût*, Abidjan, CEDA-NEI

Introduction

Inclusivity is an established theme in popular culture in Africa, from song lyrics to home entertainment videos, in television series, drama sketches on radio and novel narratives. Collective success is emphasised, and individuals may not begin to consider themselves to have succeeded unless they can demonstrate the extent to which they have actively included intimate and even distant others: family members and friends, fellow villagers and even fellow nationals, depending on one's stature and networks – in the success in question. If elsewhere millionaires and billionaires are men and women with tangible personal assets to substantiate their claims to riches, the logic of collective success in many an African circle means that no one can truly be considered successful, if they have not involved themselves in *ad infinitum* redistribution of their accumulations, spreading them broadly and deeply in rhizomic fashion.

In such contexts, a truly rich person, quite paradoxically, is one engaged in an on-going process of material impoverishment, someone with an infinite capacity to reach out and involve others in their material possibilities and promise. A gift from them to others is a gift not just in material terms, but also and more importantly, an extension of themselves – their very nature and substance, essence or soul – and the possibilities they embody for the lives of others. To give abundantly in material terms might impoverish a person in things or material resources, but it enriches them abundantly in spiritual terms and also in terms of the relationships they are able to activate and maintain through relentless sharing. Marcel Mauss calls this "an intermingling," whereby "Souls are mixed with things; things with souls" and "Lives are mingled together" (Mauss 1990 [1950]: 20). Put differently, things are activated by people who in turn are activated by things.

There is a capacity for presence in simultaneous multiplicities[1], a Godlike attribute attainable through the art of selflessness and altruism or genuine concern and compassion for the well-being of others (Ricard 2015). Reality is seldom confined to sensory perception or to dualistic rationality. One has to partake of a cosmological epistemology of infinite possibilities of forms and transformations of being to see things in people and people in things, without reducing this capacity to religion, belief, magic, witchcraft, superstition or animism (Nyamnjoh 2015). This capacity for the same reality to assume multiple forms in multiple places concurrently was poorly understood and even unfathomable in many regards and in many parts of the world blinkered by ambitions of dominance or *mission civilisatrice* prior to the proliferation of technologies of presence in simultaneous multiplicities such as the internet, the cell phone, smartphones and social media (Chinweizu 1975; Feibleman 1975; Burrows 1986; Chafer 1992; Elias 2000; Bessis 2003; Ferguson 2011).

Within the logic of presence in simultaneous multiplicities, personal success must be inclusive of all the multiple presences and forms of the successful individual. Personal profit should not blunt "the godly virtues of self-discipline and charity"[2]. Indeed, a successful individual can only prove their good fortune – activate themselves to a level of social visibility and recognition so to speak – by spending and sharing out their fortune (Mauss 1990[1950]: 38). Fortune in itself can never really substitute the ultimate gift of all – the gift of oneself, one's soul or one's essence – because things are only a substitute or proxy for the gift of self – which is what others really desire and appreciate.

This idea of gifts and giving is very prominent in many religions. In Christianity for example, the Bible urges self-abnegation through selflessness in giving, promising salvation for humility and making a virtue of poverty: Matthew 5: 42 –

2

"Give to the one who asks you and do not turn away from the one who wants to borrow from you"; Proverbs 19: 17 – "The one who is gracious to the poor lends to the Lord, and the Lord will repay him for his good deed"; Psalm 41: 1-3 – "Oh, the joys of those who are kind to the poor! The Lord rescues them when they are in trouble"; Luke 6: 38 – "Give, and it will be given to you"; Luke 19: 21 – "If you want to be perfect, go, sell your possessions and give to the poor and you will have treasure in heaven"; Acts 3: 4-6 – Peter said, "I have neither silver nor gold, but what I do have I give"; Psalm 112: 5-7 – "Good comes to those who lend money generously"; Acts 20: 35 – "It is more blessed to give than to receive"; Proverbs 28: 27 – "Whoever gives to the poor will lack nothing"; Corinthians 9: 7 – "God loves a cheerful giver"; Deuteronomy 15: 10 –"Be sure to give to them without any hesitation"; Deuteronomy 15: 7-8 – "Don't be hard-hearted or tight-fisted toward your poor relative… be sure to open your hand to him and lend him enough to lessen his need". Appearance as epitomised in the body and its needs is perceived and related to as nothing but the clothes of the soul. The less one focuses on the body the more time and energy one is able to devote to the nourishment of the soul and the purity it seeks.

These biblical urgings that promise supreme happiness as a reward for selfless giving and poverty, are the subject of Giorgio Agamben's *The Highest Poverty*, a study of monastic rules, asceticism and a form of life in Europe (Agamben 2013), in which monks exemplify the beatitudes reserved for "the poor in spirit," "the meek," "those who hunger and thirst for righteousness," "the pure in heart," and "those who are persecuted because of righteousness" (Matthew 5: 3). For, in the words of Jesus Christ himself, "It is easier for a camel to go through the eye of a needle than for a rich person to enter the Kingdom of God!" (Matthew 19: 24).

It is this same rigorous self-denial and active self-restraint that Max Weber highlights in *The Protestant Ethic and the Spirit of Capitalism* (Weber 2005[1930]). Fulfilment comes from single-minded religious devotion to honest, productive hard work, and not from the pursuit of wealth and worldly possessions. In Foucauldian terms, poverty and abnegation as a "technology of the self" (Foucault 1988: 16-49; Martin et al. 1988) – i.e. a means of achieving a high spiritual or intellectual state through a confining, suffocating or punishing regime of self-discipline and self-renunciation (Foucault 1975, 1995) – are the best guarantee of attaining "a certain state of happiness, purity, wisdom, perfection, or immortality" (Foucault 1988: 18) comparable to the beatitudes of Heaven. In Christianity as a salvation religion, supreme fulfilment comes through full disclosure and renunciation of the self in total obedience to God the master (Foucault 1988: 44-48). Seen in this light, it is easy to understand the degree to which personal riches can be an embarrassment, a curse or an encumbrance, especially when the rich person fails to ensure circulation by passing the riches onto others, needy or not.

Gifts are a form of postponement of the ultimate sacrifice which enables the giver to live, because, like Abraham in the Bible, they have found a ram to serve as a sacrifice so that Isaac might live. The more personal the gift and the more history it has accumulated, the more likely it is to appear and thus be accepted as a substitute, double or lookalike of the gift-giver by the receiver. It is in this sense, that the ultimate gift to one's parents or ancestors is the gift of reproducing them by opening oneself up to them as a container or vehicle to enable them to flow back into the world in the form of children (Warnier 1993a). This is a gift which money cannot buy, a debt which cannot be repaid in things. Here the only currency tolerated is for the debtor to become the creditor (Graeber 2011: 73-87).[3] To crave immortality and self-reproduction in eternity – a sort of Godlikeness or divine omnipresence, omniscience and omnipotence – is not to pursue an everlasting life as an individual on earth, but rather to creatively devise ways and forge relationships that make it possible to actively stay in circulation amongst the living even after physical death.[4]

David Graeber argues that because money is too generic to accumulate history, it cannot add to the holder's identity in the same manner that other things can, and thus "its identity does not cling to the former owner" in the way things more historically entangled with their owners intermingle or are mangled up with these owners (Graeber 2001: 213-214). Little wonder that in many an African context, successful individuals who preponderantly resort to gifts of money are likely to leave the receiver more insatiable than if they proffered gifts of more personal things. Because of its ephemeral, here-and-now character, money, paradoxical as it might seem, lacks the social-marker capacity to activate the receiver to the same degree of potency they require for social visibility as would a more personal thing that has accumulated history or that is capable of such history. Few are able to harness money (personalise and give it the beginnings of a history) through conversion into things of greater value before it evaporates like petrol, sending the exasperated receiver back to the giver to ask for more, in Oliver Twist-like fashion. As a gift, money is like a snack that seldom satisfies hunger.

In tune with Graeber's argument that debt embodies the essence of morality and informs everything we do (Graeber 2011: 89-126)[5], individuals are hardly allowed the prerogative to establish whether or not they are personally successful, as it is usually assumed that successful individuals might tend to be economical with the truth of their circumstance by seeking to absolve themselves of their obligation to reciprocate. In contexts of sociality where a person invariably leans on others to achieve something, the sentiment of one good turn deserves another is common currency. Even if a person is not in debt financially or materially, they might owe others debts of gratitude. Whatever the case, individuals are beholden to a frame of reference that does not accommodate overly personal and self-interested forms of success as an end. This raises questions of collective identity and individual agency and how the two intermingle to resolve or balance the tension between liberty and obligation, self-interest and generosity, autonomy and dependence, individual and group, nature and supernatural, visible and invisible, human and divine or God.

To deter those who might be motivated to resist or to free themselves of relationships, responsibilities and expectations, the pleasure or burden of determining success is incumbent on those who seek inclusion. It is not the responsibility of the haves to determine whom among the less fortunate they shall include and how. Often, a person's family, friends, acquaintances and unknown others even arrogate to themselves the power to determine, define and impose whether or not, and the extent to which, the person is rich in terms of material wealth, through widely shared assumptions and perceptions of success. It is thus difficult for people whose appearance and material circumstance might not immediately suggest obvious signs of ostentation and comfort to wriggle out of being labelled wealthy or personally successful.

A truly wealthy person is thus someone with little or nothing to show for their sweat and toil, not because he or she is lazy, has failed to make it in life, or has been the victim of unfair and a cruel devaluation of the local currency – facilitated by the "unholy trinity" of the World Trade Organisation (WTO), the International Monetary Fund (IMF) and World Bank (Peet 2003) –, but precisely because they have, willingly or reluctantly, sacrificed their "wealth-in-things" for "wealth-in-people" (Guyer & Belinga 1995). This is even truer in an ephemeral world of vicissitudes, where every new encounter with the ambitions of dominance of others both intimate and strange presents the risk of losing virtually everything a person has accumulated, including their freedom and dignity as a human being. In Maussian terms, they have opted for the social visibility that comes with giving in return and giving back more either because they are obliged, or have freely decided, to serve as the financial or resource guardians of their fellow and less fortunate community members (Mauss 1990[1950]: 69-75).

Writing about accumulation in Equatorial Africa, Guyer and Belinga argue that "wealth-in-people" "offers a useful descriptive term for the well-appreciated fact that interpersonal dependents of all kinds – wives, children, clients and slaves – were valued, sought and paid for at considerable expense in material terms in pre-colonial Africa. In some places they were the pinnacle, and even the unit of measure, of ultimate value" (Guyer & Belinga 1995: 92). A person who prioritises wealth-in-things over wealth-in-people can be compared to a rich man who would rather bank his money for meagre returns than invest it in property for a bumper harvest.

The philosophies of life which inform such "domesticated" understanding of personal agency and success (Rowlands 1996; Geschiere & Rowlands 1996; Warnier 2012) are replete with sayings considered sufficiently appropriate to drive home the importance of inclusivity: "A child is one person's only in the womb"; "One hand cannot tie a bundle"; "You need a hand to wash another'; "A goat eats where it is tethered"; "When your brother is up a fruit tree, you will eat the juiciest fruit"; and "I am my brother's keeper." I have written extensively on such ideas of success and domesticated agency – i.e. the freedom to pursue individual or group goals within a socially predetermined frame that emphasises conviviality with collective interests at the same time as it allows for individual creativity and self-fulfilment (Nyamnjoh 2002) – and have used many such aphorisms common to Cameroon illustratively (Nyamnjoh 1999, 2002, 2010a, 2013a; Nyamnjoh & Fokwang 2005).

In this study, I venture outside of Cameroon to look for examples from elsewhere in Africa[6] – from Côte d'Ivoire in particular – towards a trans-particular conversation on and around beliefs and practices that inspire strategic essentialisms, such as African communitarianism, or give currency to concepts such as Ubuntu, Africanness, Afrocentricity, Afrocentrism, Africanity, Afrikology, humanness, wholeness (Bell 2002; Nabudere 2011, 2012; Ramose 2014; Mawere 2014) and reciprocal altruism (Trivers 1971). Like Pan-Africanism or African Renaissance, such apparently collectivist pretensions are best seen and articulated as flexible, inclusive, dynamic and complex aspirations in identity making and belonging. Similar to the unity, solidarities and relevance craved, the micro and macro level importance of these identities in the making are simultaneously abstract and grounded, local and global. They are far less about single identities than about offering mental and fantasy spaces for disparate identities to aspire to inspire co-existence in freedom and dignity (Nyamnjoh & Shoro 2011, 2014).

Ubuntu is a Nguni word, widely used in South Africa by Zulu, Xhosa, Swati and Ndebele peoples and increasingly adopted by other groups within the country and across Africa and the world (Tutu 1999: 34-36; van Binsbergen 2001, 2003; McAllister 2009; Dolamo 2013; Enslin & Horsthemke 2004; Mawere 2014: 24-29; Praeg 2014; Praeg & Magadla 2014a&b). Among isiXhosa speaking South Africans for example, the expression is usually *Ubuntu ungamuntu ngabanye abantu*, translated roughly into "people are people through other people." The singular of which is *umntu ngumntu ngabantu*: "a person is a person through other people" (Tutu 1999: 35; Broodryk 2007: 39; McAllister 2009: 2) or "a human being is a human being because of other human beings" (Letseke 2012: 48) and more colloquially, "I am because you are" or "We are together." Ubuntu represents a philosophy of life that "espouses a fundamental respect in the rights of others, as well as a deep allegiance to the collective identity" (Mabovula 2011: 40), through compassion, interconnectedness, interdependence, and deep-rootedness in community (Broodryk 2002, 2008; Boshoff 2007; Muller 2008; Bidwell 2010; Letseka 2012; Whitworth & Wilkinson 2013; Dolamo 2013; Metz 2014). As "a philosophy of humanness that embraces unity, love, harmony and peace with each other and other beings in the environment" (Mawere 2014: 15), Ubuntu encourages those who embrace it to define and understand

8

individuals "primarily through their relationships with others rather than by their status as discrete individuals" (Whitworth & Wilkinson 2013: 121).

This philosophy, shared throughout most of the African continent (not necessarily using the same terminology), "regulates the exercise of individual rights by emphasizing sharing and co-responsibility and the mutual enjoyment of rights by all" (Mabovula 2011: 40). Broadly speaking, the notion of Ubuntu defines "humans as social beings, with human dignity central and integrated into both rationality and commonality (Christians 2004: 241). It posits that humans are "related to and depending on each other," and "are responsible for ensuring that others have everything that they need" (Whitworth & Wilkinson 2013: 125).

According to Desmond Tutu – whose articulations on Ubuntu as resilience and fortitude through forgiveness were at the heart of the South African Truth and Reconciliation Commission process (Bell 2002: 85-107) – one has Ubuntu ('*Yu, u nobuntu*') when one is "generous, hospitable, friendly, caring and compassionate" (Tutu 1999: 34). Ubuntu is sharing what one has, and acknowledging and providing for the fact that one's "humanity is caught up, is inextricably bound up" with the humanity of others – hence the affirmation: "'a person is a person through other people'" and "'I am human because I belong'" (Tutu 1999: 34-35). Tutu elaborates:

> A person with *ubuntu* is open and available to others, affirming of others, does not feel threatened that others are able and good, for he or she has a proper self-assurance that comes from knowing that he or she belongs in a greater whole and is diminished when others are humiliated or diminished, when others are tortured or oppressed, or treated as if they were less than who they are. (Tutu 1999: 35)

> You know when *ubuntu* is there, and it is obvious when it is absent. It has to do with what it means to be truly human, to know that you are bound up with others in the bundle of life. (Tutu 2004: 26)

To Tutu, Ubuntu is the quest for "social harmony" as a categorical imperative – "the *summum bonum* – the greatest good" – and "Anything that subverts or undermines this sought-after good is to be avoided like the plague" (Tutu 1999: 35). Pursuits or attitudes considered "corrosive of this good" include "Anger, resentment, lust for revenge, even success through aggressive competitiveness." With Ubuntu, to forgive is to be both altruistic and self-interested, for what diminishes or dehumanises another inexorably dehumanises or diminishes oneself (Tutu 1999: 35).

In a speech at a memorial service organised in Soweto, Johannesburg on 10 December 2013 in honour of Nelson Mandela, US President Barack Obama described the late Mandela not only as an embodiment of Ubuntu, but also as someone who taught millions to find the truth of Ubuntu within themselves. To Obama:

> … Mandela understood the ties that bind the human spirit. There is a word in South Africa –Ubuntu – that describes his greatest gift: *his recognition that we are all bound together in ways that can be invisible to the eye; that there is a oneness to humanity; that we achieve ourselves by sharing ourselves with others, and caring for those around us.* We can never know how much of this was innate in him, or how much of was shaped and burnished in a dark, solitary cell. But we remember the gestures, large and small – introducing his jailors as honored guests at his inauguration; taking the pitch in a Springbok uniform; turning his family's heartbreak into a call to confront HIV/AIDS – that revealed the depth of his empathy and understanding. *He not only embodied Ubuntu; he taught millions to find that truth within themselves. It took a man like Madiba to free not just the prisoner, but the jailor as well; to show that you must trust others so that they may trust you; to teach that reconciliation is not a matter of ignoring a cruel past, but a means of confronting it with inclusion, generosity and truth.* He changed laws, but also hearts [added emphasis].[7]

The Ubuntu suggestion that "humans depend completely on one another for their development" (Christians 2004: 244), is similar to Mauss' notion of "the gift," which encourages a

10

life of mutuality, obligation and reciprocity and emphasises a continuous act of sharing to maintain a balance of reciprocity between oneself and others. The obligatory circulation of wealth entails an obligation to reciprocate and to make oneself available to others in ways that allow for the maintenance of the giving and receiving cycle (Mauss 1990[1950]: 8-18). As Mauss puts it,

> To refuse to give, to fail to invite, just as to refuse to accept, is tantamount to declaring war; it is to reject the bond of alliance and commonality. Also, one gives because one is compelled to do so, because the recipient possesses some kind of right of property over anything that belongs to the donor. This ownership is expressed and conceived of as a spiritual bond. (Mauss 1990[1950]: 13)

From the perspective of Mauss' obligation to give, accept and return gifts, Ubuntu can be considered as a social organising principle involving the totality of society and its institutions, and touching on all aspects of social life (political, religious, cultural, economic, etc.). Ubuntu could inspire stable relationships in the communities in which it is practiced by encouraging individuals to recognise not only the interconnections that make their sociality possible, but also to "learn how to create mutual interests, giving mutual satisfaction." It encourages the redistribution of wealth in mutual respect and reciprocity as a way for members of a community to defend their mutual interests "without having to resort to arms," and to "oppose and to give to one another without sacrificing themselves to one another" (Mauss 1990[1950]: 82-83). Ubuntu seeks to socialise those who embrace it to recognise the virtues of giving, receiving and giving in turn as a deterrent to what Mauss terms "The brutish pursuit of individual ends," which is "harmful to the ends and the peace of all, to the rhythm of their work and joys – and rebounds on the individual himself" (Mauss 1990[1950]: 82-77).

11

Informed by Mauss' idea of exchange and circulation of wealth, Ubuntu could be likened to an alternative to market economies that "did such violence to ordinary people's sense of justice and humanity" (Graeber 2001: 158). Indeed, a noted tendency towards social protection in Southern Africa for example, where states provide direct cash payments to millions of previously ignored poor despite neoliberalism and the ever-growing social exclusion it champions (Ferguson 2015), could be seen as an Ubuntu variant of the welfare state. By encouraging the circulation of things, Ubuntu provides a framework where poverty and wealth are constantly on the move, changing hands and changing places, ensuring that everyone shall have their fair share of opportunity and possibility – of sunshine, rainfall, windfall, pitfall and downfall – in life. Ubuntu's subscription to interconnection and interdependence is a refusal to confine some from birth to a fate worse than death when too many things are in too few hands and mutual obligations downplayed.

As evident from references to Mauss above, the notion of Ubuntu and its ethic of caring, sharing and considerateness are not uniquely African (van Binsbergen 2001, 2003; McAllister 2009; Letseka 2012), even if African civilisations are widely understood to be governed by its philosophy (Enslin & Horsthemke 2012; Hailey, 2008). It is a significant coincidence that much of the current book was written at the Stellenbosch Institute for Advanced Study (STIAS), which is located at the Wallenberg Research Centre, a facility funded by two Wallenberg Foundations – Knut and Alice Wallenberg Foundation; Marianne and Marcus Wallenberg Foundation – based in Sweden[8]. According to Richard Milne of the *Financial Times*, the Wallenbergs – with "an empire that controls businesses worth €250bn" – are "arguably... Europe's pre-eminent business family." They are also "the second biggest donors in Europe to research, giving away about SKr2bn in 2014." Of added relevance to the idea of Ubuntu being more generic in nature and global in reach – being more than an

African birthmark that is – the three family members who currently head the Wallenberg business empire – Jacob, Marcus and Peter – do more than simply adhere to expectations of an "egalitarian Sweden." They "Strikingly ... own no personal part of the family empire," preferring instead to act through the 20 Wallenberg family foundations, which, according to Richard Milne, "have freed the Wallenbergs from the sort of bickering and fighting that often blights family businesses by the time they reach the fifth generation, when there are often hundreds of relatives as shareholders." Richard Milne captures the modesty of the Wallenbergs about personal success and commitment to collective success in these words: "While comfortably off, the trio do not even make rich lists in Sweden and insist they still have to work to make a living."[9] The Wallenbergs' urge to redistribute and to be measured, modest and collective even in screaming individual success, is an indication that the market or capitalist economy may not be as radically disconnected from economies of intimacy, obligation and reciprocity as is often instinctively assumed.

The resurgence in claims and articulations of Ubuntu "as a return to African roots and as essential to 'the African way of life'" in post-apartheid South Africa is remarkable across various spheres of life, from politics through religion and academics to business (McAllister 2009: 2-5). According to Patrick McAllister, Ubuntu is "seen as an autochthonous cultural resource and an indigenous philosophy that can be used in modern southern Africa, that will help the region to take its place in the world," by pointing to "an alternative modernity, vital for political and economic development and the construction of a contemporary African identity that contrasts with Western approaches and ideas, and which is thus also a gift to the world at large" (McAllister 2009: 2). Like van Binsbergen (2001, 2003), McAllister is critical of the essentialising and often romantic reconstructions of Ubuntu in post-apartheid South Africa. He finds little ethnographic evidence to authenticate the existence of Ubuntu as a coherent

13

philosophy of life independent of its representations (McAllister 2009: 4-6). Both van Binsbergen (2001, 2003) and McAllister (2009) conclude that Ubuntu is more of a utopian ideal than a description of reality, and is more claimed than evident even in remote villages and rural communities where the South African post-apartheid intellectual and political elite have tended to assume it resides the most.

Notwithstanding this criticism, Ubuntu should not be mistaken for the absence of conflict. Indeed, Ubuntu as an aspiration or an ideal goes hand in hand with the reality of conflict. In this regard, Ubuntu is a philosophy of learning to get by and get along despite conflict, even where conflict is a permanent and everyday dish. Writing about the same rural South Africa that informs McAllister's ethnographic insights, J.M. Coetzee, in his novel *Disgrace* observes: "Country life has always been a matter of neighbours scheming against each other, wishing on each other pests, poor crops, financial ruin, yet in a crisis ready to lend a hand" (Coetzee 1999: 118).

Reacting to an earlier draft of this book, Ayanda Manqoyi, a postgraduate South African student of anthropology at the University of Cape Town had this to say:

> As a South African from the Eastern Cape, what makes the concept of *Ubuntu-ism* attractive is the co-existence of the individual and the collective. It situates my own father, a successful business man in the late 1970s and 1980s with values rooted in the collective. While he had clearly made a lot of money by mastering the ways of running a large business, there had been no point in his journey where there was no connection to family, friends and even strangers. Many of the people employed in the family business were related to the family. But this was by no means simply an exercise of the power of money and opportunity through employment. When attending *umsebenzi* (custom related rituals), my father would oblige and bring with him 'gifts' that were particularly relevant to the sentiments and the history of Engcobo. The obligation and reciprocity by attending *umsebenzi* and contributing in socially acceptable ways demonstrates the realism of *Ubuntu-ism*. There was conflict,

jealousy and tensions. But whenever there were moments of crisis the family and friends that had not been speaking to each other would come together to assist one another. The role of wealth in things and technology made such obligations seem even more demanding at times. Having a telephone at home made it easy for relatives to call from public phones and inform about various customs related practices that would lead to my father send a van with a specific list of groceries and alcohol. To respond to such requests had become an obligation enabled further by owning a telephone which was not common during those days. My father was a strict and highly respected man, even by elders, but even he could not escape and did not make excuses about the obligations and reciprocity embedded in *Ubuntu-ism*. Instead, he insisted on passing the knowledge of individual success in tune with collective aspirations onto us.

Intimacy, reciprocity and trust are not necessarily good bedfellows (Geschiere 2013: 28-32). Ubuntu challenges us to recognise co-existence, intermingling and interdependence as a permanent work in progress that should not be abandoned in a hurry or by claiming freedoms in abstraction. It is hardly reason enough to give up on the concept of Ubuntu simply because it is assumed, in the case of South Africa, to have been hijacked and commercialised, to be too idealistic and uncritically embraced, as well as lacking coherence as a philosophy. The commercialisation of Ubuntu is hardly monolithic. There is a Linux operating system open source software platform known as Ubuntu. Similarly, in an interconnected world, there is no reason why those claiming Ubuntu in Africa should stand in the way of the Wallenberg Foundations in Sweden or the Bill & Melinda Gates Foundation in the USA claiming Ubuntu as justification for their obligations and reciprocities within the framework of the global capitalism from which they have benefitted abundantly.

Utopia or reality, African or not, Ubuntu is claimed and denied across Africa in ways that suggest an idea of individual self-interest far less predicated upon radical autonomy than dominant understandings of individual self-interest tend to portray. Like the gift economies presented by Mauss, Ubuntu could be said to challenge social scientists "to embrace the human condition in its entirety by exploring the moral relationship between concrete persons and society as a whole" (Hart 2007: 479), instead of resorting to often sterile abstractions and dichotomies between the individual and society, individualism and collectivism.

Through Ubuntu, students of sociality and the human condition recognise and provide for the complex interplay between individual freedom and social obligation (Mauss 1990 [1950]; Graeber 2001: 151-228; Hart 2007). As Hart argues, "Human institutions everywhere are founded on the unity of individual and society, freedom and obligation, self-interest and concern for others" (Hart 2007: 481). The conviviality or interdependence between individual and collective interest foregrounded by Ubuntu is claimed and denied in ways that have real implications for the lives of those involved. And as this case study of Côte d'Ivoire demonstrates, claiming and denying Ubuntu is far from being the preserve of the political and economic elite. Tutu acknowledges the social construction of Ubuntu when he admits that there is nothing "mechanical, automatic and inevitable" in the process of "honouring *ubuntu*" (Tutu 1999: 36).

With Ubuntu it is possible to negotiate and reconcile the apparent tensions between what Graeber terms an emphasis on "maintaining a permanent sense of mutual obligation" on the one hand, and "the denial of obligation and a maximum assertion of individual autonomy" on the other (Graeber 2001: 219), by providing for greater flexibility in which "closed relations can become more open, open relations more closed" (Graeber 2001: 220). Indeed, absolute freedom is "largely an illusion" in any social context, since "freedom largely means the freedom to choose what sort of obligations one wishes to enter into and with whom" (Graeber 2001: 221). The choice, if choice must be, is thus either between "maintaining the value of a timeless human commitment" or "that of a more

16

ephemeral autonomy" (Graeber 2001: 225). Since such a choice can only be articulated in principle, in abstraction or in callous disregard of the humanity of others, it is incumbent on all and sundry to proceed in a manner that recognises the truism that each right corresponds to an obligation and each obligation is tied to a right (Simmel & Jacobson 1965).

In his study of English sociality, Daniel Miller suggests that personal autonomy without obligation and reciprocity can very easily result in loneliness, isolation, social fragmentation and the very end of sociality in the private domain, even as the public domain exudes "undoubted generosity and ubiquitous friendliness" (Miller 2015: 341). This outsourcing of sociality to the public domain is as true of small villages as it is of cities (Miller 2015: 350). Although it is usually "assumed that people use social media to find, maintain, and extend relationships, both with family and friends," it is commonplace in England to use social media "to keep family and friends at a distance" (Miller 2015: 352). Related work on autonomy and isolation among the elderly in North London emphasises how reliance on pets and care of vulnerable others takes the place of troublesome family and dependents who make demands. It is also common to surround oneself with photos and objects which one touches often emotively and as aide-memoires emphasising virtual sociality through the power of touch as a way of being in touch (Rowlands 2007).

The use of social media simultaneously to enhance and contain sociality is a tendency not unique to the English, as studies of cell phone use in Africa have attested (Nyamnjoh 2005a; de Bruijn et al. 2009; Powell 2012, 2014; Nyamnjoh 2014). As a South African clergyman puts it, "social media is like a stranger who pretends to be your friend but sleeps between you and your wife."[10] Social media may have been creatively appropriated to contain sociality. Old and new information and communications technologies (ICTs), however unequal and hierarchized, have enabled greater mobility, encounters and interconnections that make intimacies

17

possible across the narrow confines of cultural and physical geographies in a manner that challenges conventional distinctions between local and global, insider and outsider, family and stranger, gift and market economies (Nyamnjoh 2005a; de Bruijn et al. 2009; Brinkerhoff 2009; Powell 2012, 2014; Tazanu 2012; Hudson 2013; Nyamnjoh 2014; Nkwi 2015; Obijiofor 2015).

Graeber notes that those seeking more just and more decent ways of organising economic and political life often turn to anthropology for ideas and inspiration. He challenges anthropologists to do more than warn that "gift economies too have been known to trample people underfoot" (Graeber 2001: 228). As an example of a gift economy, Ubuntu is far from being vague, stifling of human freedoms, an oversimplified romanticised "humanizing counterweight to the impersonality and social isolation of modern capitalist society" (Graeber 2001: 226). Ubuntu is not something to be relegated to small-scale village communities. Ubuntu is capable of serving as a moral theory of human rights in any context, however modern, by which the human capacity for community calls for identifying and exhibiting solidarity with others, such that the violation of human rights and dignity are egregious degradations of that capacity for community (Metz 2011).

Mogobe Ramose invites us to understand Ubuntu "as a lived and living philosophy of the Bantu-speaking peoples of Africa," with a past, a present and a future project (Ramose 2014: 121). Central to Ubuntu as a philosophy, Ramose argues, is the recognition that "motion is the principle of being" and that "Since everything is in incessant flow – a perpetual exchange – it is necessary to remain open to change and not to block it by imposing an arbitrary finality to life" (Ramose 2014: 133). To Ramose Ubuntu is "be-ing human (human-ness)" and is characterised by "a humane, respectful and polite attitude towards others" (Ramose 1999: 52). It demands recognition, protection, promotion and respect of the right to be a human being, and is thus against all forms of exclusion, indifference

18

and marginalisation of peoples such as occasioned by slavery and colonial conquest (Ramose 2014: 121-123). Key ingredients of Ubuntu as a philosophy include solidarity, mutuality, collective responsibility and the obligation to share wealth with the rest of the community (Ramose 2014: 125). Ubuntu makes an ontological point to ensure continuities, interconnections and interdependence not only among the living but also between the living, the living-dead ('ancestors') and the yet-to-be-born (Ramose 2014: 126, 134).

What, in the everyday lives of those implicated, for example, does it mean to live out the claim that a man is a man because of others? In other words, what are the challenges, and how are these challenges negotiated, to ensure fulfilment of the maxim that "to be a human be-ing is to affirm one's humanity by recognising the humanity of others and, on that basis, establish humane relations with them" (Ramose 1999: 52)? In this connection, the blogger C. Joybell writes, "I'm not in search of sanctity, sacredness, purity; these things are found after this life, not in this life; but in this life I search to be completely human: to feel, to give, to take, to laugh, to get lost, to be found, to dance, to love and to lust, to be so human."[11]

These shared understandings of Ubuntu frame the discussion in this study of relationships in which inclusion, obligation and reciprocity are emphasised. Equally significant in the discussion is my quest for interconnection between ethnography and fiction. As I have argued and demonstrated elsewhere, fiction and ethnography have more in common than meets the eye, and that challenges us both to assume mutual obligations and reciprocity in the interest of more heuristic perspectives on the social (Nyamnjoh 2011, 2013b&c). With regard to the current theme of mobility of Africans, transnational fiction can tell us much about the nature of boundaries and the grammar of identities (Clingman 2009). This study provides a thick description of a popular TV drama in Côte d'Ivoire – *C'est l'homme qui fait l'homme*[12] ["a man is a man because of another" or "it takes a man to make a man"][13].

19

This analysis show how drama captures the complexities, intricacies and tensions implicit and explicit in the relationships that popular beliefs engender between purportedly successful nimble-footed individuals and their kin, circles of friends, acquaintances and networks.

The central character in the series, Gohou, is also a well-known character in the most famous, longest running and highly regarded Ivorian television series in Francophone Africa, *Ma Famille*[14]. How does *C'est l'homme qui fait l'homme* reproduce, contest or challenge prevalent ideas of success as an inclusive pursuit? To what extent is the philosophy and way of life that underpins inclusive success justified, questioned, threatened or jeopardised by those who claim it? *C'est l'homme qui fait l'homme* offers an ethnographic context (albeit without background and history enough to reflect the fullness and intricacies of the processes of their cultivation and subjectivities) of social roles and actualities played out through the tensions of opportunity and opportunism in *Ubuntu-ism* and inclusivity, and in the discourses and practises of remittances and development in an Africa caught between and betwixt the material and visceral intersections of global and local hierarchies of being and becoming. The study is also a conversation on consumerism, the unfolding and complex relations between supposedly metropolitan centres and peripheries and the forms of sociality in Africa within the context of contemporary globalisation.

The themes highlighted above are developed in six parts, namely: treasure-hunting beyond familiar shores; one good turn deserves another; shared intricacies and entanglements; Ubuntu-ism and the seesaw of opportunity and opportunism; the zombies are back at their risk and peril; and conclusion.

Notes

[1] That is, a capacity for presence in different forms and places at the same time.

[2] See David Priestland's review of John Plender's *Capitalism: Money, Morals and Markets,* www.ft.com/intl/cms/s/0/ff835d9e-2fb0-11e5-91ac-a5e17d9b4cff.html, accessed 28 July 2015.

[3] See also David Graeber's "The Theology of Debt" www.bbc.co.uk/programmes/b0544243#auto, accessed 27 May 2015.

[4] See Philip Ball on the elusive pursuit of dreams of physical immortality through scientific innovation and related myths, "The God quest: why humans long for immortality," www.newstatesman.com/culture/2015/07/god-quest-why-humans-long-immortality, accessed 02 August 2015.

[5] See also David Graeber, "The Moral Power of Debt" www.bbc.co.uk/programmes/b05447pc, accessed 27 May 2015.

[6] Nigerian music and home entertainment video industries are full of relevant examples – for instance, Nkem Owoh's film *"Osuofia in London"* and song *"Know Me When I am Poor,"* as well as Mama-G's song *"National Moi-Moi"*

[7] See The White House Office of the Press Secretary, "Remarks of President Barack Obama – As Prepared for Delivery Remembering Nelson Mandela, Johannesburg, South Africa December 10, 2013," www.whitehouse.gov/the-press-office/2013/12/10/remarks-president-barack-obama-prepared-delivery, accessed 24 July 2015; see also www.youtube.com/watch?v=4vUB363cRqE&spfreload=10, accessed 24 July 2015.

[8] http://stias.ac.za/funding-and-sponsorships/, accessed 18 July 2015.

[9] Richard Milne, "Meet the Wallenbergs," www.ft.com/cms/s/0/4f407796-0a35-11e5-a6a8-00144feabdc0.html, accessed 18 July 2015.

[10] Presenter of the South African Broadcasting Corporation SAfm "Devotional Message" of 29 May 2015, which focused on the effects of social media in South Africa.

[11] cjoybellc.blogspot.com/2011/10/you-can-quote-me-1-30.html, accessed 15 March 2014

[12] I am most grateful to Achille Kouhon, a doctoral student in Social Anthropology at l'Université Félix Houphouët Boigny de Côte d'Ivoire, for the following detailed comment elaborating on the origin and popularity of *C'est l'homme qui fait l'homme* in Côte d'Ivoire, when he read an earlier version of this study:

"It takes a man to make another" is an adage commonly used in Côte d'Ivoire. It pervades such musical styles as the *"Zouglou"* – a musical style of the 1990s in Côte d'Ivoire, started on university campuses and used by students to denounce societal ills – or the *"Coupé décalé,"* which, for the Ivorian population are a means to express a sort of "truth," the "reality" of the masses. In the context of Côte d'Ivoire, this expression can even be equated to a theory to explain that socio-economic success cannot be achieved without the help and support of others.

Ivorian success, as expressed in such popular wisdom, is also identified as possible through an honest approach, still however, supported by someone else. The song that popularised *"C'est l'homme qui fait l'homme"* is about Donmayer, a young man who lived with his "old man," Chinto, whose business he ran skilfully (see Meleke, *"C'est l'homme qui fait l'homme,"* chanson Zouglou available on, www.youtube.com/watch?v=9Kiq0Gv_Rr8). Chinto, happy with his work, would reward him by opening a kiosk, the money spent on which would have to be reimbursed by Donmayer at a later stage. Donmayer would manage his business quite well and would reimburse Chinto the full amount that was required to open the kiosk in no time, later even opening 20 kiosks, 2 large pubs and a nightclub. He would remain grateful to Chinto, but the latter would quickly become envious of his success and his notorious reputation among the people of the region, Donmayer would reply: "I know it's because of you that I achieved success, but in life, it takes one man to make another. If someone is president, it is thanks to the people. If someone is a minister, it is thanks to the President. If someone is director, it is thanks to the Minister. If someone is s secretary, it is thanks to the Director. So, in conclusion, it takes one man to make another, thanks to someone we become somebody." Donmayer will acknowledge the support from Chinto unequivocally, explaining that the latter is the one who "made" him, and in turn, he would "make other men" because, after all, "it takes one man to make another." He adds that "in life, it takes one hand to wash another ... I know you're my saviour, but such is life."

"If anyone has succeeded in the transport business (a type of businessman commonly called *Doulacthê* in Côte d'Ivoire)," continues the song, "owning several vehicles, it is thanks to passengers boarding his buses. If someone is the driver of these vehicles, it is thanks to *Doulacthê*. If someone is an apprentice driver, it is thanks to the driver. So in conclusion, "it takes one man to make another." This adage reveals what socio-economic success in Côte d'Ivoire entails – whether achieved honestly or not, it takes a man to make another.

[L'expression « C'est l'homme qui fait l'homme » est beaucoup utilisée en Côte d'Ivoire. Vous l'entendrez assez souvent, s'il vous arrive d'écouter du « *Zouglou* » ou du « Coupé décalé », styles musicaux servant à la population ivoirienne, à exprimer une certaine forme de « vérité » ou de « réalité ». Dans le contexte de la Côte d'Ivoire, on peut même égaler cette expression à une sorte de théorie, qui expliquerait que la réussite socioéconomique ne peut se faire sans l'aide d'autrui, sans soutien.

Dans celle-ci, la réussite est aussi identifiée possible à travers une démarche honnête, soutenue par autrui. La chanson parle de Donmayer, un gentil jeune homme qui vivait chez son « vieux père », Chinto, les affaires duquel il gérait presqu'expertement. Chinto, content du labeur de celui-ci, le récompensera en lui ouvrant un kiosk, prix duquel il devra rembourser ultérieurement. Donmayer gérera bien son argent et en peu de temps, remboursera Chinto la totalité de la somme qui avait été nécessaire à l'ouverture du kiosk. Etant un très bon homme d'affaires, Donmayer ouvrira plus tard 20 kiosks, 2 grands maquis et une boite de nuit. Il restera reconnaissant envers Chinto, mais celui-ci très vite deviendra envieux de sa réussite et de sa réputation notoire auprès des gens de la région, oubliant que « C'est l'homme qui fait l'homme ». A sa rancœur, Donmayer répondra : « Je sais que c'est grâce à toi que j'ai gagné ma vie, mais dans la vie c'est l'homme qui fait l'homme. Si quelqu'un est président, c'est grâce au peuple. Si quelqu'un est ministre c'est grâce au président. Si quelqu'un est directeur c'est grâce au ministre. Si quelqu'un est secrétaire c'est grâce au directeur. Et donc, en conclusion, c'est l'homme qui fait l'homme, grâce à quelqu'un on devient quelqu'un." Donmayer, ici, reconnaitra le soutien de Chinto sans équivoque, expliquant que c'est celui-ci qui l'a « fait, » et qu'à son tour, il « ferait d'autres hommes » car, après tout, « C'est l'homme qui fait l'homme ». Il ajoutera que « dans la vie, ce sont les deux mains qui se lave … je sais que tu es mon sauveur mais ainsi va la vie."

«Si quelqu'un a réussi dans le transport en commun (cet homme est communément appelé Doulacthê en Côte d'Ivoire)," continue la chanson à laquelle nous nous référons ici, « en ayant plusieurs véhicules, c'est grâce aux passagers qui montent dans ces véhicules. Si quelqu'un est chauffeur de ces véhicules c'est grâce au Doulacthê. Si quelqu'un est apprenti chauffeur, c'est grâce au chauffeur. Alors en conclusion, c'est pour te dire que « c'est l'homme qui fait l'homme ». L'expression « C'est l'homme qui fait l'homme » révèle, en simplicité, la réussite socio-économique, approchée par voie honnête ou malhonnête.]

[13]See www.youtube.com/watch?v=iXxnsazdxBY, accessed 15 March 2014. It was produced in October 2005 by Les Guignols d'Abidjan, a theatre troupe of which Gohou and Nastou are founding members. Les Guignols d'Abidjan are mostly famous in Francophone Africa, and their plays and TV drama series seek to bring to the stage and on television the ups and downs of the everyday life of Africans. Their popularity extends beyond Francophone Africa into Europe, especially among African immigrants. With the advent of the internet, smartphones, Facebook, YouTube and related forms of social media and kindred technologies (high capacity giga- and tera-bite flash and external hard disks) the circulation of the series has accelerated remarkably, according it a fascinating ease to cross borders and navigate frontiers with far greater flexibility than the mobile Africans whose realities it represents. In this regard, it is a TV drama series that has taken up a whole new transnational global character and capacity for presence in infinity and simultaneous multiplicity, thanks to new information and communication technologies. Tellingly, it was not by being physically present and watching Ivorian national TV that I came to know of and develop interest in the series. Rather, the flexible mobility of the series brought it my way in Dakar, Senegal, shortly after it was released in 2005.

[14]   See   for   example   this   episode: www.youtube.com/watch?v=sIA1vRPcedk. The series focuses on the family in its various dimensions, intricacies, intrigues and sagas, and involves many families and the complex social relations that influence them and which they in turn shape. The two main families involved are Bohiri's and Gohou's. A key aspect of the series is love, polygamy, affairs with sugar daddies and sugar mummies, and social life in all its contours seen through the perspective of families in motion.

2

Treasure-Hunting Beyond Familiar Shores

Africans are up against a limited and limiting logic that guides practices of inclusion and measures of belonging, regardless of the fact that they are and have always been mobile or implicated in mobility. Today, they experience globalisation from above, as part of the global conglomerates of frequent flyer movers and shakers, and from below, as those immobilised by the mobility of others. Even Africans who may never be mobile beyond their place of birth connect with the rest of the world through encounters with the mobile among them. This is especially the case with the proliferation of new ICTs – such as the Internet, cell phones and social media – as flexible enablers (Appadurai 2000; Castles 2002; Urry 2004; Nyamnjoh 2005a; de Bruijn et al. 2009; Brinkerhoff 2009; Powell 2012, 2014; Tazanu 2012; Hudson 2013; Nyamnjoh 2014; Nkwi 2015; Obijiofor 2015). Conviviality between mobility and immobility makes possible otherwise unlikely cultural and economic conversations, just as it makes possible the playing out at local levels of global tensions and power struggles.

Our worlds, big or small, would not work the way they do, were it not for mobility. Peter Adey, a social geographer, invites us to conceptualise mobility as the vital relationship through which we live, understand and engage with a world increasingly on the move (Adey 2010: xvii–xviii). Our very sociality, humanity and survival depend on mobility, which is seldom a singular process, as we always tend to carry our worlds along, and are confronted with the mobilities of our and other worlds (Adey 2010: 18). As he puts it, "Our life-worlds are mobile for us, with us, and sometimes they are against us" (Adey 2010: 4). To facilitate our mobility to the extent that we are able, we mobilise and immobilise things and others as we see fit. Our mobilities make waves and embed themselves on landscapes. Fixities, argues Adey, are physically, socially, politically and economically engineered as "enablers" to make possible particular forms of mobility and thus provide "a sort of backdrop for us to distinguish mobility against." The process is similar to the chicken and egg conundrum, for "As mobilities are enabled by fixities, mobilities construct and create further fixities" (Adey 2010: 18–23).

How we make sense of the world and of one another depends on how we mediate mobility. People who are seemingly "immobile" also form relationships and make sense of the world based on interactions with mobile others (Adey 2010: 18–23). Mobility generates encounters, and encounters shape relationships. Mobility is "almost always meaningful, political, practised and mediated" (Adey 2010: 14), as it occasions various degrees of transformation and meaning-making of the contexts, places and spaces where it occurs (Adey 2010: 12). We are always differently (Adey 2010: 3) and differentially (Nyamnjoh 2011; Alpes 2011; Owen 2011; Nyamnjoh 2014) mobile. Mobility, whatever its form, is not a monopoly of any particular place, race, class, gender or generation (Clifford 1988). Any one's mobility can only be accommodated to the extent it is accommodating.

If the global tendency is to be "mobile with," as Peter Adey (2010) has argued, people on the move behave like dogs. Like dogs, we tend to mark and demarcate or signpost everywhere we go, to familiarise or domesticate the unknown and affirm our authority over particular territories. The signposts of male dogs are most imposing, almost as if female dogs were without signposts of their own, immobile, non-existent or irrelevant. Yet women are mobile as well, and their experiences, expectations and encounters are significant (Nyamnjoh 2006, 2010b). The marking of places and spaces by mobile men may be more imposing, compared to the mostly subtle and discrete mobility and presence of women, but men do not have the monopoly of seeking to tame and name the unfamiliar (Amadiume 1997: 183-198; Blixen 1999 [1937]; Magubane 2004, 2007; Nnaemeka 2005: 55). In place of reeking signposts by dogs, humans are mobile with their social backgrounds, positions and habitus – that to which they are habituated, and which they seek to reproduce even as they are open to improvisation and adaptation to varying degrees (Bourdieu 1996; Wacquant 1996; Calhoun 2000). We are mobile with the ideas, beliefs, practices, and social and material culture we are used to, and which we usually try to reproduce or adapt on our own terms.

People, far from travelling in disembedded ways as isolated individuals, often and mostly travel with their cultural values and ways of life, and are very eager to re-enact, reactivate or reignite these values in their host communities, however hostile. It is in this sense that some have used the notion of 'travelling cultures' (Clifford 1988; de Bruijn et al. 2001a&b) or 'cultural mobility' (Greenblatt et al. 2010) to indicate the specific features or situations where forms of mobility are combined with a mobility of social forms and institutions. Dogs might be obedient and follow the 'leader of the pack' in the main, but they are also stubborn and could behave in unpredictable and uncontainable ways. People are not dissimilar; they might accommodate, adapt, subvert or, like the Rottweiler, savage certain tendencies, but they are seldom passive even in victimhood.

The current dominant approach to studying and relating to mobile Africans is problematic. Nationals, citizens and locals in communities targeted by African mobility are instinctively expected to close ranks and fight off the influx of barbarians who do not quite belong and must be "exorcised" so that "insiders" do not lose out to this particular breed of "strangers," "outsiders" or "demons," perceived to bode little but inconvenience and savagery. If and when allowed in, emphasis is on the needs, priorities and convenience of their reluctant hosts, who tend to go for the wealthy, the highly

27

professionally skilled, the culturally bleached and Hottentot Venuses of the academy, even at the risk of accusations of capital flight and brain drain. Such mobile others – usually whites and/or frequent flyer black international professionals, from within and outside the continent – are believed to be higher up the hierarchy of "purity" of humanity, which is often constructed in terms of belonging to racial, cultural, geographical, class, gender and generational categories (Gupta & Ferguson 1992, 1997; Stolcke 1995; Geschiere 2009). There is need for conceptual flexibility and ethnographic empirical substantiation in the study of African mobility. Social scientists need to look beyond academic sources for ethnographies and accounts of how a deep, flexible and nuanced understanding of mobility and interconnections in Africa play out in different communities, states and regions of a world permanently on the move (Nyamnjoh 2015).

This study of *C'est l'homme qui fait l'homme* serves to argue that the mobility of Africans is more appropriately studied as an emotional, relational and social phenomenon as reflected in the complexities, contradictions and messiness of their everyday encounters as physically and socially mobile or immobilised beings. *C'est l'homme qui fait l'homme* depicts the thrills and tensions, possibilities and dangers, and rewards and frustrations of social, cultural, political and physical boundary-making and boundary-crossing. It highlights the drama of being, belonging, and becoming that bring together different worlds, and explores the various dimensions of aspiration, servitude, mobility and marginality, as well as being in transit or transition as an individual, a people or a way of life. It offers layered textures of the complexities of relationships individuals encounter in their mobility and daily living spaces, and explores the dramas that accompany the mundane. The characters involved in *C'est l'homme qui fait l'homme* are layered in speech and action, often using metaphors and allusion to custom, tradition and modernity to imply things rather than spelling them out, leaving the listener or viewer to fill in the gaps, using assumptions drawn from a shared humanity. The story provides space and scope to tackle ethical concerns pertaining to claims and denial of Ubuntu with greater complexity and nuance. Within the framework of globalisation and the histories of unequal encounters that have shaped relations under global capitalism, *C'est l'homme qui fait l'homme* provides a compelling framework to argue that mobility and identities in Africa should be understood not as an investment in the elusive and illusive quest of purity and authenticity, but rather as an enrichment of conversations and perspectives in recognition of the creativity and innovativeness that come with the entanglements and messiness provoked by social encounters and ambitions of dominance.

If there is any lesson mobile Africans could learn from their European and Western counterparts, it is how to comb the world with imperial ambitions of dominance, hunting with relentless greed for riches and resources in distant lands, and using coercive violence to dispossess and indebt without being indebted (Graeber 2011; Biel 2000; Bessis 2003; Boron 2004; Petras & Veltmeyer 2005; Duffield & Hewitt 2013). It is thanks precisely to this logic and approach that "Third World debtor nations are almost exclusively countries that have at one time been attacked and conquered by European countries – often, the very countries to whom they now owe money" (Graeber 2011: 5). For those Africans who have borrowed a leaf from Europe, uncontested success comes from hunting for opportunities in distant unfamiliar lands, among distant unfamiliar others, who should not be close enough to appeal to one's scruples and conscience. Ideally, the lands should be distant enough to constitute hunting grounds and the people unfamiliar enough to be prey and be preyed upon. Ruthlessness and detachment are the name of the game, as it permits one to freeze the humanity of those one seeks to take advantage of.

This sentiment is superbly captured by the Nigerian actor and musician, Nkem Owoh, in his song "I Go Chop Your Dollar," in which he argues, inter alia, that the infamous

29

scamming[1] for which Nigeria is renowned is just a game, and no one should seek to moralise unduly about it. He warns "Oyibo" [whites]: "I go chop your dollar, I go take your money disappear. 419 is just a game in which everyone is fair game to everyone else. You are the loser, I am the winner."[2]

In Cameroon the phenomenon of *bushfalling* documents how Europe, North America and other fruitful zones of accumulation have served as hunting grounds for mobile young Cameroonians seeking to free themselves from the frustrations, pressures and stress of underachievement and the paucity of prospects and opportunities in the homeland – the widely depleted hunting grounds of yesteryear European hunters (Nyamnjoh 2011; Alpes 2011; Tazanu 2012; Nfon 2013; Pelican 2013; Nyamnjoh 2014; Alhaji 2015; Nkwi 2015). What goes around comes around, prey today, predator tomorrow. Indeed, like the Nigerian *419* scam and Cameroonian *feymania* (Apter 1999; Benzon 2011; Malaquais 2001, 2002; Ndjio 2006, 2008, 2012), hunting and being hunted is just a game, and the hunter's village is as much a hunting ground for the hunted as the apparently wild forests, hills, valleys and grasslands of those defined and confined as game have been hunting grounds for hunters from villages far and near, African and European. As the African saying goes, no one has the monopoly of defining what constitutes a hunting ground and of who can or cannot hunt, just as no one has the exclusive prerogative to tell the story of the hunt. Until the lions [prey] produce their own historian, the story of the hunt will glorify only the hunter. By going hunting in the distant villages and towns of the hunters of yesteryears, mobile Africans are challenging the predators of imperial and colonial times to desist from their zero sum games of eternal dominance.

Mobile Africans by no means confine themselves to Europe or North America. Increasingly, they are moving to China, Japan, the United Arab Emirates and elsewhere in Asia and the Middle East (Li et al. 2009; Bodomo 2012; Lonkog 2013; Nkwi 2014; Pelican & Tatah 2009; Pelican & Şaul 2014).

On the continent, pockets of opportunity such as Botswana, South Africa and Equatorial Guinea are attractive destinations. The experience of the Cameroonian bushfallers is shared by others across Africa, as various accounts of migrants in Botswana and South Africa from elsewhere on the continent – Democratic Republic of Congo, Somalia, Kenya, Zimbabwe, Malawi, Nigeria and Senegal, to name but a few –, attest (Nyamnjoh 2006, 2010b; Sichone 2008; Neocosmos 2010; Owen 2011; Landau 2011; Brudvig 2014; Hay 2014; Powell 2014; Mangezvo 2014; Steinberg 2015; Adam & Moodley 2015).

As *C'est l'homme qui fait l'homme* shows through the characters of Daou and Amélie, Côte d'Ivoire is no different. It also shows that, if hunting is the name of the game, hunters can be game and game hunters – a relationship well epitomised by the predatory attitudes of Gohou and Nastou towards their hunter cousin and friend in Europe. These examples demonstrate as well the fluidity of social roles and how they regenerate according to context and positionality – conceptions that do not always conform to linear understanding. The theme of mobility – that Africans escape from poverty and humiliation in quest of dignity through mobility ("bushfalling") to the West or elsewhere where they can "chop dollars" (compared to visiting a forest to harvest plants, fruits, leaves, roots, backs, etc. for sustenance) is what makes the difference that violence is the means to regain humanity. In the logic of *nyongo* (Ardener 1996 [1970]; Geschiere 1997: 139–168, 2013: 1-68; Nyamnjoh 2001, 2005a, 2011 – discussed further under Chapter 6, pp.87-125 below), a form of witchcraft which privileges keeping one's victims alive for long term gratification rather than resorting to disposing of them through instant and violent death, Africans who resort to migration instead of violent destruction would rather poke and prick the conscience of their Western debtors to assume their responsibilities, obligations and debts.

If mobility has always been part and parcel of humanity, today, new technologies of communication and transportation allow for more frequent and multidirectional flows of people, ideas and cultural symbols (Castles 2002). Such acceleration and complexification simultaneously facilitates and impairs the formation of transnational communities, multiple identities and multi-layered citizenship, and the blurring of boundaries between different categories of mobility and the mobile (Appadurai 2000; Nyamnjoh 2006; Comaroff & Comaroff 2009; Geschiere 2009).

The more borders appear threatened by or reinforced against the accelerated mobility of people with "nostalgia for the future" (Piot 2010), the more people crave for and invest in rootedness and nostalgia for an imagined past (Geschiere 2009). Thus, we may be more nimble-footed today than ever before, while also being drawn to fixities. Obsessions with purity, authenticity, primary and often parochial identities coexist with notions of nation state and its logic of large-scale, exclusive communities. In Africa as much as elsewhere, people are busy rediscovering cultural identities as heritage and as commodity, in an 'identity economy' where, as Jean and John Comaroff (2009) argue, the sale of culture is rapidly replacing the sale of labour, and in certain cases, the very survival of particular groups depends on self-parody and self-devaluation as cultural spectacles to fee-paying strangers on "cannibal tours."[3] Such an economy is proving profitable to long-marginalised, impoverished populations, who increasingly realise that they can "turn the means of their exclusion into sources of profit without alienation, estrangement, or a loss of 'true' selfhood" (Comaroff & Comaroff 2009: 52). This "traffic in difference" or in "culture-as-commodity" is "driven by a burgeoning desire at once to endorse difference and to transcend it" (Comaroff & Comaroff 2009: 148). It combines with political and social policing of borders to simultaneously endorse and contest dominant ideas of globalisation as a process that encourages flexible mobility and open-ended cosmopolitan identities (Geschiere 2009).

Mobility of humans, ideas and things entails encounters and the production or reproduction of similarities and difference, as those who move or are moved always tend to position themselves or be positioned (hierarchically) in relation to those they meet and to one another. While every cultural community is mobile within itself, technologies make possible movement between places and cultural spaces. Thanks to technologies of mobility, cultural encounters informed by "interconnecting local and global hierarchies" are possible (Gupta & Ferguson 1992, 1997), and have been so throughout the histories of local and global encounters. Who gets to move, or whose mobility is privileged, shall determine whose version of what encounter is documented, how it is documented, and the extent of its visibility in the marketplace of ideas. As John Urry (2007: 9) puts it, "Moving between places physically or virtually can be a source of status and power, an expression of the rights to movement either temporarily or permanently. And where movement is coerced it may generate social deprivation and exclusion."

Ultimately, globalisation is a process not only of accelerated flows but also of accelerated closures (Appadurai 2000), for, as James Ferguson (2006: 38-41) argues, the metaphor of flows ignores the reality of global inequalities, marginalisation and disconnection, and the fact of an uneven playing field that make the process more one of global hopping than global flows.

Notes

---

[1]   See   his   film,   *The*   *Master*, www.youtube.com/watch?v=0KqesD2JU88&list=TLCp8r9ZZwvHU, accessed 10 March 2014

[2]   www.sweetslyrics.com/727896.Nkem%20Owoh%20-%20I%20go%20chop%20your%20dollar.html, accessed 06 March 2014

[3] A 1988 documentary film by Dennis O'Rourke.

One Good Turn Deserves Another

A mutually beneficial relationship is one characterised by open-ended mobility, compassion, conviviality and interdependence. Hundreds of thousands of Africans who go paddling and knocking on the doors of Europe through risky boat journeys, perilous treks across the Sahara, by flights and other means, are convinced that it is only appropriate for Europe to return the favour of the *Ubuntu* they have shown Europeans since colonial times (Nyamnjoh 2010; Lucht 2012; Triulzi & McKenzie 2013). In most dehumanising terms, European media and politicians are rather hysterical in their categorisation of the influx of those they brand as illegal immigrants, tending to see them as tidal waves or floods of epidemic proportions that must be contained before swamping Europe. It does not seem to matter that Europe needs migrants and that the jobs migrants do are jobs few European citizens want to do. It does not seem to matter that the contributions by migrants to the economies of their host communities are more than what they derive from those communities in the form of remittances.

European states, which should know better, behave as if the world were basically a fair place where hard work is consistently rewarded, laziness punished and debts dutifully repaid or serviced. They behave as if the world and its resources, migration and mobility were a European prerogative and monopoly, as they tend to gloss over or explain as normal the fact that Europeans have systematically left their countries in millions to other parts of the world. Endogenous populations did not always have the option to choose whether or not to accept their European strangers[1] (Messina & Lahav 2006). Such one-dimensionalism in claiming and denying entitlements is increasingly contested by African migrants who expect Europe and its extensions in the Americas and elsewhere to "discharge their debts and satisfy their obligations to Africa" (Shoichiro 2015) which between the 15th and 19th century lost 12 million of its sons and daughters as slaves to the coerced migration imposed by the transatlantic slave trade (Eltis 2000; Eltis & Richardson 2008).

Just as no amount of potential slaves swallowed up by the Atlantic Ocean was deterrent enough for Europeans involved in the transatlantic slave trade, today no amount of swallowing up of boatloads of migrants by the Mediterranean Sea is deterrent enough for Africans seeking restitution[2]. Those who target France in particular want France to prove its worth as an orchard to its constant gardeners in Africa – those who since colonial times have rarely seen the benefits of their countries' riches because their leaders have been too busy serving and servicing restless French hunger for raw materials from Africa. In Maussian terms, they want France and the French whose amassment of wealth has been actively and abundantly sustained by Africans and resources from Africa since the time of slavery and colonialism to embrace the logic of obligation and reciprocity by giving back and giving more to Africans who come knocking at the doors of its borders (Mauss 1990[1950]: 65-83).

If France were only to relinquish its position of power in favour of the modest status of an equal, France would understand why its success and riches would not have been possible without Africa and Africans turning a blind eye on France's greedy accumulation of the wealth of its colonies and postcolonies. By taking their resources and labour throughout the period of colonial encounters, France emptied Africa and Africans of their souls, the very essence they needed to remain human. Only a reunion with their beleaguered souls would do justice to their quest to be human and live in dignity. In other words, if France can speak of a social contract between the French state and the citizens of France, it should have the moral obligation of recognising the rationale for such a contract between the French state and the citizens of its former colonies for whom independence has not delivered more than continued neo-colonial exploitation with impunity by France, the French and French corporations. This is the sentiment captured in popular music such as *Travailleurs immigrés* by Douleur and *Ayo... Africa, Privatisation* and *Affaire Kaolo* by Longue Longue, all stingingly critical of the misery, exploitation and dependency of Africa and Africans trapped in one-dimensional relationships with France, Europe and the West (Nyamnjoh & Page 2002; Nyamnjoh & Fokwang 2005). The perception is widespread on the continent that Africans would live in dignity in their own countries if these countries had not been unduly underdeveloped by centuries of unequal encounters and unequal exchange with Europe, with or without the collusion of local leaders reduced to facilitating the penetration and debasement of their own populations by external corporate and foreign interests (Rodney 2012 [1972]; Chinweizu 1975; Plumelle-Uribe 2001; Mentan 2010a&b, 2013; Branch & Mampilly 2015).

France's hunter-gatherer approach to its presence in Africa since first encounters, has been the subject of critical interrogations from the days of its displays of Sara Baartman "the Hottentot Venus" as a freak show or as a caged tigress (Crais & Pamela 2009) and El Negro – whose body was stolen by two French taxidermists from a grave beyond the Cape Colony frontier in 1830-31 (Parsons 2002), through its colonial excesses to postcolonial scandals involving corporations such as ELF Aquitaine (Beti 2010 [1972]; Agbohou 2000; Koulibaly 2005; Nubukpo 2011; Verschave 1998, 2005). According to world peace activist Mawuna Remarque Koutonin, 14 former French colonies in Africa continue to pay a colonial tax to France, apparently in recognition of the benefits French colonialism supposedly brought them.[3] It is the debt they owe for having had the privilege of being colonised by France – i.e. for having benefited from France's *mission civilisatrice*[4]. When in

1958 Sékou Touré of Guinea dared to opt out of the French colonial empire, preferring "freedom in poverty to opulence in slavery," he and his country were taught a lesson by the French who systematically destroyed infrastructure constructed under colonial rule, and who deliberately flooded the country with fake banknotes in order to undermine the new currency which Guinea had created to mark its aspirations for freedom in independence. Others who were not as courageous or as foolhardy as Sékou Touré of Guinea yielded to a mirage of independence that did not even pretend to disguise the continuation of French dominion in every sphere of postcolonial economic, cultural and political life. It was within this framework of the illusion of independence that the leaders of the 14 former colonies agreed to "to pay an annual debt to France for the so called benefits ... got from French colonization."[5]

France maintains a pervasive presence in these countries, through a variety of mechanisms, knowing, from the repeated articulations of its political leaders, the centrality of Africa to its leadership position in the world. To maintain a stronghold on its former colonies and their resources such as oil, gas, gold, uranium and wood, France remains ready to dispose of and impose leaders even by means of sponsored coup d'états. Bob Denard, a notorious French mercenary and professional coup maker, always enjoyed the tacit support of various French governments in the coup d'états he staged in Africa, while never claiming any official involvement. According to Koutonin, of a total of 67 coup d'états in 26 African countries in the past 50 years, 16 of those countries have been ex-colonies of France, amounting to 61 percent of all the coups in Africa. Other impositions include the fact that 14 Francophone African countries are obliged to put 85 percent of their foreign reserves into the French central bank under the control of the French Ministry of Finance; respect a cap imposed by France on the amount of money they may borrow from the reserves; guarantee France the right of first refusal on any raw or natural resource discovered in their countries; accord France the first right to buy their natural resources; give priority to French interests and companies in public procurement and public biding; consider French companies first in the award of government contracts; reserve for France exclusive right to supply military equipment and train their military officers, as well as the right to pre-deploy troops and intervene militarily in their countries to defend French citizens and interests; desist from entering into military alliances with any other country unless authorised by France; ally with France in situations of war or global crisis; make French the official language of their countries and the language of education; and use the French colonial currency – the CFA Franc, even when France itself has migrated to the Euro where it has negotiated a fixed exchange rate between the Euro and the CFA Franc. Koutonin concludes by affirming that "France is severely addicted to looting and exploitation of Africa since the time of slavery"[6] (see Beti 2010 [1972]; Agbohou 2000; Koulibaly 2005; Nubukpo 2011). It is no wonder that France and its neighbours have vociferously protested China's inroads into the continent.

France's long history of intervention and interference in its former colonies in Africa continues with the traffic in mutual influence between French politicians and multinational corporations on the one hand and on the other African heads of states who readily waste away African resources and wealth on the French power elite with callous disregard to the plight and predicament of ordinary Africans. This corruption was the subject of a 2014 documentary film by Patrick Benquet on the changing fortunes of President Charles de Gaule's policy initiative, "*La Françafrique*," its patron-client networks, entanglements, co-implications, complicities and reversible patterns of power and influence broadcast on Al Jazeera. Independence was not to be mistaken for freedom, as France left no one in doubt that it would go to any length to secure its interests through overt and covert networks of influence and by putting in power or ensuring the election of only those unequivocally subservient to French economic, cultural and political interests. Masterminds such as Jacques Foccart spearheaded the complicity and connivance between French and African leaders. The French political elite did not hesitate to put policy and self-interest before morality. The African dictatorships they propped up knew they could ignore accusations of collusion and complicity with France over resources for personal gain and employ violence with impunity against their poverty stricken compatriots to stay in power[7] (see also Verschave 1998, 2005).

If so many African leaders can "ignore their constitutions, cling to power, and get away with it,"[8] Helen Epstein argues, the West is often largely to blame. As she puts it, in order to understand such impunity:

> ... it's important to appreciate how much influence the West has over these countries – either through foreign aid given bilaterally, via institutions such as the World Bank, or in the form of clandestine military support. For example, Western aid pays for half of Burundi's budget, roughly 40 percent of Rwanda's, 50 percent of Ethiopia's and 30 percent of Uganda's. All these countries receive an unknown amount of military aid as well. This money enables African leaders to ignore the demands of their own people, and facilitates the financing of the patronage systems and security machinery that keeps them in power.[9]

This impunity can be traced back to the debt crisis in the 1970s, which resulted in structural adjustment programmes which Western countries initiated and coordinated through the World Bank and IMF. These austerity programmes demanded the devaluation of local currencies and large public spending cuts, resulting in huge layoffs, and deepened instead of alleviating poverty, corruption and indebtedness (George 1990; Gibbon & Olukoshi 1996; Olukoshi 1998; Peet 2003; Graeber 2011: 1-19). The tough conditionalities or strings attached to loans by the World Bank, IMF and related lenders, and the predicaments that ensue are astutely captured in *Life and Debt*, a documentary film produced in 2001 by Stephanie Black, on how structural adjustment programmes devastated the economy of Jamaica and reduced able-bodied, hardworking citizens to human rubbish, instead of bringing about growth and poverty reduction[10]. Almost everywhere such programmes have invariably worsened the very conditions they were designed to remedy, leading to them being described in many an African circle as a drug often more dangerous than the illness it is meant to cure.[11]

Today, Africans are watching with bemusement how the very same stringent measures are incurring the wrath of jobless and uncertain citizens across Europe – from Greece to Spain, Portugal, Italy, Ireland and beyond – as severe economic downturn threatens (Varoufakis, Halevi & Theocarakis 2011)[12]

Like an African head of state on a bed of nails in the 1980s being force-fed standardised and routinized austerity measures – or like the Greek "Odysseus … forced to choose between two routes for his ship: one that passed close to a sea monster (Scylla) and another that skirted a whirlpool (Charybdis)"[13] –, on 27 June 2015 Greece's Prime Minister Alexis Tsipras called a referendum on 5 July for voters to decide whether to accept a bailout deal offered by international creditors, after a television address in which he described the bailout plan as "humiliation" and the austerity measures as "unbearable"[14]. The snap call for a referendum was seen by C. J. Polychroniou as a political move by the government "to take the pressure off its shoulders, a refusal to accept responsibility for having dragged the country into five months of never ending negotiations with its lenders with disastrous consequences for the economy"[15]. Tsipras' request for an extension of the current bailout plan before it expired on 30 June to allow for the referendum was rejected by the Euro zone finance ministers, increasing the prospect of a default on the 1.7 billion dollar loan owed the IMF by Greece.[16]

When Greece effectively defaulted, it became the first advanced economy ever to go into arrears with the IMF. By

41

failing to make a due payment, Greece had put itself at par with African countries such as Zimbabwe, Sudan and Somalia. Used to compliance without resistance from miserable Third World debtors or dictators with begging bowls outstretched, "Europe's elites, who detest nothing more than to be reminded of the will of the people," must have been "outraged" by Tsipras' call for a sudden referendum.[17] They must have been even more outraged when Greek voters, angry and disillusioned after five years of austerity[18], overwhelmingly rejected the bailout offer by 61.3 percent of the vote, leading Prime Minister Tsipras to declare that democracy had conquered fear and blackmail, arguing that Greeks had made "a very brave choice" for a "Europe of solidarity and democracy." Hopeful that he now had the mandate from his citizens to negotiate a better deal with the creditors, he declared in a televised address: "As of tomorrow, Greece will go back to the negotiating table and our primary priority is to reinstate the financial stability of the country"[19]. In a comment in the *NewStatesman*, a day after the 'No' vote by the Greek electorate, Slavoj Žižek writes:

> Their [the Greeks'] No was a No to the eurocrats who prove daily that they are unable to drag Europe out of its inertia. It was a No to the continuation of business as usual; a desperate cry telling us all that things cannot go on the usual way. It was a decision for authentic political vision against the strange combination of cold technocracy and hot racist clichés about the lazy, free-spending Greeks. It was a rare victory of principles against egotist and ultimately self-destructive opportunism. The No that won was a Yes to full awareness of the crisis in Europe; a Yes to the need to enact a new beginning.[20]

It is uncertain the extent to which the results of the referendum would lead to a softer or more conciliatory approach by the creditors, some of whom have accused Tsipras of tearing down the bridges between Greece and Europe.[21] Indeed, if past experiences are anything to go by, claims of inextricable links, mutual dependence and a common humanity do not seem reason enough for compassion and more humane policies between creditor and debtor countries. Dogs bark, but the caravans move on. It is possible that little would change even with the resounding 'No' vote by the Greek electorate, as there is always the likelihood that Greece's debt providers and caretakers of debt would accuse the Greeks of "not feeling enough guilt ... of feeling innocent."[22]

Few would be surprised if the creditors resume business as usual, where the more compromises Greece makes from its subordinate position as a poor, weak debtor country, the more compromises its rich and powerful creditors would demand.[23] Already, it does not bode well that that the Greek Finance Minister Yanis Varoufakis had to resign, despite the government's decisive victory in the referendum, citing pressure from Eurozone leaders infuriated by his recent comments comparing Greece's creditors to terrorists. "I shall wear the creditors' loathing with pride," were his parting words[24]. Shortly after his resignation Yanis Varoufakis, in an article titled "Germany won't spare Greek pain – it has an interest in breaking us," declared:

> After the crisis of 2008/9, Europe didn't know how to respond. Should it prepare the ground for at least one expulsion (that is, Grexit) to strengthen discipline? Or move to a federation? So far it has done neither, its existentialist angst forever rising. Schäuble is convinced that as things stand, he needs a Grexit to clear the air, one way or another. Suddenly, a permanently unsustainable Greek public debt, without which the risk of Grexit would fade, has acquired a new usefulness for Schauble ... Based on months of negotiation, my conviction is that the German finance minister wants Greece to be pushed out of the single currency to put the fear of God into the French and have them accept his model of a disciplinarian eurozone.[25]

Nothing, especially democracy, must be allowed to stand in the way of the need to discipline and punish those guilty of perceived fiscal delinquency, so the screws must continue to turn deftly, predictably and routinely, with as little compunction as possible. What is needed are not an informed electorate capable of making choices in freedom, but rather self-regulating docile bodies that can be used, manipulated, subjected, and purportedly improved and transformed by the austerity measures dictated to governments that have failed the test of fiscal discipline (Foucault 1975, 1995).

Interestingly, Nobel Prize winning economist Joseph E. Stiglitz remarks,

> ... almost none of the huge amount of money loaned to Greece has actually gone there. It has gone to pay out private-sector creditors – including German and French banks. Greece has gotten but a pittance, but it has paid a high price to preserve these countries' banking systems. The IMF and the other "official" creditors do not need the money that is being demanded. Under a business-as-usual scenario, the money received would most likely just be lent out again to Greece.[26]

States and governments reduced to such ridiculous levels of dependency are weakened beyond the point of claiming to be relevant to their own citizens in any meaningful way. Called upon to preside over structural adjustment programmes that are almost guaranteed to fail from the outset, "turning downturns into recessions, recessions into depressions,"[27] such states and governments are virtually tasked with overseeing a programme of dying by design for their citizens. Even those with visions are hardly in a position to realise their visions, with their hands and feet literally shackled by the whims and caprice of foreign capitalist interests and their institutions of legitimation such as the World Bank and the IMF – institutions in which voting rights are in proportion to the size of one's economy (Peet 2003). "Given the weakness of African states (and by extension every borrowing state) in relation to the interests of rich nations, international financial institutions and multinationals, and their peripheral position in the global economy and politics, the only real authority or semblance of power that is affordable to African governments is that which is aimed towards their own populations, which are often too poor and too vulnerable to organise and mobilise effectively against exploitation and repression" (Nyamnjoh 2013a: 39-40). The West is thus able to effectively claim democracy, peace and prosperity by systematically outsourcing its poverty, violence and dictatorship to Africa and other purportedly underdeveloped (increasingly including within its own ranks – e.g. Greece) regions of an interconnected world.

Poor as they may be, it is not charity African migrants request from France or Europe, even as little of so-called foreign aid may trickle down to them (Hancock 1989). Nor do they seek what some have termed "imperialism in reverse: the revenge of the once-colonized" (Collier 2013: 11-12). They have enough sense of history to know that France and the rest of imperial Europe are in their debt (Graeber 2011: 307-360).[28] They loath the tendency in the media and among scholars to categorise them merely as poor and destitute Africans begging for sustenance from rich Europeans and behaving as if they have a divine right and entitlement to alms (Hollaway 2000; Sachs 2005; Chabal 2009; Lewis 2014). If not force-fed with justifications for their migration and predicaments, these Africans do not seek to prey on Europeans by portraying their poverty as "an injustice of the cosmic order" that deserves the attention of any individual or society in better circumstances (Simmel & Jacobson 1965: 119-120). It is recognition of their humanity and dignity that they seek through their insistence on reciprocity and obligation from those who have harvested their labour and resources abundantly in slavery and colonialism at different points in time (Rodney 2012[1972]; Plumelle-Uribe 2001; Bwemba-Bong 2005; Lovejoy 2011; Eltis 2000; Eltis & Richardson 2008). They seek and insist on recognition of the silences in African history and for the West to acknowledge, account and compensate for its excesses in Africa (Depelchin 2005, 2011; Diop 1991; Obenga 2004).

In seeking restitution through migration to the land of their former colonisers in Europe,[29] they are not dissimilar to African-Americans currently seeking the righting of past wrongs, especially in the form of reparations for slavery. In a recent interview Molefi Kete Asante, foremost proponent of Afrocentricity, captured this preoccupation thus: "I would like to see politicians open the discussion on reparations for 246 years of enslavement."[30] The recognition of African humanity and dignity means freedom from economic slavery and the payment of historical debts. By opting to send migrants to Europe to seek redress for histories of unequal encounters and unfair transactions and exchange between the West and the rest (Chinweizu 1975; Ferguson 2011), Africans are not unaware that other forms of redress exist. They simply know too well to seek to compound the celebration of coercive violence as the dominant form of influence which their Western debtors have tended to privilege (Nyamnjoh 2015).

Those with capitalist ambitions of dominance do not expect Africans to be mobile, especially beyond their continent, even as mobility is celebrated in principle and practice for others (Collier 2013: 11-26)[31]. When not savaged with envenomed razor-sharp territoriality, mobile Africans are often perceived by the nationals and citizens of the host countries at whose borders they clamour for inclusion as an invasive and predatory inconvenience. This was especially the case after the high-income societies of the West witnessed the largest increase in migration from poor countries from 1990-2000, an increase which coincided with deceleration in the growth of their high-income economies, thereby forcing them to respond by "retightening their immigration controls," even if what followed as migration policies were "based on neither an understanding of the process of migration and its effects nor a thought-through ethical position" (Collier 2013: 51-52). Since then, those who countenance African mobility do so *selectively*[32] (Bergson & Ngnemzué 2008; Foé 2008; Nyamnjoh 2013b; Collier 2013: 57-142), with Paul Collier citing "new and highly rigorous research" to suggest that "for many of the bottom billion," of whom Africans are a large part, "current emigration rates are likely to be excessive" (Collier 2013: 23), but "set to accelerate" for the foreseeable future (Collier 2013: 50).

African musicians in France – some of whom, like Papa Wemba[33] have been accused of using their position as musicians to smuggle hundreds of people from Africa who disappear upon arrival – have often composed songs to decry the arrest and deportation of fellow Africans. Petit Pays of Cameroon is said to have named his band *Petit Pays et Les Sans Visa* because he was once deported from France for not having a visa.[34] African immigrants in France and Africans seeking to emigrate to France would argue that it is not without their exploitation and dispossession under French colonialism and neo-colonialism that "between 1945 and 1975 French per capita income tripled," resulting in what the French nostalgically refer to as "'The Golden Thirty Years'" (Collier 2013: 28).

It is against this background of unequal encounters and the policing of African mobility, that Daou and Amélie journey to France and Germany, respectively. *C'est l'homme qui fait l'homme* starts with hardworking Daou who, although relatively successful by local standards, has decided to leave for France to seek greener pastures. He has invested in seven plots of land and a car, but his ambitions and aspirations are apparently much higher. He needs someone he can trust to take care of his affairs locally, while he is abroad making money to construct houses on the plots he has acquired. He chooses his cousin, Gohou, to look after his plots of land and to erect buildings on the land. Apart from being family, Gohou is not exactly an inspiring choice. It is difficult to comprehend why Daou would choose to entrust his land and a car to his cousin who is admittedly incapable of managing his own affairs. Perhaps Gohou is chosen because Daou has a small family[35], or perhaps because, despite the fact that he is lazy, sleeps right into the day, and lives in a tiny modest ramshackle one-room

47

cubicle of a house close to a nearby bush, Daou seems to trust him.

When Daou meets Gohou sleeping right into the day, this provokes the question: "Why are you this lazy?" Gohou looks shabby. Daou is unimpressed with how dirty and unattended everything around him seems. "This is inconceivable. ... and look at all that!" Daou points to the overgrown grass, adding: "Huh, look! You live with grass around! You cannot even take a machete to clear it." Gohou lacks initiative, as he keeps intending to cement his house, an insistence which makes Daou point out that "tidying up" must not wait until cementing has been done. Daou challenges Gohou: "But cousin, why don't you want anyone to come into your house? After all, it is your house! You have to tidy up." Gohou comes across as a man of excuses and prevarication. "Look at the planks over there," Daou draws his attention. "You should paint them or else the rain will rot them all." To which remark, Gohou seeks to reassure: "I know, I'm going to lay bricks."

Despite these signs, Daou asks Gohou to follow him all the same, so he can show him the plots of land he has bought at different locations in the city of Abidjan. Gohou promises: "The family's lands, they are my lands. So I'll take care of them, as if they were my own, my personal matter. Maurice is a fraud... He sold everything, but the money did not last long. He messed everything up." From this statement by Gohou it seems Daou has been disappointed by another family member before, Maurice. But one is perplexed why Daou should turn to Gohou, knowing how lazy and unambitious the latter is. This exchange between the two men concluded the presentation:

> Daou: You know that I am leaving tomorrow?
> Gohou: Yeah.
> Daou: And you know very well why I am leaving, right?
> Gohou: I know.
> Daou: You know we are not many in the family.
> Gohou: I know that.

48

Daou: You know that. If both of us were to stay together nothing would be accomplished.

Gohou: Oh, it's not good.

Daou: The plot that I've just shown you, it is the family's land. So, it is close to my heart.

Gohou: No, no! It is close to our hearts.

Daou: Yeah, our hearts.

Gohou: Yeah, our hearts.

Daou: You understand, right? If I leave, as soon as I start working, I'll send money for you to start building.[36]

Daou promises to leave Gohou with his car to "look for a buyer," saying: "If you find someone, sell it, and you will start to build on the Rivera plot." Daou promises as well to hand over the certificates of entitlement to the seven plots.

It is generally understood that those leaving Africa to seek greener pastures in Europe or elsewhere are often too single-mindedly committed to succeeding at all costs, and cannot afford to pick and choose what to do to earn money. Everything and anything goes, even if it means reducing oneself to an expendable and dispensable zombie at the beck and call of those who call the tunes in the business of getting by in Europe while staying relevant to Africa (Nyamnjoh 2005a, 2011; Newell 2005; Tazanu 2012; Nyamnjoh 2010, 2014). This understanding is widely shared. Thus, although not having been to Europe himself, Gohou gives Daou advice on how difficult life in Paris is, and the reason why Daou must not be picky once there. Interestingly, this is indicative of a level of authority that Gohou claims and assumes as opposed to being asked. "Whatever you find, you do. Even if you have to break down tar, break it," he tells Daou. This includes doing the most menial and degrading of jobs – things one would ordinarily not do, in order to safeguard one's dignity and integrity. Desperate situations call for desperate measures. "Even if you have to wash corpses for money, do it. You should not be afraid of the work to be done,"[37] Gohou indicates how low he expects Daou to go in hunting for money in Europe. Daou's preoccupations are here and now. He wants to be sure that he can count on Gohou. "I count on you," he tells Gohou who replies: "Yeah, yeah, okay. No problem. Count on me, Daou. No problem." Daou is tacit and unquestioning in his acceptance of the responsibility Gohou assumes.

Going to Europe to fend for oneself is not the monopoly of the African male. Women are just as involved as are their male counterparts – even as their hunting techniques may differ –, and equally preoccupied with delegating important matters in the hands of those they can trust, family or friends (Alpes 2011; Nyamnjoh 2014). In *C'est l'homme qui fait l'homme*, we should understand *l'homme* more appropriately as "person," in order to accommodate women leaning on other women to succeed, just as much as they lean on men and are leaned on by others. Thus, the arrangements and negotiations going on between Daou and his cousin, Gohou are paralleled by developments between two friends – Amélie and Nastou –, months later (perhaps two years even), following a chance encounter at La Gourmandine, a fast food restaurant that symbolises the ease with which Ivorians embrace the tastes of others and their taste for otherness (Newell 2012a).

Amélie is an Ivorian woman based in Hamburg, Germany, which she fondly calls home. She has returned briefly to Abidjan and met Nastou, an old friend. In the scene at La Gourmandine, Amélie is recounting her experiences in Europe, which she considers largely superior to Côte d'Ivoire, and is enjoying the way her friend marvels at everything she recounts about Europe. To Amélie, it is evident that going abroad to seek greener pastures is an investment in superiority and in development, vis-à-vis those she has left behind. She ridicules Nastou for being ignorant of the "civilised" things of Europe, and sees Côte d'Ivoire as lacking in development. Insistently Amélie makes the point that the situation in Europe is positively different from that in Africa. She tells Nastou, "You know, there, it's not like here huh! …. Not at all! There, there is the subway, there is the tram, there is the tunnel and

50

everything." The English Channel which links France and Britain is mentioned for Nastou to marvel at the idea and superior technology of being able to tame the sea with an underwater tunnel, so trains may run underground.

Visiting Europe is an important rite of passage in an African's quest for civilisation, Amélie believes, implying the broader assumption that success lies in western notions of the idea. Nastou absolutely must "come to Europe" to experience development, despite the inconvenience of winter when one cannot afford to dress as lightly as one dresses in Côte d'Ivoire. Indeed, winter is so harsh, cold and wet that one simply "cannot have fun at all in winter." She mimics the accent of a white French woman, an accent which in popular Ivorian French would be termed *chocobi* (meaning, to mimic or to want to pass for a white person).[38]

Although clearly of limited formal education just as her friend Nastou, Amélie displays the mannerisms of many an African immigrant who believe they have succeeded because they live and work in Europe, even if the jobs they do are unenviable and menial. Like Daou, Amélie is a symbol, if not of success, then of those who have managed to escape the challenges and hardships of life in Abidjan, especially among the young and unemployed. Amélie's addiction to Europe and its attractions are widely shared by youth in Abidjan, who aspire to European lifestyles through speech, dress, food, mannerisms and the latest and cutest technologies of communication and sociality such as fancy cars, cell phones, smartphones and iPads, internet, Facebook and other social media (Bahi 2010: 51-56; Newell 2009a, 2012b, 2013).

Amélie's expectations of modernity position Africa in the shadow of global forces and constantly needing to catch up with the depoliticised, ahistorical technicised development logic and practice of Europe and North America (Ferguson 1990, 1999, 2006). This feature and attitude is common among Africans who live abroad, who often come back on short trips looking down on their states of origin, the supposedly backward lifestyles and primitive thinking of locals, always complaining about how ridiculous their countries are, compared to the developed world.

It is a mark of civilisation, it seems, if those who return from France, England or the U.S. for example, have forgotten how to speak the indigenous and endogenous languages or have mastered the art of speaking a European language with the appropriate European accent. They have the latest gadgets and show off their foreign, purportedly modern clothing to their less mobile or less frontier-crossing compatriots. Dervla Murphy depicts the yearnings for things European by George Charles Akuro – a Hamburg-based migrant from Cameroon– in these terms:

> "Cameroon is *very* bad," insisted George. "All these bush people, they don't know how to live –they are backward stupid people! In Hamburg I have everything – big home, big car, deep freeze, fridge, cine-camera, television, stereo-system, swimming-pool for my kids. See! I show you!"
>
> He drew a thick wallet of photographs from his briefcase and the children crowded eagerly around to marvel yet again at his achievements. There was George, leaning nonchalantly on the roof of a Mercedes by the open driving door – and George removing a silver-foil-wrapped dish from a face-level microwave oven – and George posing by an open refrigerator taller than himself and packed with colourful goodies – and so on. There were dozens of photographs, all of a professionally high standard and looking remarkably like advertisements for the objects illustrated. [....] (Murphy 1989: 56).

Some African diasporans like Amélie and George would claim that they have forgotten how to be African, and express this often in a joking manner: "Oh, I have spent so much time away that I do not remember how to speak properly (followed with giggles)." But their "forgetfulness" is exaggerated as if to prove how much they have distanced themselves from the heart of darkness Africa is generally perceived to be by "civilised Others," or how "foreign" they are, as if to endorse a "tourist identity" in the country of their birth.[39] It seems a better identity to be a foreign tourist than a local.

With the West as the only standard of measure that seems to count, the only currency that matters to most of those who embrace its values, should it surprise Africans abroad that the money they send back home for development is never truly used as expected by kin and friends who aspire to the foreign lifestyle, without necessarily putting much effort to this aspiration, and expecting family members and friends abroad to help them instead (Nyamnjoh 2005a, 2011; Tazanu 2012; Newell 2005, 2012b, 2013; Nfon 2013; Nyamnjoh 2014; Nkwi 2015)? This begs other questions. Why, despite the problems of trust often encountered with relations and friends, do Africans abroad feel obligated to or continue to prioritise investments back home? What is it that keeps many diasporic Africans glued to their communities of origin, especially after the often turbulent and dangerous journeys some of them have had to make across inhumane geographies such as the Sahara, the deadening hostility of the Mediterranean Sea and the fortresses of Europe or the other islands of prosperity in the midst of global dispossession? Could they – for those who can afford to – not invest in the stock exchange of their host countries? Why are they so reluctant to outgrow their connections with Africa? Is it because, however successful they become abroad, they never truly feel at home? Could it be that the world of binary oppositions, hierarchies and the zero sum games of exclusionary logics of belonging make it impossible for Africans to ever truly feel at home away from their places of birth? Perhaps Africans have grown wary of zero sum games of belonging, and would rather seek to reconcile various geographies and identity margins, as a way of mitigating the delusions of grandeur that come with ambitions and claims of purity. Through this tendency to reconcile frontiers and identities, mobile Africans are able to reach out, encounter and explore ways of making themselves more efficacious in their relationships and sociality with the added potency brought their

53

way by others. By refusing to outgrow Africa even when they are able to, Africans who seek to make intimate strangers of myriad identities across multiple geographies suggest alternative and complementary modes of influence over and above the current predominant mode of coercive violence and control.

Notes

[1] See "The Longest Journey: Europe's Migration Crisis," www.bbc.co.uk/programmes/p02w8y7y, accessed 14 July 2015.

[2] See for example, "Italy rescues 3,300 migrants in Mediterranean in one day," www.bbc.com/news/world-europe-32940557, accessed 26 June 2015.

[3] See Mawuna Remarque Koutonin, Silicon Africa January 28th, 2014, "14 African Countries Forced by France to Pay Colonial Tax," www.ocnus.net/artman2/publish/Africa_8/14%20African%20Countries%20Forced%20by%20France%20t.shtml, accessed 4 July 2015.

[4] See Chinweizu 1975; Burrows 1986; Chafer 1992; Elias 2000; Ferguson 2011 for some of the purported benefits of the savagery of colonialism.

[5] See Mawuna Remarque Koutonin, Silicon Africa January 28th, 2014, "14 African Countries Forced by France to Pay Colonial Tax," www.ocnus.net/artman2/publish/Africa_8/14%20African%20Countries%20Forced%20by%20France%20t.shtml, accessed 4 July 2015.

[6] See Mawuna Remarque Koutonin, Silicon Africa January 28th, 2014, "14 African Countries Forced by France to Pay Colonial Tax," www.ocnus.net/artman2/publish/Africa_8/14%20African%20Countries%20Forced%20by%20France%20t.shtml, accessed 4 July 2015.

[7] See "The French African Connection," www.youtube.com/watch?v=uOambdQnCdw, accessed 06 July 2015.

[8] See also Helen Epstein's "Who's Afraid of African Democracy?," www.nybooks.com/blogs/nyrblog/2015/may/21/burundi-whos-afraid-african-democracy/, accessed 31 May 2015.

[9] See also Helen Epstein's "Who's Afraid of African Democracy?," www.nybooks.com/blogs/nyrblog/2015/may/21/burundi-whos-afraid-african-democracy/, accessed 31 May 2015.

[10] See www.youtube.com/watch?v=8WyIUIJjFmg and www.lifeanddebt.org/about.html, accessed 26 June 2015.

[11] See also Amartya Sen's general critique of such austerity measures, in "The Economic Consequences of Austerity,"

www.newstatesman.com/politics/2015/06/amartya-sen-economic-consequences-austerity, accessed 7 June 2015; and for a comparative angle, Peter Dolack's "The Destruction of Jamaica's Economy Through Austerity," https: //systemicdisorder.wordpress.com/, accessed 7 June 2015.

[12] For a report on desperate top level meetings between Greece and its international creditors to avoid Greece defaulting on its debts and its possible exit from the eurozone, see "Greece debt talks: Crisis deepens amid deadlock," www.bbc.com/news/world-europe-33265923, accessed 26 June 2015. In Spain, where privatisation is the order of the day in the midst of the crisis, 'Madrid's regional government and city administration are hawking their treasures and altering ordinances in order to make the Spanish capital more attractive to investors. The Spaniards are even selling the names of subway lines.' See report by Helene Zuber at www.spiegel.de/international/business/madrid-takes-dramatic-steps-to-curb-red-ink-in-crisis-a-911438.html, accessed 19 July 2013. See also "The Global Minotaur: The Crash of 2008 and the Euro-Zone Crisis in Historical Perspective," www.youtube.com/watch?v=iVxaTC7Qp44, accessed 26 June 2015.

[13] See Buttonwood, "Debt and democracy: Greeks caught between Scylla and Charybdis," www.economist.com/blogs/buttonwood/2015/06/debt-and-democracy, accessed 28 June 2015.

[14] "I call on you to decide - with sovereignty and dignity as Greek history demands - whether we should accept the extortionate ultimatum that calls for strict and humiliating austerity without end, and without the prospect of ever standing on our own two feet, socially and financially," he told his Greek compatriots on television, adding, "The people must decide free of any blackmail." See "Greece debt crisis: Tsipras announces bailout referendum," www.bbc.com/news/world-europe-33296839, accessed 27 June 2015.

[15] See C J Polychroniou, "Greek referendum is a Machiavellian plot," www.msn.com/en-za/news/featured/greek-referendum-is-a-machiavellian-plot/ar-AAceKx9?ocid=SKY2DHP, accessed 29 June 2015.

[16] See "Greek MPs back referendum on bailout," www.bbc.com/news/world-europe-33302526, accessed 28 June 2015. See also Nicolás Cachanosky, "Understanding the Greek Crisis," www.atlasnetwork.org/news/article/understanding-the-greek-crisis, accessed 06 July 2015.

[17] See Ian Martin, "There's method in Greece's madness – it could pay off," www.telegraph.co.uk/news/worldnews/europe/greece/11703745/Theres-method-in-Greeces-madness-it-could-pay-off.html, accessed 28 June 2015.

See also Joseph E. Stiglitz, "Europe's Attack on Greek Democracy," www.project-syndicate.org/commentary/greece-referendum-troika-eurozone-by-joseph-e--stiglitz-2015-06, accessed 30 June 2015.

[18] See a Bloomberg YouTube video by Jonathan Jarvis, "The European Debt Crisis Visualized," www.youtube.com/watch?v=C8xAXJx9WJ8, accessed 06 July 2015.

[19] See "Greece debt crisis: Greek voters reject bailout offer," www.bbc.com/news/world-europe-33403665, accessed 06 July 2015.

[20] See "Slavoj Žižek on Greece: This is a chance for Europe to awaken," www.newstatesman.com/politics/2015/07/Slavoj-Zizek-greece-chance-europe-awaken, accessed 08 July 2015.

[21] See "Greece debt crisis: Tsipras says voters made 'brave choice'," www.bbc.com/news/world-europe-33404881, accessed 06 July 2015.

[22] See "Slavoj Žižek on Greece: This is a chance for Europe to awaken," www.newstatesman.com/politics/2015/07/Slavoj-Zizek-greece-chance-europe-awaken, accessed 08 July 2015.

[23] See C J Polychroniou, "Greek referendum is a Machiavellian plot," www.msn.com/en-za/news/featured/greek-referendum-is-a-machiavellian-plot/ar-AAceKx9?ocid=SKY2DHP, accessed 29 June 2015.

[24] See www.theguardian.com/world/2015/jul/06/greek-finance-minister-yanis-varoufakis-resigns-despite-referendum-no-vote, accessed 08 July 2015.

[25] www.theguardian.com/commentisfree/2015/jul/10/germany-greek-pain-debt-relief-grexit, accessed 12 July 2015. See also the full transcript of his first interview since resigning as the Greek Finance Minister, www.newstatesman.com/world-affairs/2015/07/yanis-varoufakis-full-transcript-our-battle-save-greece, accessed 14 July 2015.

[26] Joseph E. Stiglitz, "Europe's Attack on Greek Democracy," www.project-syndicate.org/commentary/greece-referendum-troika-eurozone-by-joseph-e--stiglitz-2015-06, accessed 30 June 2015.

[27] See Joseph. E. Stiglitz, "Greece, the Sacrificial Lamb," www.nytimes.com/2015/07/26/opinion/greece-the-sacrificial-lamb.html?_r=0, accessed 27 July 2015.

[28] See also David Graeber, "The Birth of Capitalism" www.bbc.co.uk/programmes/b054qf7d, accessed 27 May 2015.

[29] See Manthia Diawara's film entitled "Whole Soyinka in Conversation with Senghor's Negritude"

[30] See Molefi Kete Asante: Why Afrocentricity? By George Yancy and Molefi Kete Asante opinionator.blogs.nytimes.com/tag/philosophers-on-race/?_r=0, accessed 26 May 2015.

[31] See also Mawuna Remarque Koutonin, "Why are white people expats when the rest of us are immigrants?," www.theguardian.com/global-

development-professionals-network/2015/mar/13/white-people-expats-immigrants-migration, accessed 29 July 2015.

32 See French President Nicolas Sarkozy's provocative speech in Dakar on July 26, 2007 for his idea of "immigration choisie" – "chosen and not endured immigration" – and the reactions it elicited from African and Africanist intellectuals, the first of which by Achille Mbembe can be accessed from the following link: www.ldh-toulon.net/spip.php?article2057 (accessed 20 April 2012).

33 See news.bbc.co.uk/2/hi/europe/3497837.stm, accessed 7 March 2014

34 See en.wikipedia.org/wiki/Petit-Pays, accessed 7 March 2014

35 Although this raises the question: Why would Daou's having a small family convince him to choose Gohou, knowing that he cannot manage his own affairs? Would not the fact that he is a family man make him search for a trustworthy family member? After all, he would not want to jeopardize his family.

36 [« Daou: Tu sais que c'est demain le départ!

Gohou: Ouais.

Daou: Et tu sais très bien aussi pourquoi je pars, n'est-ce pas?

Gohou: Je sais.

Daou: Tu sais que nous ne sommes pas nombreux dans la famille.

Gohou: Ca je sais.

Daou: Ça aussi tu sais. Si nous deux on devait rester ensemble ici-là, on ne pourra rien réaliser.

Gohou: Ouh, c'est pas bon.

Daou: Ce terrain que je viens de te présenter la, c'est le terrain de famille. Donc, ça me tient beaucoup à cœur.

Gohou: Non, non! Ça nous tient à cœur.

Daou: Ouais, ça nous tient à cœur.

Gohou: Ouais, ça nous tient à cœur.

Daou: Tu as compris, non? Si je pars, dès que je commence à travailler, je vais te faire venir de l'argent pour que tu commences à construire. »]

37 While the Ivorian singer Zouglou Espoir 2000 claims that Ivorians go to France to wash corpses because corpses back home are not good ["ils vont laver les cadavres en France, parce que ici (en Côte d'Ivoire) il n'y a pas de bons cadavres..."], it is clear from Gohou that washing corpses in Europe is much better paying than doing so in Côte d'Ivoire.

38 For a related discussion of the creative appropriation and usage of language in Abidjan, see Sasha Newell (2009).

39 For an example of such attitudes in popular culture, see Nkem Owoh's film "Osuofia in London"

4

Shared Intricacies and Entanglements

If a person is a person because of another, this emphasises human life as a network of interconnected and interdependent socialities in which agency is both an aspiration and a constantly negotiated or domesticated reality, for individuals and collectivities alike. If humans pride themselves with the capacity to harness nature, it is only appropriate to make human nature part of the bargain. How can greed as creed be left untamed when no one individual has a monopoly of greed? Mauss, to whom we referred earlier, is worth quoting here again, when he asserts that the brutish pursuit of individual interests is not only detrimental to the peace, rhythm of work and joys of all, but has the tendency to rebound on the individual in question (Mauss 1990[1950]: 77). It is through a simultaneous recognition of one's capacity to act on others as well as to bear the actions of others that the sort of conviviality implicit in *Ubuntu-ism* is made possible (Nyamnjoh 2015).

This is in tune with the Foucauldian recognition that – technologies of self-cultivation and self-activation notwithstanding (Foucault 1988: 16-49; Martin et al. 1988) – no one is self-built, that every single human being is the result of billions of actions of other human beings that have converged in producing a subject and shaping it while making it possible for him/her to take oneself as the object of his/her own actions (Foucault 1975, 1995), and thus, the self-managing, self-made individual of neoliberal and neo-Kantian Western thought is a complete delusion (Warnier 2013: 101-105). Subjects are not subjects in abstraction and do not act alone. Subjects act in accordance with their particular surrounding sets of circumstances and relationships that bind them. This is in tune with the following excerpt of a thank-you-email I received from Murray Stanford, a former postgraduate student of mine:

> The term 'self-made' is something which I believe is a myth. I believe our successes are based on those around us who supported us and believed in us. I would never be the man I am today without friends like you who treated me with kindness and believed in me. That is what a true educator should be, and sadly many professors (in my experience) lose sight of that, and are blinded by their own egos.

While *Ubuntu-ism* is as much a reality as it is an aspiration, an ideal or a discourse (van Binsbergen 2001, 2003), only the absolutely selfish, self-centred and dictatorial determined to tyrannize all else into compliance and passivity can make a creed of greed with total indifference to the prospects of the competing greed of equally capable others (Nyamnjoh 2002). It is often because one trusts that one will be given back to, that things one gives to others are going to circulate *ad infinitum*, that one is interested in giving to others. By giving, one is challenging others not only to accept one's gifts, but to prove their humanity and sociality by giving back and giving even more than they received (Mauss 1990[1950]). Trivers (1971: 35) suggests that several factors regulate a system of human reciprocal altruism: "friendship, dislike, moralistic aggression, gratitude, sympathy, trust, suspicion, trustworthiness, aspects of guilt, and some forms of dishonesty and hypocrisy."

With this idea of sociality as recognition of an individual's dynamism and inextricable entanglements and interconnections with others – shaping and acting on others as much as being shaped and acted on by others –, few would be surprised that in the course of their conversation, it surfaces that Nastou now has a new boyfriend, having dumped[1] the one Amélie knew before she left for Germany. Daou's Gohou is Nastou's new boyfriend. Much has changed in two years or less. Gohou has become an extremely well to do businessman – which, as we gather later, is only possible through defrauding unsuspecting and trusting others, including and especially relations and friends abroad in Europe such as Daou. "Sometimes he sells petrol; sometimes he works with people who make tar. And he also sells land,"[2] reveals Nastou. "At first it was a bit difficult, but now it's going well," she adds. On her cell phone, she asks Gohou to come over to La Gourmandine, his favourite place, and meet her friend, who lives in Europe. Gohou arrives soon after. Nastou introduces them.

Gohou is keen to know about Europe and Amélie is keen to show how well she knows Europe, and how much better than Africa Europe is. "My brother[3] lives there too," he tells her. "It's been two years since he left," he volunteers. Daou works in Europe as "a maintenance technician" ["*technicien de surface*"], he adds proudly. Amélie laughs this off, saying to work as a cleaner means Daou is not doing much in Europe; he offers himself for whatever jobs call for little or no skill or are too menial to catch the attention of bona fide citizens and documented migrants. Gohou is clearly taken in by the pompous title that Daou has fed him in an attempt to translate local Ivorian professional and occupation hierarchies into European ones. This is a common practice among Africans doing menial jobs to get by in Europe and North America, who cannot bring themselves to bear the shame of telling the truth of their lowly circumstance abroad.

Asked where in Europe his brother is, Gohou replies vaguely but confidently: "Where Didier Drogba[4] lives. Last time, they even had a photograph taken together and sent it to me"[5] This was at the time when Didier Drogba, the renowned Ivorian footballer and advocate of national reconciliation (Bahi & Dakouri 2009), was a Chelsea football club player and based in England, not France, as Gohou imagined. Amélie ridicules Gohou for thinking that Europe is one big village where everyone knows everyone else, just as Africans often do when uninformed Europeans speak of Africa as though it is a country. "Europe is a continent, like Africa," she lectures him. "And in Europe, there are countries such as those in Africa," she reiterates, but Gohou's attention has migrated to Amélie's cell phone. He is attracted by the cuteness of the size, and asks her what it is, then if he could touch it and feel it, and finally, if he could use it to make a call. Amélie obliges, reluctantly, alerting him to the fact that she is on roaming. He must therefore keep his call short, for she would not bear the cost of a long call. Gohou fumbles with the phone he cannot operate. Anxious he might damage a "very expensive phone," Amélie elects to show him how. The call Gohou makes reveals much about the *419*-like and *feymania*-like (Apter 1999; Benzon 2011; Malaquais 2001, 2002; Ndjio 2006, 2008, 2012)[6] – albeit small time and local level – businessman that he has become: "Hello? Valentin? This is Gohou... Your position? Ah you're already there? But you had to call me, yo! No, you should have called me! Huh? Okay, do not move, you stay there, I'll be there in two minutes. Ok? Okay, okay!"[7] "I'll leave you because I have to attend to business," he tells the woman, turning down the ice cream they have ordered him. Amélie's verdict: Gohou "is modern. I like him already." "Careful, this is my guy," Nastou warns.

Soon after Gohou's departure, the two women leave La Gourmandine, to do business. Amélie has brought along from Europe fancy cosmetic products and other trendy consumer items for sale from door to door, and office to office. Potential customers with whom she has taken prior appointments are waiting impatiently at various points in the city to sample and purchase her goods. Pacesetter Africans aspire to consume European products and Amélie and others who straddle Europe and Africa have found in such consumer desires and fantasy a lucrative niche worth their while. Indeed, the business is so successful that Amélie proposes to send, upon her return to Germany, more products for Nastou to sell for her. "Of course I can. It will be faster that way," replies Nastou, warming up to the prospect of being an agent for her friend.

As they go about the city doing their rounds, a magnificent building catches Amélie's attention. "Oh, it feels like I'm in

Hamburg. What a beautiful building! What an amazing architecture! Stunning! Ooh la la...!"[8] she exclaims. "Everyone who goes past this house falls under its spell,"[9] Nastou confirms. "We do not have money to build that kind of house, so we go past, we look at it only to rinse our eyes and that's it,"[10] she adds with a touch of envy. When Amélie would not relent with her "It's like being in Hamburg,"[11] Nastou retorts, "Ah in Hamburg. You thought that we would not have that kind of house here? There are houses prettier than this one."[12] At this point, Amélie confesses her interest in owning a house like this in Abidjan. She asks Nastou to find out whether the house is for rent or for sale. Nastou shows how familiar she is with the landscape and goings on of Abidjan by informing her friend that the house belongs to a young man who lives in Europe. The young man built the house so "When he comes back from Europe, that's where he stays,"[13] hailing the young man as an example of from-rags-to-riches and for his foresightedness. Europe, it seems, is clearly worth the risk of a perilous journey, if it translates into investments such as the magnificent house by the young man.

Nastou: Those that are overseas should do the same. They could build houses here so that when they come back, they have their own place to stay, instead of living with relatives, friends or in hotels.

Amélie: Oh yes, that's great. I'm telling you! Black people, huh! Black people are starting to have brilliant ideas. I still cannot believe it...oh la la. Oh, I'm so interested, I'm interested. You know, about what you just said... uh... I thought of it, but I know not to whom to entrust the management of my business, you know. And my brother, you know, he is difficult, huh! He has nothing, nothing, nothing in the head. This kid, as soon as I send money to our mother, he will steal it. And then, it's the girls, the nightclubs... well, no, no! I cannot entrust the management to him. Oh no, you see?

Nastou: Oh no, we are aware of this little fellow.

Amélie: Oh yes, this kid, he drains me, I promise you, he drains me. [....] Are you interested in helping me build a house here? Huh? You'll take care of it, you know?

Nastou: Girlfriend, you know, you know it's complicated, huh?

Amélie: What is complicated?

Nastou: I don't like anything that has to do with money. It scares me.[14]

Having succeeded in Hamburg, presumably (relatively speaking, of course), Amélie would like to lean on her friend to succeed in Abidjan as well. She does not trust her younger brother with money, as he has repeatedly wasted away in the company of young girls all the money she has sent him before. It is not clear what Nastou stands to gain in the arrangement envisaged, beyond the satisfaction of showing concern and compassion – Ubuntu – for a friend in need. Such deals are usually ambiguous, with the person in Europe counting either on the fact of the kinship or the friendship of the person they would like to rely on in Africa. This evokes a feeling of precarity that those who are "left behind" in Africa are required to deal with. The fact that the terms of such dealings are not always clearly established in terms of mutual benefits could account for the tensions that often characterise such arrangements. In the present case, tempting though the invitation is to combine the role of agent and caretaker for Amélie, Nastou resolves the only way she can help her friend is to assist her in purchasing a plot of land from Gohou her boyfriend, who sells land, and whose land is "guaranteed," coming "With all the papers and everything" that makes for a bona fide land deal. Gohou, she advertises, is unlike other land dealers who are known to sell the same piece of land to several buyers simultaneously.

Amélie takes her friend at her word: "Works for me, works for me... It's a deal...." Nastou promises to see Gohou on her behalf, and Amélie in turn indicates she will put Nastou in charge of any future building project on the land she finally procures. Again, it is not clear what the terms of her proposed arrangement would be, and how Nastou stands to benefit from coordinating and facilitating the erection of her Hamburg-style house. All Amélie tells Nastou is: "Ok! Oh thank you! You know, well, when this project takes shape, when it starts, I'll start sending you money, not a word to the family huh! You know that old witch, huh? I do not want them to eye my... you see what I mean?"[15]

Although Amélie hints at why she would rather entrust her money in a friend to the exclusion of close kin, one wonders whether it is enough to tell Nastou "I trust you." What is the price of that trust? Should not trust be valued and rewarded? Nastou is not drawn in. She remains reluctant to assume the role of Amélie's right-hand person, especially if it involves money, for she hates to have trouble with people over money. She strikes one as an honest person who knows the temptations of trust and money only too well. When she later shares this concern with Gohou, his response shows he is far less scrupulous, more ruthless, self-interested and selfish in his dealings with family, friends and acquaintances. To borrow from Nkem Owoh, he would not hesitate to *chop the dollar* of whoever crosses his path in the name of family, friendship or business ties. He tells her upfront: "You know, when it comes to money, you should not think for too long. No! What are you afraid of? You know that you can become rich, huh?"[16] Gohou promises to help show her "how to take care of the affairs of people who are far away,"[17] as there is a lot of money in it. "You never know where happiness comes from,"[18] he tells her. "It comes to your door and hits you like that, in the chest... BOOM! And you want to say no to it?"[19] Converted, however reluctantly, Nastou agrees: "You'll tell me how to do things, and then I'll do them for her."[20]

Unlike Nastou who appears to have a conscience initially and to want to give her friend a fair deal, Gohou the land seller, is no less dubious than others who sell the same piece of land to more than one buyer. He moves around with a tall, well-built, muscular bodyguard, whose appearance contrasts remarkably with Gohou's diminutive size and frail build. We meet him soon after trying to sell what he calls a "six hundred metres square" plot to a buyer, without papers and insisting on payment even before he has clearly demarcated the land to the satisfaction of the buyer.

> Buyer: I said, I want the land titles.
> Gohou: What land titles?
> Buyer: This plot! The title deeds for this plot!
> Gohou: You've never bought a plot?
> Buyer: No. This is the first time.
> Gohou: Ah, I can see that it is the first time. I am not new to this, huh! I am in my fifth sale.
> Buyer: For this plot?
> Gohou: What do you mean, 'this plot'? What does that mean? What are you trying to teach me? If it's land titles that you ask, we will not go far, huh!
> Buyer: No, no, no. What's the point of bickering over land titles? Okay, okay. I can trust you!
> Gohou: You're not the only buyer, huh!
> Buyer: Okay, good! Goodbye gentlemen.
> Gohou: Goodbye. So, call me, and then I'll give you the papers, huh! Good![21]

The buying and selling of urban and peri-urban land in Abidjan is not dissimilar to elsewhere in Africa, where the state has not always succeeded in standardising and institutionalising the processes and procedures that regulate access to land (Onoma 2009; Lentz 2013). In his study of commodification of peri-urban land in Blantyre, Malawi, Jimu (2012) questions and debates how and why peri-urban villages have become the locus of the selling and buying of customary land, the practices and also the relations involved. He provides rich ethnographic insights on the disputes and social relations between land sellers, land buyers, traditional leaders, and intermediaries. The transactions draw strength from the growing peri-urbanisation and monetisation of social relations, processes which affect land decisions at family and individual levels, steeped as they are in the broader globalised monetisation of relationships.

Given the prevalence of disputes and the tendency for sellers to sell to more than one person, the buyer in the above transaction has every reason to worry about buying a plot of land without the official title deed, as it is risky to build on land one does not own in a properly recognised manner. Gohou makes the buyer understand that he is an experienced hand at selling land, and that he is at his fifth sale of a building plot. If, as we recall from the beginning, Daou left him in charge of seven plots, Gohou has two plots left. But then, given that he has since become a businessman, perhaps he buys and sells land more regularly. On the other hand, could he be one of those who sell the same plot to several buyers simultaneously? Or who claim to own plots that they do not actually own? The buyer above is not alone in worrying about title deeds or sales certificates from Gohou. Amélie, Nastou's friend, has bought a plot from Gohou and is having a house constructed on the land on her behalf by Nastou. But she is yet to be given the sales certificate for the land by Gohou; without which papers it is always a possibility that Gohou might seek to sell the same piece of land to another buyer, or turn around to deny that he ever sold the land to the person claiming it. In the following telephone conversation in which Amélie is communicating the money transaction number for the funds she has sent through a mobile money transmission service, it surfaces that she is worried about not having the documents for the land she has acquired:

Nastou: [On the phone]: "My girlfriend, hmm, how are you? Yes, everything is fine here. Huh, alright. Ok, I will write the number down. Zero... 05, 07 hmm, 90, 08, 87, 13, 29. Okay. Question: Europe. Answer: Africa. Ah it's like the other times, right? Huh? No, for the papers, no, he will give them to me...I'm at his place right now. Once he is back, I'll go withdraw the money. No, I have already told him about the papers. He is only waiting for the money to give me the papers. [....] As soon as I withdraw the money, I'll call you. I will call you to tell you. Later."[22]

In the game of opportunity and opportunism, the mobile or cell phone is a great enabler (de Bruijn et al. 2009), and the accelerated mobility of money – "Money, Real Quick" – the order of the day (Omwansa & Sullivan 2012). Mobile money agencies have mushroomed across the continent, with harvesting diasporic remittances a lucrative line of business among others (Ake & Mbiti 2010; Etzo & Collender 2010; Demirgüç-Kunt & Klapper 2012). Relations between African migrants and their relations back home in Africa have been transformed remarkably through the instant availability and reachability that the cell phone affords (Archambault 2012; Tazanu 2012; Frei 2013; Nyamnjoh 2014; Obijiofor 2015). Prior to the cell phone, migrants had greater choice and control over the communication process with relatives and friends back home, but since the advent of the cell phone, the long arm of the home country and home village reaches out in ways and with demands that cannot always be ignored – often threatening migrants as they do, with tradition and custom ("*kontri fashion*") and the anger, disappointment and possibly "witchcraft" one risks when one fails in one's responsibilities and obligations vis-à-vis family and relationships (Geschiere & Nyamnjoh 1998; Nyamnjoh 2005a, 2011; Geschiere 2013). The necessity to remember and be reminded about those back home is brought to the fore in a way that has never been more palpable. The cell phone also allows migrants exploited by one another to communicate their grievances to the wider family and social networks left behind, in a bid to seek their intervention and obtain redress.

Gohou uses the cell phone to literally inundate Daou with impossible requests. He is constantly on the phone asking Daou to send over more money for the buildings he has been assigned to erect by the latter. One such phone call with Daou goes thus:

Hello? Hello? Yes. Hello, Daou? Yes, it's Gohou, here. Daou, you must send money now. No, send money. What are

68

you waiting for? No, you must be kidding, you are kidding. You must send the money now. No. The sand is finished, the cement is finished, there's no more...there's no more water... everything had to be stopped. Even the men have started complaining. You must send money. No, when you cannot finish things, do not start them! You do not start. We need the money to finish the job. ... But if there's no money how do we complete the job...if there's no money? Yes...okay! Okay. You find a way of sending the money tonight, tonight. Daou, I'm counting on you, I'm counting on you. Send money so that I finish the job here. Good. Okay. Thank you, goodbye.[23]

Communication is the reward but the inclusivity that it necessitates is the price.

As I have noted elsewhere (Nyamnjoh 2005a), it seldom crosses the minds of relatives and friends of migrants back home that those they seek to reach abroad might not have as much money or resources as they seem to suggest in how they relate to them. If they are not *beeping* or *flashing* [24] and calling to ask for money, they are requesting for other consumer items, including cuter and smarter phones.[25] Gohou uses similar tactics. If he is not complaining of poor reception on his cell phone because of poor network connections, he is asking Daou to call him back because airtime is too expensive, or to send him a better quality phone capable of better reception. "Call me back. Ah, that one! He'll finish my units" After his phone call to Daou, he turns to his bodyguard and curses: "What type of mobile is this? That's out of style. And then the bastards there, they think that we are ignorant, huh! But they are surprised when they come here and see how stylish I am, and how much we are ahead of them."[26] Many a migrant has expressed frustration and disappointment with how family and friends back home in Africa misappropriate or misuse the money and resources they send home for building and related projects (Nyamnjoh 2005a, 2011; Tazanu 2012; Nyamnjoh 2014).

Similarly, the money sent by Daou is seldom used for what it is meant. Gohou, who has become quite a big shot in town, his humble beginnings and poor formal education notwithstanding, wastes the money away in bars, nightclubs, casinos, café-theatres, and other entertainment outfits, often in the company of young women. In nightclubs, Gohou is to be found dancing in an exclusively reserved "private" area, often with several girls who are delighted to have him stick money into their bosoms, and in the company of expensive champagnes, wines and spirits, smoking expensive cigars, heavily jewelled and in expensive and trendy outfits. When he dances, he throws banknotes to people dancing alongside him or who show appreciation for his trendy dance styles. He regularly checks his cell phone for missed calls, and makes a point of displaying it with ostentation. He would open a bottle, applauded by those surrounding him with attention and adoration, and serve champagne to everyone, spilling as much as he retains[27]. Gohou's *joie de vivre* and predilection for ostentatious or conspicuous consumption (Veblen 1979[1899]) combines the attributes of the Cameroonian frequenter of *carrefour de la joie* (Ndjio 2005) and *bushfaller* on holiday (Nyamnjoh 2011)[28], as well as the Senegalese *thiof* (Nyamnjoh 2005b).

The nightclub and bar context and behaviour depicted in *C'est l'homme qui fait l'homme* resonate with Newell's observation on particular types of economic and sexual relationships in Abidjan, where men and women attempt to seduce each other through what he terms the *bluff*, and exploit the relationship for material gain (Newell 2009b). As an embodiment of social parasitism, Gohou is a charmingly opportunistic, unscrupulous, cunning and selfish anti-hero or trickster who seems all too familiar in his extravagant and thoughtless existence made possible by the sweat and toil of intimate and distant others. Gohou strikes one as a wasted man afflicted by wastefulness who delights in wasting away others and their hard-earned resources. In this regard, he is not dissimilar to the *bluffeurs*,

70

who, according to Newell, are young urban men in Côte d'Ivoire whose reputation and pride nationally are measured by familiarity with and access to fashionable and expensive clothing, accessories, technology, and a robust nightlife, and who express their cultural mastery over modern (and often so-called "Western") taste by indulging in wasteful expenditure as a means of accumulation. To the *bluffeurs,* appearing modern is so important for success that they are ready to deplete their already meagre resources to project an illusion of wealth in a fantastic display of mimicry of mass mediated consumerism (Newell 2009a&b, 2012b, 2013). This consumer culture of young Ivorian men is a common trend throughout the continent (Gott & Loughran 2010). In Congo Brazzaville, for example, it is known as *La Sape* and practised by *Les Sapeurs* (Gandoulou 1989; Friedman 1994: 120-134; Gondola 2010; Picarelli 2015). The Nigerian film industry – Nollywood – proliferates with films depicting such lifestyles, where films such as "Glamour Girls" indicate that the craving for prestige through ostentatious consumption is not a male preserve (Krings & Okome 2013; Ugor 2013).

In his study of entrepreneurialism among Bamileke of the Cameroon grassfields, Jean-Pierre Warnier depicts how people such as Gohou afflicted by wastefulness and the incapacity to accumulate or what he terms *Atchul* and *Balok* tend to contaminate those they encounter with their affliction (Warnier 1993b: 139-158). There is a great sense of humour in Gohou's unscrupulous wastefulness however, even though it is not necessarily to be condoned. The indication of his laziness and all-day sleeping pattern gives a clue to his sense of reality. One can assume that he is a man whose sense of reality is completely altered by the illusions of European ideas of being but without a desire to take personal responsibility for his life. However, what makes his story enjoyable is the humorously conniving ways in which he demands and commands this and that from Daou. It is easy to sympathize with his deplorable ways because of the humour around his story.

In Gohou's wasteful consumption of money intended for Daou's building projects, one incident stands out. We meet Gohou at a café-theatre playing competitive pool despite his startling mediocrity at the game. To worsen his mediocre performance, he insists on drinking champagne as he plays. Little wonder he loses every single game dismally, just as he loses the huge amount of money he places as bet. While his fellow contestants in the game of pool decline his offer of champagne with "party later, play the game first," Gohou laughs them off with "I start the party before anyone else does." The game does not end until Gohou has gambled away the very last bank note on him. He regrets too late: "Oh, today is not a good day for me! Oh la la la la la la, I should not have, I should not have...."[29] Comforted by champagne, Gohou is philosophical in defeat:

> [To the winners] Well, I lost today... I lost today too. But anyway, it's not money that interests me. It's the entertainment that interests me, the pleasure one gets from it. That's what interests me; not the money. Money...I have money. If I don't have enough, I just need to snap a finger and more money comes through, huh. Money... You know, huh, in life, when you have money, you must, you must live. Otherwise, when you die, it is other people who benefit.[30]

It is hardly surprising that soon after gambling away all his money playing pool, we meet Gohou at the parking lot of the café-theatre, desperately trying to contact Daou – his zombie toiling away selflessly abroad (see Nyamnjoh 2005a, 2011 for related examples) – on his mobile phone to send him more money. And as usual, claiming to be too poor to make a normal phone call, Gohou flashes or beeps Daou with the words: "Hello Daou? Daou? This is Gohou, call me, call me!"[31] As he waits for Daou to call him back, Gohou turns to his bodyguard and insults Daou in these words:

That bastard! You are fine over there, and you think that here... that here, what do you think it is like here? It's been raining out here huh... so it was raining? Wait, you think the kids in there...they think that this is what money is. That's nothing! That, that, that... is not money![32]

This shows how little regard Gohou has for Daou, as well as the fickle nature of his attitude towards his cousin. He treats Daou more like a milk cow or a wallet on legs than as flesh and blood. Again, this is not uncommon, if one takes into account the various ethnographic studies on the predicament of the migrant, who feels exploited abroad and at home, by strangers and by kin alike. Gohou's bodyguard, who follows him everywhere, reacts to his insults of his cousin with absolute silence. Instead, he continues to follow Gohou devotedly, as the latter paces about in the parking lot. At one point Gohou complains: "Oh stop following me like that! What is this? What are these manners? You're not my shadow!"[33]

Daou calls back dutifully and Gohou screams instructions into his cell phone. This is interesting because of the power dynamics that are at play. Realistically, Gohou does not hold the power – Daou has the monetary, social and geographical advantage. But Gohou is able to manipulate the situation in such a skilful way that he plays on Daou's emotions by bringing up his past and the importance of collectivity:

Hello Daou? Is that you? …. Send me money because the items are finished. Daou, do not mess with me! Daou, don't joke around. I said the supplies are over. So if money is not sent soon, suppliers will strike. Once the strike starts here, it's over! I will not be able to do anything. But it is not only one plot that we are building on Daou! Send me the money! Send me the money! Daou, do not forget your past, do not forget your past. Remember that *it takes one man to make another*. That's it! *Man makes man*. Daou! That's it. Send me the money tonight, huh! I'm waiting on the money to complete the job, did you understand? Daou what is that mobile phone that you sent me? Huh? This is an outdated phone! Here, people no longer use that! Here, we are advanced when it comes to technology! Well, send me

73

another phone. Huh? I want the latest phone, the latest phone! Yeah, dual screen, colour screen, with camera, camera... everything, huh, digital sound, with a Bluetooth system. Send this to me! It is important to me. Okay, okay, okay! I'll speak with you tomorrow... Daou. Daou, I'm counting on you. Man makes man. Do not forget your past. That's it. Okay... I... thank you very much [added emphasis].[34]

It is perplexing that Gohou should use the aphorism *It takes one man to make another* or *Man makes man*, to persuade Daou to remit resources for the construction of a house that is not Gohou's. There is no equivalent reciprocity in the relationship. While this aphorism is normally used to express collectivity in the Ubuntu sense of communitarianism, it can also be abused or capitalised upon to show how in a fast changing economy, relationships of interdependence are stressed more than they are practiced, as people exploit one another in order to get rich. Little wonder that proverbs exist – such as the Shona (of Zimbabwe) proverb that says: "*Kashiri kununa kudya kamwe*" which literally means "one bird becomes fatter by feeding from the fellow bird or one can never be rich without exploiting others" – that encourage greed as creed.

Notes

---

[1] [« J'ai cassé son cou, » « Je l'ai zappé, » « je l'ai laissé tomber »]

[2] [«Des fois il vend du pétrole, des fois il travaille avec les gens qui font le goudron. Et puis, il vend aussi des terrains »]

[3] Gohou uses "brother" and "cousin" interchangeably. He is probably from a region of Côte d'Ivoire where the concept of brother outweighs that of cousin, and accusations and counter accusations of witchcraft are used as a mechanism to encourage collective or inclusive success within extended families, as we discover later when Daou meets his elder kin to complain about Gohou's misuse of his money and investments.

[4] Apparently, Drogba's mother, Clotilde Drogba, has, like the mother of all Ivorian football fans, cooked and served "chicken and fish with rice, plantains and spicy sauces to fans, while her Chelsea star son eats at the

hotel with the other players," successively at the 2006 World Cup in Germany and also at the 2012 African Nations Cup in Equatorial Guinea, see: www.bbc.co.uk/news/world-africa-16799368, accessed 14 March 2014

[5] [« Où Drogba Didier habite. La dernière fois même, ils ont fait photo avec et m'ont fait venir ça »].

[6] See also www.dibussi.com/2010/02/donatien-kouagne.html/, accessed 7 March 2014

[7] [« Allo? Valentin? C'est Gohou...Ta position? Ah t'es déjà sur le terrain? Mais fallait m'appeler yo! Non, fallait m'appeler! Ein? D'accord, ne bouge pas, tu restes là, j'arrive dans deux minutes. Ok? D'accord, ok! »].

[8] [« Oh, on se croirait à Hambourg. Mais quelle belle bâtisse! Quelle architecture! Pharamineuse. Ouh là la...! »]

[9] [« Cette maison-là, tous ceux qui passent la tombent sous son charme »]

[10] [« Nous on n'a pas l'argent pour construire aussi, donc, on passe, on regarde pour se rincer les yeux et puis c'est tout. »]

[11] [« On se croirait à Hambourg »]

[12] [« Ah à Hambourg. Vous pensez que nous on n'a pas les bonnes choses ici aussi quoi! Y'a des maisons plus jolies que ça aussi »]

[13] [« Maintenant, quand il vient ici-là, il habite dedans »]

[14] Nastou: Les parents qui sont là-bas là, ils devaient faire des choses comme ça ein! Ils devaient construire des maisons ici, comme ça, quand ils viennent, ils habitent dedans, au lieu de rester chez des parents, chez des amis ou à l'hôtel.

Amélie: Oh oui, mais c'est génial. Mais j'te dis pas ein! Les Blacks, ein! Les Blacks commencent à avoir des idées géniales. C'est pas vrai ca...oh là là. Oh beh, ça m'intéresse ça, ça m'intéresse. Tu sais, c'que tu viens de dire...euh...j'y pense mais je sais pas à qui confier la gestion de mes affaires, tu vois. Beh le frangin, lui, tu sais, lui, il est très moche ein! Il n'a rien, rien, rien de la tête. Ce petit, dès que j'envoie des sous à la vieille, il te le pique. Et puis, c'est les nanas, les boites de nuit...ah beh non! A celui-là, j'peux pas confier la gestion. Ah non, tu comprends?

Nastou: Ah non, on est au courant de ce petit-là.

Amélie: Ah beh, ce petit, non il me fatigue, je t'assure, il me fatigue, et dans le crane. [....] Est-ce que ça t'intéresse pas que je t'apporte de l'argent pour que je puisse construire une telle bâtisse ici? Ein? Tu vas t'en occuper, tu sais?

Nastou: Ma copine, tu sais la, tu sais que c'est complique, ein?

Amélie: Complique en quoi?

Nastou: Moi, tout ce qui est affaire d'argent-là, je n'aime pas...j'ai trop peur de ça.

[15] [« Ok! Oh merci beaucoup! Tu sais, bon, quand ce projet va prendre forme, quand ça va commencer, que je vais commencer à t'envoyer des

75

sous, pas un traitre mot a la famille ein! Tu connais ce vieux sorcier d'ici, ein? Je veux pas qu'ils aient l'œil sur mon...tu voies ce que je veux dire? »]

16 [« Tu sais, quand il s'agit d'argent, on ne réfléchit pas longtemps. Non! T'as peur de quoi? Tu sais pas que tu peux devenir quelqu'un d'argent [de riche] ein? »].

17 [« Comment on s'occupe des affaires des gens qui sont loin comme ça là. »]

18 [« Tu sais, on sait jamais d'où vient son bonheur. »]

19 [« Ça vient te frapper à la porte comme ça, en pleine poitrine...BOUM! Et puis tu veux refuser? »].

20 [« Toi tu vas m'expliquer, et puis moi, je vais faire ça pour elle. »]

21 [« Acheteur: Ouais. Je veux les titres fonciers.

Gohou: Pardon?

Acheteur: Je dis, je veux les titres fonciers.

Gohou: Quels titres fonciers?

Acheteur: Ce lot! Les titres fonciers de ce lot!

Gohou: Tu n'as jamais acheté un terrain?

Acheteur: Non. C'est la première fois.

Gohou: Ah, ça se voit que c'est la première fois. Je suis pas nouveau dans ce domaine, ein! Je suis, je suis à ma cinquième vente.

Acheteur: De ce lot?

Gohou: Comment ça, de ce lot? Ça veut dire quoi ça? Vous voulez m'apprendre quoi? Si c'est titres fonciers que tu demandes, on va pas aller loin ein!

Acheteur: Non, non, non. Ça sert à quoi de se chamailler dessus? Ça va, ça va. Je peux te faire confiance pour ça!

Gohou: Tu n'es pas le seul client, ein!

Acheteur: D'accord, bon! Au revoir messieurs.

Gohou: Au revoir. Donc, tu m'appelles, et puis je te donne les papiers ein! Voilà!"]

22 Nastou: (au téléphone): « Ma copine, hmm, ça va? Oui ça va ici. Ein, ou d'accord. Ok, je vais prendre le numéro. Zéro...05, hmm 07, 90, 08, 87, 13, 29. D'accord. Question: Europe. Réponse, Afrique. Ah c'est comme les autres fois, quoi! Ein? Non, pour les papiers, non, il va me donner la, là je suis chez lui comme ça. Dès qu'il arrive, je m'en vais retirer. Non, je lui ai déjà parlé des papiers. Il attend l'argent seulement pour me les remettre, quoi. [....] Tout à l'heure, dès que je retire, je t'appelle. Je vais t'appeler pour te dire. A plus. »

23 [« Daou, Daou, Daou. Allo. Allo? Oui. Allo, Daou? Oui, c'est Gohou, voilà. Daou, voilà, mais envoie l'argent là, maintenant. Non, mais envoie l'argent. Tu attends quoi pour...? Non, tu déconnes, tu déconnes. Mais fais venir l'argent la maintenant. Non. Le sable est fini, le ciment est fini, bon bon, y'a plus de, y'a plus d'eau...tout est calle. Même les hommes

se plaignent a tort et à travers, n'importe comment. Mais fais venir l'argent. Non, mais quand on peut pas faire des choses, on commence pas! On commence pas. Mais il faut l'argent pour terminer le travail. …. Mais si y'a pas l'argent comment on peut terminer si y'a pas l'argent? Oui mais…d'accord! D'accord. Tu fais venir l'argent, ce soir, ce soir même. Daou, je compte sur toi, je compte sur toi. Fais venir l'argent, je finis les travaux là. Vila, voilà. Ok d'accord. Merci, au revoir. »]

24 To beep or flash someone's cell phone is to make a call without letting them answer, as an indication that you would appreciate if the person calls back. This practice is common among those who do not have enough prepaid airtime to make a call.

25 Honorine Express, a US-based Cameroonian bushfaller, renowned for her critical YouTube video postings castigating opportunistic relationships among bushfallers and between bushfallers and their family relations and friends back in Cameroon, provides excellent illustrations of these tendencies in two of her postings: "Demanding and ungrateful family members," www.youtube.com/watch?v=OJ3wZ97Ab0w and "Feel free to go home," www.youtube.com/watch?v=cBK-yqs9ETI, both accessed 07 August 2015.

26 [« C'est quel portable ça? Ça, c'est démodé. Et puis, ces salauds là, ils pensent que nous on est Gaou ici, ein! Mais ils sont surpris quand ils arrivent et ils voient comment j'suis stylé là, nous on est devant eux. Ceux-là ils sont battus. »]

27 This corresponds to the Coupé Décalé mode started by the singer Douk Saga, whom incidentally, Gohou imitates in his dressing and also in the practice of splashing banknotes, popularly known as "travaillement" [workingness] (see Newell 2006, 2009a&b, 2012, 2013).

28 Honorine Express, a US-based Cameroonian bushfaller, is renowned for her critical YouTube video postings castigating opportunistic relationships among bushfallers and between bushfallers and their family relations and friends back in Cameroon. Her postings include: "Demanding and ungrateful family members," www.youtube.com/watch?v=OJ3wZ97Ab0w; "Bushfaller flew," www.youtube.com/watch?v=hB7H6q_tIzQ; "Feel free to go home," www.youtube.com/watch?v=cBK-yqs9ETI – all accessed 07 August 2015.

29 [« Oh là là, je suis pas dans mon grand jour aujourd'hui ein! Alors la…Ah la la la la la la…fallait pas, fallait pas… »].

30 [(Aux vainqueurs) « Bon, j'ai perdu aujourd'hui…C'est perdu aujourd'hui encore. Mais de toutes les façons, moi, ce n'est pas, ce n'est pas l'argent qui m'intéresse. C'est le loisir qui m'intéresse, le plaisir qu'on a dedans. C'est ça qui m'intéresse, ce n'est pas l'argent. Sinon l'argent, j'ai déjà l'argent. Si j'en manque, il suffit de claquer le petit doigt et ça tombe ein?

L'argent…Vous savez, ein, dans la vie, quand on a l'argent, il faut, faut vivre, sinon, le jour où tu meurs, c'est d'autres personnes qui en profitent. »]

³¹ [« Allo Daou? Daou? C'est Gohou, rappelle-moi, rappelle-moi! »].

³² [«Ce salaud la! Vous êtes tranquille là-bas, et vous pensez que…ici-là, c'est, c'est quoi…Il a plu dehors ici ein…donc il pleuvait la…Attends, tu penses, les enfants-là, ils pensent que c'est l'argent-là, je joue comme ça. Ça c'est rien! Ca, ca…ca ce n'est pas l'argent ça! »].

³³ [« Oh arrête de me suivre comme ça! C'est quoi ça? Quelles sont ces manières la? Tu n'es pas mon ombre la!»]

³⁴ [« Allo Daou? C'est toi? …. Fais-moi venir l'argent parce que les éléments sont finis. Daou, faut pas déconner! Daou, ne décorne pas. J'ai dit les nécessaires sont fini. Et donc, si l'argent ne vient pas maintenant, bientôt, les commerçants seront en grève illimitée. Une fois la grève commence ici, c'est fini! Je pourrai plus rien. Mais c'est pas seul chantier Daou! Fais-moi venir l'argent! Fais-moi venir l'argent! Daou, n'oublie pas ton passé, n'oublie pas ton passé. Mets-toi dans l'idée que c'est l'homme qui fait l'homme. C'est ça! C'est l'homme qui fait l'homme. Daou! Donc, voilà. Fais-moi venir l'argent ce soir ein! J'attends l'argent pour faire le travail, tu as compris non? Mais Daou, c'est quel portable tu m'as fait venir comme ça la? Ein? C'est un portable dépassé! Ici même les gens n'utilisent plus ça! Ici-là, nous, on est en avance ein! Bon, fais-moi venir un autre portable. Ein? Je veux un portable dernier cri, dernier cri! Ouais, double écran, écran couleur, avec appareil photo, camera ein… tout ça, son digital, avec un système Bluetooth. Voilà, fais-moi venir ça! C'est important pour moi. …. Donc, a demain Daou. Daou, je compte sur toi. C'est l'homme qui fait l'homme. N'oublie pas ton passe. Voilà. D'accord… je… merci beaucoup. »]

5

Ubuntu-ism and the Seesaw of Opportunity and Opportunism

When are claims of *Ubuntu-ism* an opportunity for collective success and social inclusivity, and when are they a mere ploy for opportunism? An individual toiling away in a distant land might be a victim of various claims by family, friends and acquaintances who are not themselves ready to reciprocate when s/he or others come knocking with claims and demands of their own (Nyamnjoh 2005a, 2011). How then does one differentiate opportunity from opportunism? When should relationship claims be taken seriously, and when should they be ignored?

To the Nigerian, Nkem Owoh, one should be beware of those who come claiming relationships only when one's circumstances have improved. In his song "Know me when I'm Poor,"[1] he argues that poverty is a good litmus test for genuine relationships. A friend, brother or sister in need is one indeed. It is when a person is poor that he knows those who clearly care about him, thus his appeal for family, friends or acquaintances to relate to him as a human being and with humanness when he is poor, and not to wait until he is rich to come claiming that they are related to him. The chorus of his song is worth quoting:

> Know me when I'm poor not when I am rich
> You claim relationship (claim relationship)
> Know me when I'm poor not when I am rich
> You claim relationship (claim relationship)
> My father is your aunty's brother (claim relationship)
> My great-grandfather senior your mother (claim relationship)
> We come from the same village together (claim relationship)
> That time I no go remember eh (claim relationship)

The song speaks to Daou, Gohou and their relationships in profound ways. As cousins, Daou and Gohou obviously knew each other prior to the former's departure to France, but the land and car left behind by Daou and the money he regularly remits to Gohou towards his projects in Abidjan have brought the two closer in ways that might not have been possible otherwise. The opportunity created by Gohou's relationship with Daou has in turn resulted in opportunism on the part of Gohou, of which he may or may not be aware. Daou's land, car and money propel Gohou to dream and live a life of sterile consumption that would otherwise not have been possible. The attention and company his extravagant and playboy lifestyle in turn attract is going to last only for as long as he pretends to be rich, or misappropriates Daou's money to prop up his ostentatious pretentions. Thus, when things fall apart and his schemes and ploys are uncovered, those who used to flog around him vanish, making Nkem Owoh's song ring through for him as well.

One could very well imagine Gohou, destitute, meeting one of his girlfriends with her new boyfriend, using the following words from Nkem Owoh's "Know Me When I am Poor,"[2] to address the new boyfriend in question:

> You think you have [a] sweet thing. Accept my sympathy because you are the next victim. That she has this symmetry is because of my money. See me I eat and grow tiny. This person is a store. Look! She will drain you and finish you and then go. She is taking you to the cleaners. By the time they ... dry clean you there will be no moisture left in you. You are in a haste to go to hell! That is hell oh with you! That's the specimen of hell!

If Gohou's girlfriends end up like hell to him, Gohou is clearly hell to Daou. It is not clear why he should insistently ask for money from Daou to build a house, not for himself, but for Daou. He seems more committed to Daou's cause than Daou himself, a state of affairs that should normally raise suspicion. Is Gohou so selfless that he seems more concerned about

Daou's future than Daou is himself? So why does Daou continue to send the money when Gohou's phone calls are so blatantly phoney and he, Gohou, so obviously commandeering vis-à-vis land? Not only is Gohou overly enthusiastic about being of service, his attitude on the phone is bullish and disrespectful of Daou.

Nastou may have been initially honest and respectful vis-à-vis Amélie and her hard earned money, but Gohou has converted her to his callous indifference and unscrupulous ways. Indeed, she shows she can learn fast and in some respects, she proves a more astute player of Gohou's game of opportunism when presented with an opportunity. The next time we meet Nastou, she is at a building site, inspecting the house she is building with the money Amélie sends. What immediately strikes one is how much she has learnt from Gohou in terms of ruthlessness and dishonesty. She is inspecting the house as if it was her own, and she is not pleased with what the builders have done in her absence. They have made a mess of many things: "Look at all that. Pipes...lying around everywhere; the pipe is broken, the water is just flowing. This month, it is they who will pay for water..."[3] She is consumed by her monologue when her phone rings, Amélie at the other end of the line:

Who's calling me again? Hello? Ah it's good that you are calling. I was waiting for you! What does that mean? Huh? You must send money. I am here, waiting. And then you are sitting there. What is this? You know what? Never start something when you are not ready for it! You are putting me in uneasy situations. I do not even know how to do it. You know what? It is not easy? But wait, it's not easy? What does that mean? What I'm trying to do...am I doing it for myself? This is for you, huh! I am doing it for you! For our friendship! You cannot tell me "no, it's not easy," because I'm doing it all for you! Do you think I have nothing else to do here? No, no, no, no! No, I am not getting angry! Darling, I am not getting angry. But it is your behaviour...I do not like it! You are making me wait like that, unnecessarily. Ah? You sent it? You too... you should have told

81

me! You, you... you put me on edge like that. Yes, no, no, no, that's not it. That's not it. That's because I have been waiting for a while. Ok hmm, it's the 05, 06, 77, 98, 09, 19. Question: Euro. Answer: CFA. Hmm, CFA, I wrote it. It's as usual, huh? Yes! Ok, here I am at the construction site right now. Yes. Hmm hmm....[4]

Much later, when the current mess with the building will have been corrected, Nastou would, thanks to the money freshly remitted by Amélie, go shopping for equipment for the new house. She buys from a shop that sells only the most expensive things imported from Europe to the most elitist of consumers in Abidjan. Nastou buys the cutest bathtub, sink, toilet pots, and floor tiles. She is too choosy and overly personal in her taste to be shopping with her friend in Hamburg in mind. Not once in the exchange with the shop attendant does Nastou mention Amélie or contemplate whether or not the latter would like what she has bought for the house. This demonstrates an unadulterated desire to conform to a standard that she deems to be relevant in her context.

Those abroad who invest in land and building projects back home, trusting as they may be, do require a second measure of proof to reassure them that their money is being well spent, and not diverted into other projects or misused by the likes of Gohou and Nastou. The latter, equally, invest their efforts at keeping one step ahead of their kin and friends abroad. They know that photographic evidence is good evidence, and familiar as they are with the landscape of the city and what building projects are ongoing where, Gohou and his likes are able to take glossy coloured photos of buildings under construction that resemble the projects of which they are in charge, which they then send to relatives and friends abroad as evidence of progress on their own specific projects. In this way the gullible migrants can continue to make funds available for those in charge of projects at home to continue misappropriating or diverting onto other ends. Thus, it is hardly surprising that the next time we encounter Gohou, he is desperately inventing photographic proof for Daou, who has obviously sent home enough money to begin to feel entitled to evidence that something is actually going on. Gohou invites a photographer to a building site that is obviously not his own, for he has no building going on, to invent the evidence Daou needs. To Gohou, it is important that Daou does not turn off the tap of remittances flowing in, given the flashy lifestyle he has become used to. All must be done to reassure and contain Daou.

In his characteristic abrasive manner, Gohou calls to reassure Daou that the photos are on their way, and with that proof should come more money:

> Hello? Daou? Daou? Yeah, that's Gohou! Well, now, Daou... uh, you know, you must send more money! No, send me more money. I'm working. I'm working. Your building is finished. Yes! No, no. Anyway, I'll send the photos. When you see the pictures, you will know what kind of a huge job I did for you here. That's it. But no, well...the money to send you the photos...I will sacrifice my money to send you the pictures! Let it go, let it go. No, you have to send some more money because I've found a gardener for the flowers around the building, and then the flowers in it... anyway, it will be fabulous. Fabulous. Fabulous. Here! But Daou, Daou! You will have to increase the amount of money you send because we need to build a wall. We need a wall, because... when people go past....the building is so beautiful... they do not stop screaming "Wooo... wooo... ooooouuu." That will attract the attention of the witches on you. Oh, I don't want the witches to eat you. Well, that's it. So I am sending you the pictures tomorrow, huh? Ok, but you must be quick, you have to hurry to send the money, huh? Ok, thank you.[5]

To argue for inclusivity, domesticated agency, conviviality or *Ubuntu-ism* and the opportunities it affords individuals and collectivities does not imply the absence of opportunism and conflict in societies that subscribe to such aspirations. Indeed, opportunism and conflict are the products of inclusivity. It is thus an invitation to embrace the challenge that no humanity is complete if it entails wasting away the humanity of others, however justifiable that might be in the short term.

Notes

[1] www.youtube.com/watch?v=z0JGB0PV0mE, accessed 9 March 2014

[2] In "Susanna" another of his songs, Nkem Owoh deals with a similar theme, when a destitute businessman tells his girlfriend who has moved on, "Money go love go [….] Money go woman go." Indeed, this is a widespread theme among musicians the continent over – for another example, see Cameroon's Tchaya Stoppeur in "Money Di Finish."

[3] [« Qu'est-ce qu'ils m'ont fait comme ça? Ein? Ma chambre est si pale…quand c'est moi à cote…ou je vais déposer la coiffeuse? Il ne le faut pas! Ou je vais déposer mes maquillages? Et même le salon, le deuxième salon…agrandissez-moi un peu ce deuxième salon! Mais vraiment! Oh, c'est là où je dois recevoir mes visiteurs de marque. Ça aussi, ils ne le font pas. Regarde-moi tout ça la! Je fais du travail, je fais du travail…en deux jours seulement d'absence, ils foutent tout en l'air derrière toi! Ils vont m'entendre! Si c'est chez moi ils ont trouvé travail-là, ils vont m'entendre. »]

[4] [« Qui m'appelle encore? Allo? Ah voilà, ah beh ça tombe bien! Je t'attendais! Mais qu'est-ce que ça veut dire? Ein? Tu dois faire venir l'argent. Depuis je suis-là, je t'attends. Et puis, tu es assise là-bas. C'est quoi ça? Tu sais quoi? Quand on est pas prêt là, on ne commence pas! Là tu me mets dans des situations-là. Je sais même pas comment m'y prendre. Tu sais quoi? C'est pas facile? Mais attends, c'est pas facile? La ça veut dire quoi? Ce que je suis en train de faire la, est-ce que c'est pour moi-même? C'est pour toi ein! Je le fais pour toi! Pour notre amitié! Tu peux pas venir me dire « non, c'est pas facile," parce que je suis en train de faire tout ça pour toi! Tu crois que je n'ai rien d'autre à faire ici? Non, non, non, non! Non, je m'énerve pas! Chérie, je ne m'énerve pas. Mais c'est par ton comportement. Je n'aime pas ça! Tu me fais attendre comme ça, inutilement. Ah? Tu as envoyé? Toi aussi…fallait me dire ça! Tu, tu…tu me mets sur les nerfs comme ça. Oui, non, non, non, c'est pas ça. C'est pas ça. C'est parce que…y'a longtemps je t'attends. Ok. Hmm hmm, c'est le 05, 06, 77, 98, 09, 19. Question: Euro. Réponse: CFA. Hmm hmm, CFA, J'ai écrit. Ok. C'est comme d'habitude ein? Oui! Ok, là la même je suis sur le chantier comme ça. Oui. Hmm hmm…. »]

⁵ [« Allo? Daou? Daou? Ouais, c'est Gohou! Bon, voilà, Daou…euh, tu sais, faut que tu fasses venir l'argent encore! Non, fais-moi venir l'argent. Moi je suis en train de travailler. Je suis en train de travailler. Ton bâtiment, il est fini. Oui! Non, non. De toutes les façons, je vais te faire venir les photos. Quand tu vas voir les photos, tu sauras que j'ai abattu un travail énorme pour toi ici. Voilà. Mais non, bon. L'argent pour faire venir les photos. Moi-même je vais sacrifier mon argent pour te faire venir les photos! Laisse, laisse. Mais non, il faut faire venir un peu plus d'argent parce que j'ai déjà vu un jardinier pour les fleurs autour, et puis les fleurs dedans…en tout cas, ça sera fabuleux. Fabuleux Fabuleux. Voilà! Mais Daou, Daou! Il va falloir que tu augmentes l'argent parce que…parce qu'il faut un mur. Il faut un mur, parce que…quand les gens passent comme ça la, le bâtiment est tellement beau…quand les gens ils passent comme ça, ils n'arrêtent pas de crier. « Wooo ou…wooo…oooouuu ». Ça, ça va attirer l'attention des sorciers sur toi. Oh moi, je veux pas que les sorciers te bouffent. Voilà, c'est ça. Donc, demain je te fais venir les photos, ein? Ok. Mais faut faire vite, faut faire vite pour l'argent, ein? Ok. Merci. »]

6

The Zombies Are Back at their Risk and Peril

As I have argued in relation to Cameroon, migrants abroad can be compared to zombies in a form of witchcraft – *nyongo* – which privileges zombification of its victims over instant gratification through instant and total death. Regardless of nomenclature, throughout Cameroon the distinctive feature of this type of witchcraft is that its witches are less keen on making an instant meal than a short-, medium- or long-term investment by transforming their victims into zombies who are then made to slave for them on invisible plantations, invisible supermarkets and other avenues of accumulation serviced by devalued and largely undocumented labour. In such witchcraft, the emphasis is less on blood dripping violence or death as on keeping one's victims alive and taxing them hard.

In other forms of witchcraft that privilege instant gratification, victims are more like sheep, denied the possibility of old age by the violent appetites of others. Like sheep they own themselves and their lives only in principle, and seem to exist only to be violated and eaten by others. In *nyongo* the option to postpone instant gratification is a risky one of course, because the zombie could turn out to be a bad investment by provoking inquisitions that claim the lives of those who plant them in *nyongo*, and/or by being stubborn and unpredictable.

One is accused of *nyongo* when he or she is believed to have appropriated or attempted appropriating the life essence of another person, resulting in a mysterious temporary death. Those capable of *nyongo* are claimed to benefit from the afflicted by harnessing the abilities to slave for them as zombies after the presumed death. Cameroonian migrants abroad sometimes consider themselves as victims of *nyongo* by family and friends back home in Cameroon (Nyamnjoh 2001, 2005a, 2011; see also Geschiere 2013: 1-68).

In our present case, Daou and Amélie may well liken themselves to zombies in similar fashion, forced by duplicitous family and friends back in Côte d'Ivoire, such as Gohou and Nastou, to slave away and remit hard earned money towards imaginary projects. Zombies are usually zombified by their temporary death forever, and are neither in a position to return to the world of the living on a permanent basis, or to seek justice through speaking out, as their tongues are often severed (Ardener 1996 [1970]; Geschiere 1997: 139–168). But given that migrants abroad are only like zombies, they sometimes complain and even return occasionally, only to be met with disappointment and shattered dreams. To the likes of Gohou and Nastou, zombies return at their own peril.

The surprise call from Daou caught Gohou completely off guard, although it came in the presence of his bodyguard. Gohou was dancing at his favourite nightclub in his favourite company of beautiful girls, responding to the whim and caprice of his ever generous wallet, when Daou called to say that he was heading back home with immediate effect:

> What? You are coming back? You're coming back, huh? But why, why are you coming back? Already? Wait, when did you leave?[1]

To be utterly without a conscience might be an aspiration for many attracted by opportunism as a way of life, but few actually succeed in killing their conscience or at least muffling it. Even Gohou did not succeed in doing so. Later that night, in bed with Nastou, Gohou has a nightmare that makes him cry out in his sleep: "Thief thief thief, thief, thief, thief,"[2] forcing Nastou to wake him up. In the morning, Nastou demands to know why he was crying out "thief, thief" in his sleep. But Gohou is not in a mood to share, and asks Nastou to forget it, for it was just a nightmare. Just then, his phone rings. He asks Nastou to answer in his place, saying: "Take it. It's, it's, it's Daou. I'm not here! I'm not even here. Answer!"[3] Nastou answers the phone and speaks to Daou, while Gohou tells her in whispers what to say. He tries to lie to Daou through Nastou, but not having agreed on what lie to tell a priori, they contradict each other, leaving Daou in no doubt by the end of the call that things are amiss:

> Nastou: Hello? Yes? Daou. How are you? Yes, I'm well! Ah, Gohou? Uh... yes huh. Go, he's travelling huh! He lost his uncle, huh!
> Gohou: NO NO! Which uncle?
> Nastou: Well, he left a week ago.
> Gohou: No! No, yesterday! Yesterday!
> Nastou: Oh no, I forgot! He left two days ago.
> Gohou: No! Yesterday, yesterday, yesterday, yesterday!
> Nastou: He left two days ago.
> Gohou: YESTERDAY!
> Nastou: (turns to Gohou) What is it now?
> Gohou: Well, I left last night... last night...
> Nastou: Hello Daou? Yes! Hmm hmm... Oh, you spoke to him? Oh okay. It's true. He left yesterday.
> Gohou: Night, night...
> Nastou: He left last night...
> Gohou: Night, night... Ooooh!
> Nastou: You say you've spoken to him? Ah?[4]

When Daou makes Nastou understand that he spoke to Gohou on the phone the day before, their attempt to lie falls apart. "When he comes back, I will tell him that you called," Nastou tells Daou. But to Gohou's shock, Daou announces he is returning home from France, and coming straight from the airport to see Gohou. The latter tries in vain through Nastou to dissuade Daou from coming. To him, any lie would do, as long as it keeps Daou from coming back home.

> Nastou: Yes, we will pick you up from the airport.
> [....]
> Gohou: Oh, no! You should have told him I was not there.

Nastou: Goodbye, Daou. See you soon.
Gohou: Soon, where? Why are you doing that?
(Nastou hangs up the phone and turns to Gohou)
Nastou: What is up with you? Hey! Your phone!
[....]
Gohou: Oh, you're spoiled. Couldn't you tell him that the country is at war?
Nastou: What war?
Nastou: But why don't you want him to come back?
Gohou: The nightmare... the nightmare...
Nastou: What nightmare?
Gohou: Last night's nightmare... it was him...
Nastou: Look, your nightmare stories, family, witches... huh! I'm not into any of it, huh! Don't give me the phone again when he calls.[5]

If Daou is giving Gohou nightmares by contemplating a return to Abidjan soon, Nastou's nightmare is already a reality. Amélie has returned to Abidjan, and is busy tracking down Nastou. She visits La Gourmandine, where they met when she was last in town, to look for Nastou. She is told by the cashier her friend has made a big jump up the social ladder: She lives in the millionaires' district; she built a beautiful house there. It's the Rivera.[6]

Off Amélie goes to look for Nastou in the millionaires' district. When she finally arrives and introduces herself where Nastou lives, the guard asks her to wait, and goes to inform Nastou of her arrival. The guard returns and lets her in through the gigantic gate. "Oh! It's beautiful, it's beautiful! Oh, my friend! She has good taste. That's why we are friends, huh! Oh well thank you Mister," she tells the guard, who asks her to sit down and wait.[7] Nastou arrives, condescendingly, and her cold reception of Amélie snaps the latter's enthusiasm, replacing it with perplexity. Here is an excerpt of the encounter:

Amélie: Oh dear... oh it's beautiful. As you are beautiful... Oh dear. How are you?
Nastou: Hello.

Amélie: It's... it is just like... you are covered in gold... darling! Oh. You look fantastic! Oh you're like a princess. Oh! All your jewels...gold. Tell me, have you won the lottery?
Nastou: Well, why the lotto?
Amélie: Well, because of all this? It is an absolute palace. You have very good taste! You never told me!
Nastou: Listen, huh, everyone has their little secret.
Amélie: (laughs) It's unbelievable. Did you find a man with money?
Nastou: Well, why would you think that it's always up to the man to make the woman? Huh? We women, we can also make ourselves huh! [8]

This is significant, an assertion of independence by Nastou. If the tradition has been that a woman is a woman because of a man, it is also possible, and indeed to be encouraged, for a woman to be a woman because of a woman – such as Amélie – or simply because of herself as a woman, which is what Nastou is claiming in this encounter. Noticing that her friend was about to go out, Amélie asks to go along to see the house Nastou has constructed on the plot of land she supposedly acquired with the money she has been remitting:

Amélie: Ok. What if we took the opportunity to visit my house?
Nastou: The house?
Amélie: Yes, my house! The one...
Nastou: Ah! You want to show me your house?
Amélie: Ah ha... oh dear, there are only us here, we are friends. Stop being so formal!
Nastou: Uh, I don't know what you mean.
Amélie: Ha back to earth. Huh? My home? I've sent you money, remember...so that you build my house? Ok?
Nastou: Listen lady, I am neither an architect nor builder or a contractor. So this story about building a house...I do not understand it at all.
Amélie: Wait, I am not understanding it either. I don't understand. I don't understand. Did I not send you money?
Nastou: I do not know what you mean.
Amélie: But it's not possible... Listen...
Nastou: I do not know...[9]

Unable to believe what she is hearing, Amélie needs to remind herself that her eyes are not deceiving her as well. She asks if she is indeed standing face to face with Nastou:

> Nastou: Yes, I am Nastou.
> Amélie: Oh, so I'm not mistaken... I am asking you where my house is. Ok? Do you get it?
> Nastou: Your house?
> Amélie: Yes, my house...
> Nastou: No, actually, I do not get it; I do not understand.
> Amélie: [....]You must not joke like that. Give me my house, or give me back my money. That's what I'm asking, huh!
> Nastou: This house is mine. But hey, your house must be around...it must surely be somewhere. I don't know...
> Amélie: What are you saying? ... So you are telling me that the money I gave you to build the house, my own home, you took it to build your own house? Ah, no, no, no, no, no. Things won't end like that!
> Nastou: You are telling lies.
> Cold-bloodedly, as if she has never seen or had any dealings with Amélie before, Nastou, outdoing Gohou in her callous indifference as the scammer that she has become, orders her houseboy to kick Amélie out of her house:
> Nastou (to Greg): Madam is not feeling well, she must be accompanied to the door.
> Amélie: You know what? No, no, no, no. Things won't end that way! Nastou, will you give me my money, yes or no? Do you hear me?
> Greg: If you do not leave, I will be obliged to use force to get you out.
> [....]
> Amélie: ... Listen, let go of me, let go, let go... FRAUD! IT IS NOW UP TO THE POLICE OR JUSTICE TO JUDGE! ....
> Fraud! Oh let go of me! Let go of me! This is unreal! You are nothing but a bunch of crooks...frauds![10]

This accusation brings up questions of possession – who owns what, who is owned and how socially acceptable it is to claim ownership. Greg pulls Amélie out of Nastou's house. He closes the gate on Amélie. Nastou, still indignant, sighs: "There are all kinds of people in this world... that come bother us."[11]

The phone rings and we know that not only has she firmly embraced Gohou's unscrupulous way of life and line of business, she seems set to beat him at the game of fraudulently enriching herself off the toil and sweat of her friends in Europe. This is how the phone call goes:

> Hello, yes? Christelle, darling? How are you? Ok? So listen, your house, is almost finished! Yes, and you know that it is the end that is the most expensive huh! So you're going to send lots of money. Hmm hmm... yes. We need to finish it for you as fast as possible, huh! You know mine, uh... I finished it really quickly. Yes. Huh tomorrow? Send me money tomorrow. Ok. So I'll be expecting the money tomorrow. Anyway, you have been very kind and fair thus far. Ok. Kiss my darling. See you soon, I kiss you.[12]

The next to surface is Daou. In his characteristic modesty, he rents a car upon arrival from the airport, opting for a small car at a lesser fee than the bigger one with a more powerful engine proposed by the car hire service. He is on a short visit to find his cousin, Gohou, before returning to Europe, so he hires the car for one week. Gohou is so popular that even the car hire saleswoman knows him. She tells him, "...you can find him in the underground parties... the nightclubs of Abidjan... everybody knows him. It's not even a problem." Daou drives straight to Gohou's old and dilapidated house-cabin, thinking Gohou still lives there. The new occupant of the place has never heard of Gohou, who probably abandoned the place as soon as Daou left for France, making him in charge of his land and car. Daou goes off, in pursuit of Gohou who is at a nightclub, enjoying himself as always. Daou arrives at the construction site, where the building under construction is a pale image of the photographs he was fed by Gohou. Daou is infuriated: "This is not what he showed me in the photographs! Damn, what's going on? Look at that! What is this? On top of it, I've looked everywhere and I still cannot find him."[13] Daou drives off again, stopping here and there, now and again to talk to friends and acquaintances, in the hope that some might know where Gohou is.

When he finally meets his relatives, he lays his complaint against Gohou, hoping for their support in his quest for justice. "He tells them: Did you see what Gohou did to me? Did you see what he did to me? He completely screwed up my life. I went through all of our land. And everything is lost. I've seen bad things, but not like that. And it's very serious. Some people have shown me acquisition papers. It proves that he sold everything. But this one, if I catch him, I catch him; I'll send him to prison."[14] However, their reaction is not what he expected. Both relations, elderly men, attempt to dissuade him by evoking the witchcraft accusations that his violent retaliation against a close family member is likely to provoke.[15] One of these relatives says: "Do you have the courage to send your cousin to prison? Well, we are here; we see everything and know everything. And you know, Gohou, he is unscrupulous. Honestly, he is problematic. You see, when the money was coming through, it was about the nightlife, nightclubs, with the girls, it worked on everyone."[16] And when Daou asks him: "But why did you not call me? Why?"[17] The relative answers: "It's Gohou who knows the paperwork. He is the one who had the paperwork, and he managed it. That's it."[18] Here the relative demonstrates that they could do nothing as Daou himself chose to disrespect collectivity by leaving everything in the hands of only one relative, Gohou. The second relative reminds Daou: "You know Daou, Gohou is your first cousin, and you know that very well. Even if he has committed a serious offense, you cannot send him to prison. You're going to dishonour the family."[19] The insinuation that he could be guilty of dishonouring the family stuns Daou. "Dishonour the family?" he asks, in total disbelief. "I had to work hard for the money that he wasted,"[20] he reminds the two family members. "And you are asking me not to react? Ok, I'll dishonour the family, right? But if I catch him, I kill him and then kill myself. It's easy."[21] The two men try in vain to dissuade him from such an extreme reaction, and when they fail in their attempt, they give up, saying: "When he sent the money, did we know about it? Oh what is happening is his problem!"[22] It would appear, if Sasha Newell's study of thieves in Abidjan is anything to go by, that even theft is ruled by relationships of exchange and obligation and social relationships are prioritized over financial gain (Newell 2006).

The above interpretation of Ubuntu and its emphasis on sociality, conviviality and interdependence does not seem to have adequate answers for the opportunism of some to the detriment of others within its framework (van Binsbergen 2003: 450-454; McAllister 2009: 7-8). Such opportunism falls within factors such as anger, resentment, lust for revenge and success through aggressive competitiveness, which Tutu (1999: 35) considers corrosive of Ubuntu as "the greatest good." As active and creative beings, Ivoirians are not defined and confined by the real and imagined traditions of Ubuntu, nor are they bound down by the diktats of modernity and its often abstracted index of freedoms. They negotiate and navigate the possibilities and tensions of tradition and modernity in ways that do not reproduce either as unchanging or in accordance with the winner-takes-all logic of zero sum games.

Daou finally catches up with Gohou, who is still partying with the girls, showering them with banknotes. Daou recognised his old car. He stops and sees Gohou through the windows of the club where he is enjoying himself. Gohou is surprised and stops dancing. "Take a step and I'll yell that you are a thief," Daou warns. Gohou tries to run but his own bodyguard stops him. Daou approaches and asks Gohou: "Where were you going to?" "Pissing," says Gohou, timidly. Daou does not believe him:

> Daou: Really? Did I not call you before coming back?
> Gohou: There was a network problem.
> Daou: There was a network problem... I asked for you and was told that you had sold all the plots.

Gohou: Who said that?

Daou: But what did you do with the money?

Gohou: Daou, do not forget your past, huh! Daou, I'm your cousin!

Daou: No, Gohou, you disappointed me.

Gohou: The money you have sent me was used to build the house. Have you not seen the photos?

Daou: What did you build? I went to the construction site. What I saw has nothing to do with the photos you sent me.

Gohou: Daou! I swear in the name of God, huh! Those who say that I have stolen your money are bastards!

Daou: We'll go to the construction and you'll show me what you have accomplished.

Gohou: We can go huh, we can go.

Daou: Let's go.

Gohou: You'll see for yourself!

[....]

Daou: Well, let's go.

Gohou: Your money, your money...

Daou: You think, you think I went for a stroll in Europe to get money?

Gohou: No, I'll, I'll, I'll explain... no, I'm going to...

Daou: We are taking that car. We are taking my car. Go on... (He forces Gohou into the red car)

Gohou: Daou gently, gently.

Daou: A bastard like that...[23]

Gohou has been caught in his lies. They arrive at the purported construction site. Daou hustles Gohou out of the car, and challenges him to show him the house:

Daou: You go through here. And you will show me the house.

Gohou: Well slowly, Daou, gently. Gently and... this not the house?

Daou: This is not the house that I saw in the photographs!

Gohou: But that's because the house was not finished! This is because the house was not completed. Now that is finished, the house looks different. It looks different. It is the same house.

Daou: And from what I know about water... we never had water in this area.

96

Gohou: Do not try to find out where the water is coming from. Are you looking for a house or for a plot of land? And Daou, this, this is the house that you saw in the photograph. The house was not completed. But here, it is almost finished. Daou, do not forget your past.

Daou: Oh no, Gohou, never say that word again. Do you understand? Do not ever say this word again. Do you remember your past? When I left, is that how you were dressed?

Gohou: No, but… It takes a man to make another in life.

Daou: It is I, Daou, who'll do that? What is wrong with you? Nonsense!

Gohou: Go look inside the house, go. You'll be surprised.

Daou: Okay. I will visit the house... What does that mean?[24]

Daou approaches the house, as Gohou escapes. It does not take him long to discover that Gohou has devastated him completely. He has been thoroughly dispossessed. The owner of the house chases him away, with the chilling words: "Listen sir, I am the owner. I have work to do, and if you have nothing to do, go elsewhere…" Daou turns around to face Gohou, but the latter has taken to his heels. "It's unbelievable!" Daou exclaims. *L'homme ne fait pas l'homme; l'homme fait lui-même*[25] was all that went through his mind, knowing how much he had slaved away in sweat and toil at home and abroad to qualify as a *self-made man*, barely leaning, most reluctantly, on others. If such devotedly monumental efforts at moulding the self could come crashing like a pack of cards, what did this say about often uncontextualised and unproblematised claims that it was possible to be self-made and autonomous as a social being?

There are countless examples of similar stories across Africa. This was evident from the reactions I got from sharing earlier drafts of this book with colleagues and contacts in various countries of the continent. In South Africa where rural to urban migration is very high and rural-urban interconnections resilient and active, stories such as the following account by Cape Town based Noxolo Nozuko abound:

Generally, and as a remitting person to the rural Eastern Cape, I can identify with the entire argument in the book. My own daily life is shaped by this logic of *Ubuntu-ism* and the opportunism that comes with it. Since I moved to Cape Town to pursue my education while working, when I can, I always lived with an understanding of the "collective success" or "material inclusivity" as I succeed in life as an African life philosophy. However, in my case, unlike other family members, my family knows where I draw the boundaries. They are aware and understand that I give as I can, and beyond that, they have to make their own plans to make do. I do not feel guilty for limiting my strength of Ubuntu towards my family because I usually state I do not owe them but I am giving out of good will and love. However, it would have been tricky if I had a child at home. I would have been tricked into giving to an extent I would not otherwise give.

But for some of my family members who are also remitting from big cities, and whose children are left with relatives at home, their sense of guilt overrides the logic of Ubuntu and its limits. For example, one of my distant aunts used to take advantage of her younger sister when she was working in Jo'burg. Her sister left two children with her, after she separated from her husband, and went to Jo'burg to work. The guardian aunt used to telephone her and lie about one of the children being sick when she wanted money from her before month end. This one time, she lied and said one of the boys was in the hospital from a car accident. In hearing the news, the mother took a bus and returned to the village without saying she was coming back home. When she arrived, to my older aunt's shock, the children were playing outside with no injuries. In her self-defence, my aunt claimed she wanted her to send the money she needed immediately instead of waiting for the usual month end remittance. However, that was the last time her young sister ever took her seriously for anything. All of us in the family we hardly take her seriously when she calls and tells us about bad news at home. We have to confirm with other family members, at home, before taking her news as truth. And she has become a subject of family gossip and laughter when we call each other and when we return home.

We have become used to her agitating us with "serious" news when she wants money from us. But some of us in the family never learn. About two weeks ago, one of my aunts whose child is also in her care, called me. She currently works in

Bloemfontein and lives with her husband there. We were having one of those family gossip conversations over the phone. As we were conversing, she laughingly reminded me about our aunt's strategy to elicit money from us. She told me that last year, before she went home for the Christmas Holiday, our aunt called her and asked her to send money. She wanted to 'buy' Christmas clothes for the child in her care. However, in actual reality our aunt did not need the money to buy clothes; she only wanted to have money in her bank account. However, she was later saddened to learn that her son and one of her sister's sons took her banking card and withdrew the money. They used it to buy clothes and alcohol.

On my aunt's arrival from Bloemfontein, she learned that her child's clothes were not bought and inquired why. Our aunt was crying and told her that her son and his cousin stole the money and used it. When she asked why she did not buy the clothes immediately, she replied that she wanted her bank account to have money until she got paid month end. Eventually, she had to give out more money for the second time to buy the child's clothes. It is not even that my aunt is struggling with money. She is a known business woman selling meat at home. She has livestock and lends out money. She is one of those people who love having money all the time.

This book reminds me of the same madness happening in the rural Eastern Cape today. In most cases, it is never about serious needs that need to be met, it is usually petty things like people wanting clothes or alcohol or to appear to be doing well. However, they never bother to think about the well-being of their toiling and tossing zombies they are milking for days and months on end as long as they get what they want.

The stories of the Gohous and the Daous or the Nastous and Amélies, however widespread, are not the only stories to be told about the relationship between Africans abroad and their relationships with Africans back in their home countries. To every story of disappointment and the opportunism in claims and denials of Ubuntu, there are counter stories of the solidarity, mutuality and collective responsibility that have developed through migrants responding to the obligation to share their wealth, however hard earned, with the community of family and friends left behind. This is what studies of development associations (elite and otherwise) by sons and daughters of particular villages, ethnicities or regions in town or abroad targeting the needs and needy of various home villages across the continent point to (Barkan et al. 1991; Nyamnjoh & Rowlands 1998; Platteau 2004; Fochingong & Ngwa 2005; Mercer et al. 2009; Nyamnjoh 2014). There are cases where urban-rural-remittances have sustained families especially in education and health. Indeed, diaspora and transformation of African economies should not be viewed only in terms of housing construction and conspicuous consumption. Remittances go as well to education, health and taking care of the elderly. Nothing illustrates the obligation to be inclusive in one's success better than a Gikuyu song[26] where an urban migrant is challenged that although he is rich and driving cars in Nairobi, his mother is a pauper in the village. As Rowlands reminds us in his study of the elderly in London, "Everyone to some extent has to 'care for' and to 'take care of', and expects this of others. Who or what might be the object of care, or who or what cares for you, need not matter" (Rowlands 2007: 148).

However, even when migrants bend over backwards to redistribute their wealth with mothers and other relations back in the home country and village, it is not always guaranteed that their efforts are appreciated.

Honorine Express, a US-based Cameroonian bushfaller, renowned for her critical YouTube video postings castigating opportunistic relationships among bushfallers and between bushfallers and their family relations and friends back in Cameroon, provides excellent illustrations of these tendencies. One of her postings – "Demanding and ungrateful family members" – captures the intricacies of such relentless demands by family members. Because the issues it broaches are widely shared and a common topic of conversation among bushfallers and other African immigrants, I have decided to transcript and share it verbatim here as an endnote.[27]

Another example that resonates with many issues raised by Honorine Express in her Vlog postings is the personal story of renowned Togolese international footballer Emmanuel Adebayor who has played for several top European clubs, including Monaco, Arsenal, Manchester City and Tottenham Hotspurs, and who won the African footballer of the year award in 2008. On 6 May 2015, I accessed a detailed Facebook posting in English and French by Emmanuel Adebayor[28], complaining about the catalogue of ingratitude that his Togolese family has repeatedly shown him despite his generosity with his riches in their regard. Despite taking leave from his current club Tottenham Hotspurs to attend to personal matters back home in Togo[29], the problems seemed to have persisted, resulting in him going open on Facebook with the posting.

In the Facebook posting, Emmanuel Adebayor tells his Facebook friends why he has decided to share with them stories that he has kept to himself for a long time, insisting that his reason for finally coming out in the open is less to do with "money" and more with the hope that "all families can learn from what happened in mine." Here is his story: "At the age of 17, with my first wages as a footballer, I built a house for my family" and made sure they were safe. When he was awarded the trophy of African Player of the Year in 2008, he took his mother along with him to share the honour, and "to thank her for everything." That same year, "I brought her to London for various medical check ups," but when his daughter was born and he called his mother to announce the birth the mother did not want to hear about it, as "she immediately hung up the phone." Despite their differences, he continued to support his mother, including sponsoring a trip by her to Lagos to meet with the Prophet T.B. Joshua. He also gave her "a great amount of money to start a business of cookies and different items," and allowed her to put his name and picture on them for publicity. "What else can a son do in his power to support his family?" he asks.

Doing even more does not seem to bring recognition and gratitude in his case.

A couple of years ago, I bought a house in East Lagon (Ghana) for $1.2 million. I found it normal to let my older sister, Yabo Adebayor stay in that house. I also allowed my half brother (Daniel) to stay in the same house.

It was a 15-room house. When he decided to go to the house on vacation a few months later, he was surprised to see many cars in the driveway, and to discover that:

> ... my sister decided to rent out the house without me knowing. She also kicked Daniel out of that house. ... When I called her and asked for explanation, she took about 30 minutes to abuse and insult me over the phone. I called my mother to explain the situation and she did the same as my sister. This same sister says I am ungrateful.

To be accused of ingratitude by those he considered most ungrateful was beyond comprehension. Here was a sister for whom he had bought a car and created business opportunities, and who in addition had rented out his house without as much as informing him, let alone seeking his permission.

Kola Adebayor, his brother who "has now been in Germany for 25 years," is equally disappointing. Emmanuel Adebayor "fully cover[s] the cost of his children's education," and has borne the cost of several trips Kola has undertaken back home. He provided him with "money to start a business" when he was still playing his football at Monaco, but "Where is that business today?" What is beyond forgiveness is the lack of solidarity and compassion towards him, and towards others equally in need of respect. This was the case when he sent Kola to bury his late brother Peter:

> When our brother Peter passed away, I sent Kola a great amount of money so he could fly back home. He never showed up at the burial. And today that same brother (Kola) is telling people that I am involved in Peter's death. How? He is the same brother who went and told inaccurate stories about our family to "The Sun" in order to take some money. They also sent a letter to my Club when I was in Madrid so I could get fired.

102

It would appear that Kola has been particularly disappointing. He has failed to fulfil the expectations of the family, despite his 25 years in Germany, unable to provide the family with electricity or with a phone, but ready to impose himself on Emmanuel Adebayor at the slightest opportunity. This includes unannounced visits, and expecting him to settle his bills and to take care of him and his family in Germany in sickness and in health. Repeatedly reminding himself that "blood is thicker than water," Adebayor forgave a lot of hostility from Kola, including when the latter held a knife to his throat, and threatened him to make money available so Kola could start a car business.[30]

Emmanuel Adebayor is particularly perplexed by accusations that he did little to save his brother Peter, who passed away on July 22, 2013. But he recollects how he had to drive the fastest he could from Ghana to Togo when he got news that Peter was seriously ill, only to be denied access to him by his mother who insisted "I should just give the money and she would solve everything," which he did. Although Kola neither contributed to nor was present at Peter's funeral, he accuses Emmanuel Adebayor of causing Peter's death, and of having opened a shop for Peter that was "not good enough." What is more, Kola, who "is never satisfied," even though "As a big brother, he is supposed to be doing all that I am doing for the family." Instead, he keeps "texting saying that my career would be destroyed."[31] Emmanuel Adebayor believes he gave Peter a decent burial, even in his absence, just as he buried his father in 2005. He recounts his father's passing thus:

> On April 22nd 2005, we received some bad news. I received a call and they announced that my father passed away. I was devastated. I called my big brother and told him that we all have to be there. Again, I made sure there was a flight ticket ready for him. We all went back home and I took care of everything. A long time before my dad died, he was in the hospital one day and he asked me to make sure his funeral is not a moment of sadness. He wanted us to celebrate his life. I

leave it to God to decide if the funeral I organized for my dad was what he wanted. The man who calls himself the "big man" in the family did not contribute to anything. But he still has the boldness to say I do not take care of this family.[32]

Emmanuel Adebayor does not seem to be lucky with his family. Even his brother Rotimi Adebayor, whom he sponsored into a football academy in France, resorted to stealing the phones of other players – "Within a few months; out of 27 players, he stole 21 phones." In a follow-up Facebook posting on 10 May 2015[33], Emmanuel Adebayor focused in particular on Rotimi, "a brother who keeps saying today that I am not a good support for our family." He recounts how he has supported Rotimi since the age of 13, sending the latter to school even after Rotimi had been sent by his parents to live in "a village far from the big city" as punishment for doing "something very bad." Emmanuel Adebayor brought Rotimi back to the city and put him in school. Despite many gestures of brotherly support and solidarity, Rotimi has consistently displayed his ingratitude by systematically abusing Emmanuel's generosity. Among Rotimi's excesses, Emmanuel enumerates the stealing and selling of jerseys or shirts swapped with other football superstars such as the late Marc-Vivien Foé of Cameroon and Zinedine Zidane of France. Rotimi's stealing and selling did not end with football items and forging a master key to access the room where his brother kept his precious items. Nor did it respect even what was bought by Emmanuel for their mother, as the following excerpt testifies:

> When I was in Metz, I was earning about €15,000 a month. I wanted to get something unique for my mom to thank her for all she did for me. I wanted to make her happy. So I decided to take an amount worth 3 months of my wages and I bought her a Cartier neckless for about €45,000. Rotimi and his friends Akim(@Yam Freedom) and Tao (@Sao Tao Oyawole) made a plan and stole that precious neckless. They sold it for about

€800. When my mom and I found out, my mother asked me not to bother because he is the younger brother.

His excesses notwithstanding, Rotimi has repeatedly benefitted from Emmanuel's recognition that "blood is thicker than water." But Rotimi would not give up stealing and abusing the privileges of "I am your brother." He would not apply himself as much as he was expected to with the chances he got. Emmanuel authenticates this with the following example:

> One day, my mom called me early in the morning when I was still in bed. She told me that Rotimi has gotten a Visa to go to Dubai so he can play football out there. He had to leave that day with his friend Kodjovi (@Denilson de Souza) who was in the same situation. It was either they went that day or the Visa would be suspended. I asked one of my guys at the time (@Agui Mozino) to go find tickets for my brother and his friend. We could not find any economy class ticket on that day so I had to get them both first class tickets. After all, it was an opportunity for him to make his own career in Dubai. Only 4 days later, Rotimi went back home. He explained how the lifestyle in Dubai was not made for him. He said he wasn't free to do what he wanted to do because it is a strictly Muslim place. He couldn't drink, party as much as he wanted or kiss girls in public.

We are spared Peter's stories because he is no longer alive, although Peter did join Kola in holding him at knife point to provide money for them to start a car business. When in 2005 he organised a meeting "to solve our family issues," his entire family was of the opinion that "I should build each family member a house and give each of them a monthly wage." His stories suggest that Emmanuel Adebayo is seen and related to by the rest of his family as a wallet on legs. They do not relent asking him to redistribute his wealth to them, but are hostile to any idea of him expanding the pool of those he helps. "Every time I try to help the people in need, they had to question me and all of them thought it was a bad idea." To conclude,

"Today I am still alive and they have already shared all my goods, just in case I die."[34]

There is little in the attitude and behaviour of his family to suggest that Emmanuel Adebayor owns himself, let alone his wealth. While it is normal in claims of Ubuntu to assume that one's fortune or riches does not belong to one alone, that one has the duty to share one's success with others – both intimate and distant –, in the case of Emmanuel Adebayor his family does not even appear to expect him to claim any of his hard-earned riches. They treat him like a hen that lays golden eggs, but is strictly forbidden from claiming any for itself. In the eyes of his family, however much of his riches he shares with them, he is expected to share even more – to give away until there is nothing left to give. Only then would he be forgiven and forgotten by them. After usurping his wealth, they will have usurped him completely – mind, body and soul – leaving him truly dead to them.

Despite not having been to school, Emmanuel Adebayor is proud of his achievements, and especially of what he has done for his family, ungrateful though they are. Every now and again, he feels like committing suicide, because of the family pressures he has been made to bear. "For everyone who knows me, I'd do anything for my country and my people," he concludes his story.[35] In three Facebook posts Emmanuel Adebayor has shared with us not only a story of how he went from very little to fame as a footballer, but more importantly, the selfless generosity with which he greeted his good fortune. As Antoinette Muller puts it in a commentary titled "Stranger in a Strange Land: Adebayor's Silent Struggles," Emmanuel Adebayor has "gone from having no football boots to earning enough to provide, not only for himself, but for his family, and be in a position to support a number of charity projects across Africa," and "his actions mostly suggest that he is a good egg, who cares deeply for his fellow humans."[36]

The more I discussed Adebayor's story with readers of drafts of this book, the more it dawned on me that his story

106

was more common than many reading his Facebook postings would imagine. Xolela Ntsebeza of South Africa shared with me the following personal story after reading about Adebayor in this book. I am grateful for his permission to reproduce it here.

I am reminded of my own family. This was a wealthy family with riches. Just like Emmanuel Adebayor's relation with his father, it was known that my father was particularly fond of my sister. This relation caused tensions in the family, bringing closer my brothers to my mother. When my father died, it was no surprise that my sister was left out of important business decisions. Instead, my mother leaned heavily on my brothers. Even in moments where major mistakes were made, such as selling of prime commercial property in a whim without market evaluation, and despite my sister's plea against such decisions drawing from the training she got from my deceased father, these warnings fell on deaf ears.

But Ubuntu is not only about close family. Unlike the Adebayor family, opportunists drawing from Ubuntu came from *intimate strangers*, to borrow the title of one of your books. In my family's case, we had trusted friends that used their positions as bank managers and auditors to loot millions in the form of money, property and legally owned diamonds. But at these moments, the family, despite their differences, would come together to fight off the opportunism that came from our intimate strangers. The intimate strangers took until there was nothing left to give, and only then were we forgiven and forgotten by them, at least momentarily. However slow the family's recovery has been and even though the experience has brought the family much closer, the tensions that still occur continue to take the form of the divisions that emerged in those early days. But the family knows that any evidence of this to outsiders has potential of inviting intimate strangers that continue to lurk close in opportunistic fashion. Such wolves in sheep skin bring the family back together.

Adebayor's story raises some perplexing questions. What could have provoked a renowned international footballer of his calibre to the point of washing his family linen on Facebook? Is his intention limited to what he claims – so that "all families

107

could learn from what happened"? Could this also be a way of loosening his daughter from the entrapment imposed by his insatiable family members? Adebayor portrays himself as an excellent example of an inclusive achiever through selfless contributions to others and their welfare. He would like to redistribute what he accumulates beyond the narrow confines of his immediate family, if only they disabuse themselves of insisting on the lion's share. This is evident particularly with his brother Kola, who unashamedly and actively repeatedly used kinship to guilt trip and demand money from him. Even though at various moments in the Facebook post claims were made that Adebayor was not giving back, the family members actively discouraged any attempt to spread the wealth to help other people. They would rather his Ubuntu started and ended with them. Unlike with the Ntsebezas where intimate strangers (bank managers and auditors) took advantage of the death of their father to "loot millions in the form of money, property and legally owned diamonds," in Adebayor's case the opportunism is squarely from within his own intimate family circles.

The fact that the story is told entirely from Adebayor's perspective – the perspective of the hunted and not the hunter – begs the questions: Why, given his stature and prominence, did Adebayor yield to this predatory dimension of his family? He could easily have argued, as some purportedly self-made others would, that it was within his right as an individual who had made it big to seek to protect his hard earned wealth. Why did he not take this step? Is it enough to explain his position simply in terms of blood being thicker than water?

What is evident from Adebayor's story is the special bond he had with his father (just like the Ntsebeza daughter above), particularly during his father's last days before passing away. Could this special bond have affected his relationship with the rest of the family in a manner similar to Ntsebeza's daughter? Did the rest of the family feel somehow cheated out of their share of their father's blessings by Adebayor as a result of this special bond? Could ingratitude in his regard by the family members partly be understood as claiming by force their share of Ubuntu in the form of their father's blessings? Is it possible that his father might have grown to like him more because of his success? Was it in part in guilt for the special bond between them that Adebayor accepted, literally, the request by his dying father to take care of the family? It was also possible for him to have interpreted the request as a call for him to reproduce his father by giving birth to the next generation of Adebayors. Interpreted thus, he could easily have pointed to his daughter as evidence of having fulfilled that obligation.

By seeking to take care of the family beyond mere reproduction of his father by birth, and by accommodating his family members even in their excesses, Adebayor makes a compelling case for inclusiveness, considerateness, generosity and humaneness not dissimilar to the case made by Nelson Mandela for Ubuntu to which we alluded in the introductory chapter of this book.

Notes

---

¹ [« Tu viens? Tu viens, ein? Mais pourquoi, pourquoi tu viens? Déjà? Attends, toi tu es parti quand déjà? »]

² [« Voleur…voleur…voleur…voleur, voleur, voleur…»]

³ [« Ah oui, d'accord! Tiens t…t…t…c'est Daou. Je suis pas là! Je suis même pas là. Réponds!! »]

⁴ [« Nastou: Allo? Oui? Daou. Ça va? Oui, moi aussi ça va! Ah, Gohou? Euh…ein oui. Go, il a voyagé ein! Il a perdu son oncle ein!

Gohou: NON NON! Quel oncle?

Nastou: Bon, il est parti il y a une semaine.

Gohou: Non! Non, hier! Hier!

Nastou: Ah non, j'avais oublié! Il est parti il y a deux jours.

Gohou: Non! Hier, hier, hier, hier!

Nastou: Il est parti il y a deux jours.

Gohou: HIER!

Nastou: (se tourne vers Gohou) C'est quoi maintenant?

Gohou: Beh c'était hier soir…hier soir…

Nastou: Allo Daou? Oui! Hmm hmm…Ah, tu l'as eu? Ah d'accord.
C'est vrai. Il est parti hier.

Gohou: Nuit, nuit…

Nastou: Il est parti hier soir…

Gohou: Nuit, nuit…Ooooh!

Nastou: Tu dis tu l'as eu? Ah?

5 Gohou: Nuit…

Nastou: D'accord, ok, ok. Je vais lui faire la commission de toute
façon. Bon, il faut rappeler, il faut rappeler…

Gohou: Non, non, non, non, non, non!

Nastou: Moi je sais pas. Quand il va venir, je vais lui dire que tu as
appelle. Ah? Ah d'accord! Tu arrives?

Gohou: Quoi?

Nastou: Ah d'accord! Ok. On t'attend.

Gohou: Non, non! Qui l'attend? Qui l'attend?

Nastou: D'accord, on t'attend!

Gohou: Non! Dis-lui de pas venir!!!

Nastou: Oui, on va venir te chercher à l'aéroport.

Gohou: Mais qui va aller le chercher? Dis-lui de ne pas venir.

Nastou: Mais il faut rappeler. Tu vas parler avec lui. Hmm hmm,
d'accord. De toute façon, je vais lui faire la commission. Ouais. Mais il faut
rappeler, comme ça, tu pourras lui parler.

Gohou: Ah, comme ça, fallait dire que je suis pas là.

Nastou: Au revoir Daou. A bientôt.

Gohou: A bientôt ou? Pourquoi tu fais ça?

(Nastou raccroche le téléphone et se tourne vers Gohou)

Nastou: Toi-même, c'est quoi? Tiens! Ton portable!

[….]

Gohou: Oh, tu as gâté. Tu pouvais pas lui dire que y'a la guerre dans le
pays?

Nastou: Quelle guerre?

Gohou: Toi-même, quand il va appeler, tu vas lui dire qu'il y a la
guerre.

Nastou: Mais pourquoi tu veux pas qu'il vienne?

Gohou: Il doit pas venir ici. Il doit pas…

Nastou: Mais pourquoi?

Gohou: Le cauchemar…le cauchemar…

Nastou: Quel cauchemar?

Gohou: Le cauchemar d'hier la nuit…c'était lui…

Nastou: Regarde, vos histoires de cauchemar, famille, sorciers…ein! Je
suis pas dedans ein! S'il appelle la, faut plus me le passer!]

6 [« Amélie: Vous ne savez pas ou est-ce que je peux la joindre ou la
trouver? Vous ne savez pas?

110

Caissière: Si, elle habite au quartier millionnaire.

Amélie: Au quartier millionnaire?

Caissière: Oui. Oh, elle a construit une belle maison là-bas.

Amélie: Oh, elle a construit une belle maison! Ah ça c'est super ça! Et, et c'est ou le quartier millionnaire?

Caissière: C'est à la Riviera.

Amélie: A la Riviera...Ah d'accord. Merci bien Mademoiselle. Au revoir... »]

7 [« Oh! Mais c'est beau, c'est splendide! Oh, ma copine! Elle a le même gout que moi. C'est pas pour rien qu'on est amies ein! Oh merci bien Monsieur » qui demande à Amélie de patienter, et de s'asseoir.]

8 [«Amélie: Oh chérie...oh elle est toute belle. Comme elle est magnifique...Oh chérie. Ça va?

Nastou: Bonjour.

Amélie: C'est...t'est tout à fait...comment tu es dorée...chérie! Oh là là. Mais tu es fantastique! Oh tu es comme une princesse. Oh là là! Tes bijoux...tous en or. Beh dis, t'as du gagner au Lotto toi?

Nastou: Beh pourquoi au Lotto?

Amélie: Bien tu vois tout ça? C'est un véritable palais. Mais t'as du goût chérie! Tu m'as pas dit ça moi!

Nastou: Bien écoute ein, chacun a son petit secret.

Amélie: OH...toi t'es une cochonne toi! Tu me caches beaucoup de choses... (rires). C'est pas possible. Tu as du tomber sur un bon mec qui a du fric.

Nastou: Beh pourquoi vous pensez que c'est toujours l'homme qui doit fabriquer la femme? Ein? Nous les femmes, on peut se fabriquer aussi ein! Ouais...quand même. »]

9 [«Amélie: Eh bien, dis-moi euh....tu sortais, non?

Nastou: Oui, je sortais.

Amélie: Ok. Si on profitait pour aller voir ma maison?

Nastou: La maison?

Amélie: Non, ma maison à moi! Celle que...

Nastou: Ah! Vous voulez me présenter votre maison?

Amélie: Ah ha oh chérie...c'est entre nous, nous sommes copines là. Arrête de me vouvoyer.

Nastou: Euh, je sais pas de quoi vous parlez.

Amélie: Ha reviens sur terre. Ein? Ma maison à moi! Je t'ai envoyé des sous, tu te rappelles? Pour que tu construises une maison à mon nom. Ok?

Nastou: Ecoutez Madame, je ne suis ni architecte, ni maçon, ni entrepreneur. Alors, cette histoire de construction de maison, je n'y comprends rien du tout.

Amélie: Attends, moi non-plus je comprends rien, Je comprends rien. Je t'ai envoyé de l'argent, oui ou non?

Nastou: Je sais pas de quoi vous parlez en fait.

Amélie: Mais c'est pas possible…Ecoute…

Nastou: Mais je sais pas…

Amélie: La, la, la plaisanterie a assez dure ein!

Nastou: Mais je ne suis pas une animatrice, une marionnette, ni une comédienne pour venir m'amuser…

Amélie: Je dis, c'est toi Nastou, non?

Nastou: Oui, c'est bien moi, Nastou.

Amélie: Oh, donc, je me suis pas trompée…Je dis bien, ma maison à moi. Ok? Bon tu piges?

Nastou: Votre maison?

Amélie: Oui, ma maison…

Nastou: Non, en fait, je pige pas parce que je comprends pas.

Amélie: Eh regarde, je dis, faut pas t'amuser comme ça. Tu comprends? Faut pas t'amuser comme ça. Tu me donnes ma maison, ou tu me donnes mon argent. C'est ce que je te demande ein!

Nastou: Cette maison est la mienne. Mais bon, peut-être un peu partout…votre maison doit surement se trouver quelque part. Moi, je sais pas… »]

[10] [« Amélie: Tu dis quoi? Tu dis quoi? Donc, tu me dis que l'argent que je t'ai donné pour construire la maison, ma maison à moi, tu l'as pris pour construire toi-même ta maison? Ah la, non, non, non, non, non. Ça va pas se passer comme ça!

Nastou: Mais vous dites des choses qui sont pas vraies.

Amélie: Je dis ça va pas se passer comme ça! Nastou, ma maison ou mon argent!

Nastou: Greg? Greg?

Greg: Ou Madame?

Amélie: Heyyyy! Mon sang monte.

Nastou: (A Greg) Le sang de Madame monte, alors, il faut l'accompagner à la porte.

Amélie: Tu sais quoi? Non, non, non, non. Ça va pas se passer comme ça! Nastou, tu me donnes mon argent, oui ou non? Tu m'entends?

Greg: Si vous ne sortez pas, je serai oblige d'utiliser la force.

Amélie: (A Greg) Toi là, je t'ai pas sonné! Je vais te gifler! Tu comprends? Ne me parle pas sur ce ton! Ça veut dire quoi ça? (A Nastou) Espèce d'escroc! (Elle crie et s'agite).

Greg: Madame, la porte s'il vous plait!

Amélie: Quelle porte? Ecoutez, lachez-moi, lachez-moi, lachez-moi…Ca veut dire quoi ça? ESCROC! C'EST LA POLICE OU LA JUSTICE QUI VA TRANCHER CETTE AFFAIRE! Qu'est-ce que ça veut dire? Escroc! Ah laisse-moi-toi! La, tu me laisses la! C'est pas possible la! Mais vous êtes qu'une bande d'escrocs…Fripouilles! »]

[11] [«Il y a tout genre de personnes dans ce monde…Fatiguer les gens.»]

[12] [«Allo, oui? Christelle, coco? Comment tu vas? Ok? Bien coute, ta maison, elle est en finition ein! Oui, et tu sais que c'est la fin qui coute plus cher ein! Donc, tu vas me faire venir beaucoup d'argent….hmm hmm…oui. Faut qu'on te la termine au plus tôt, ein! Tu sais que la mienne, euh…je l'ai terminé en un temps record. Oui. Demain ein? Demain tu me fais venir de l'argent. Ok. Donc j'attends demain. De toute façon, tu as été très juste jusque-là. Ok Bisou ma chérie. A bientôt, je t'embrasse.»]

[13] [«C'est pas ce qu'il m'a montré sur la photo! Bon sang, qu'est-ce qu'il m'arrive? Mais regardez-moi tout ça la! C'est quoi ça? Avec ça, je le cherche partout, et je ne le retrouve pas. »]

[14] [«Vous avez vu ce que Gohou m'a fait? Vous avez vu ce que Gohou m'a fait? Il a complètement foutu ma vie en l'air. J'ai parcouru tous les terrains. Et tout est perdu. J'ai vu des coups comme si c'était et des fois, celui-là, c'est d'autres. Et c'est des choses graves…y'a certaines personnes qui m'ont présente des papiers d'acquisition. Ça prouve qu'il a tout vendu. Mais celui-là, si je l'attrape, je l'attrape, je le fous en prison. »]

[15] According to Boa Thiémélé Ramsès (2010), belief in witchcraft and its tendency to explain all and justify all is rife in Côte d'Ivoire and among Ivorians, as they seek fulfilment and mitigation to the miseries and suffering of their individual and collective lives.

[16] [Tu as le courage de foutre en prison ton cousin? Bien nous sommes ici, on voit tout et on sait tout. Et tu sais, Gohou, c'est un cas. Très sincèrement, c'est un cas. Tu vois, au moment où l'argent était là, ses virées nocturnes, en boite, avec les filles, il travaille même sur les gens »].

[17] [« Mais pourquoi vous ne m'avez pas appelle? Pourquoi? »]

[18] [« C'est Gohou qui connait papiers. C'est Gohou qui connait papiers, et il a géré. Voilà. »].

[19] [« Tu sais Daou, Gohou c'est ton cousin directe, et tu le sais très bien. Même s'il a commis une faute grave, tu n'as pas à le mettre en prison. Tu vas salir la famille. »].

[20] [« Salir la famille! J'ai dû cravacher dur pour avoir l'argent qu'il a gaspille »]

[21] [« Et vous me demandez de ne pas réagir…Ok, je vais salir la famille, non? Mais si je l'attrape, je le tue et je me tues. C'est trop facile ça »].

[22] [« Quand il faisait venir l'argent, il nous connaissait? Oh mais tout ça, c'est son problème ça! »]

[23] [« Daou: Ah bon? Je t'ai appelle avant de venir non?

Gohou: Y'avait pas réseau.

Daou: Y'avait pas réseau…Je demande après toi, on me dit tu as vendu tous les lots.

Gohou: Qui a dit ça?

Daou: Mais qu'est-ce que tu as fait de l'argent?

Gohou: Daou, n'oublies pas ton passe ein! Daou, je suis ton cousin!

Daou: Non, mais Gohou, tu m'as déçu.

Gohou: L'argent que tu m'as fait venir, j'ai construit la maison. Tu n'as pas vu dans les photos?

Daou: Tu as construit quoi? Je suis allé sur les lieux. Ce que j'ai vu n'a rien à voir avec les photos que tu m'as envoyées.

Gohou: Daou! Je te jure, au nom de Dieu, quoi ein! Ceux qui disent que moi j'ai bouffe ton argent-là, c'est des batards!

Daou: On va aller sur le site et tu vas me montrer les réalisations.

Gohou: On peut aller ein, on peut aller.

Daou: Allons-y.

Gohou: Toi-même tu vas voir!

[….]

Daou: Bon, allons-y là.

Gohou: Ton argent la non…ton argent la…

Daou: Tu penses, tu penses que je suis allé me promener en Europe pour avoir l'argent moi?

Gohou: Non, je vais, je vais, je vais t'expliquer…non je vais te…

Daou: On prend cette voiture. On prend ma voiture. Passe ici… (Il force Gohou dans la voiture rouge, louée)

Gohou: Doucement Daou, doucement.

Daou: Un salaud comme ça… »]

[24] [« Daou: Tu passes ici-là. Eh tu vas me montrer la maison là.

Gohou: Eh doucement, Daou, doucement. Doucement…et, ca, c'est pas maison la, qui est là?

Daou: Mais c'est pas cette maison que j'ai vu sur la photo moi!

Gohou: Mais c'est parce que la maison elle n'était pas terminée! C'est parce que la maison elle n'était pas terminée. Maintenant que c'est terminé, la maison donne un autre aspect. Ça donne un autre aspect. C'est ça qui est là.

Daou: Et puis, à ce que je sache, de l'eau vers…ici, dans cette zone, on a jamais eu de l'eau.

Gohou: Ne cherche pas à savoir d'où vient l'eau ou pas. Tu cherches maison, ou bien c'est terrain que tu cherches? Et puis, Daou, la, la, c'est la maison que t'as vu sur la photo. La maison n'était pas terminée. Mais là, la, on est en voie de finition. Daou, n'oublie pas ton passe.

Daou: Ah non, Gohou, faut plus jamais répéter ce mot. Tu as compris? Ne répète plus jamais ce mot-clé. Toi, tu te souviens de ton passe? Quand je partais c'est comme ça que tu étais habile?

Gohou: Non, mais…Dans la vie là, dans la vie-là, c'est l'homme qui fait l'homme.

Daou: C'est moi, Daou, qui va te faire? Ça va pas chez toi? N'importe quoi!

Gohou: Vas voir dedans, vas voir. Toi, toi-même tu seras surpris.
Daou: D'accord. Je vais visiter la maison quoi…Ca veut dire quoi ça? »]

[25] *L'homme ne fait pas l'homme; l'homme fait lui-même* is the title of a popular song released in the early 1990s by the Cameroonian Bikutsi musician, Manga Lucky.

[26] *Mwanake uyu tiga kwi yamba ota maburi ona gutare mbura.* (Young Man stop being arrogant. Do not open up like an umbrella when there is no rain), by Queen Jane. Mwanake uyu tiga kwiyamba www.youtube.com/watch?v=yAg72kMWj3g&list=PLEF6FDD02A141FA 0E, accessed 06 May 2015.

[27] Full transcript of Honorine Express, "Demanding and Ungrateful Family Members, www.youtube.com/watch?v=OJ3wZ97Ab0w, accessed 07 August 2015.

Hi there! Thank you everybody for tuning in again to Honorine Express this bright Tuesday morning. I appreciate all your likes, your comments, your feedback. Before we go ahead, I am going to read a message form one of my fans, her name is Sanzi B and Sanzi, thanks to you. She says

"Hi Honorine, thank you so much for the brilliant messages. Finally someone stood up to talk about this. God bless my sister. Thank you."

Thank you too Sanzi for taking out your awesome and precious time to give me this feedback. I really, really do appreciate it. So thank you so much.

Today I am going to talk about ungrateful family members, demanding family members; direct mothers, brothers, fathers and uncles. This one is not about friends; this one is about direct family members. So, we all are over here, we are struggling, we are working very hard. Some of us our parents paid different kinds of money; they put their hands into so many different places to get us over here. But that is not enough for them to kill us in stress, heaven knows we are trying.

First of all, if you have any family member who is too demanding and no matter how much you try, they only want to kill you, they want to press you, they need money today, they need money tomorrow, they need money another day, tag them with this video. I know some of you are so scared you cannot talk about it. Tag them with this video, at least you are not the one who said it, it was just a random video that you found online and you tagged them with it.

However, I want to address you people who are back home, please learn when to call people who are overseas. No matter the country they are, before you people want to call us, look at your time. The way you

115

people treat some of us, it's just like we are slaves or something. 3:00 am, someone is sleeping, their phone is ringing *"briing, briing!!"* "Allo, allo, allo... is this sister Honorine?" "Yes. Vita what is it?" "Oh, sister Honorine, please call me back, call me back. I don't have credit." You don't have credit; you are calling me to beg for money, you don't have credit. Besides, you called me at 2 am. I will think that it is an emergency, I will call Vita. "Vita what is it?" "Sister Honorine, I just wanted to tell you that I don't have money for this, I don't have money for that. Please send me the money quick, quick, quick, quick. Oh, I have my *njangi* on Saturday." Before I continue, *njangi* is something like a meeting that we have in my country. People go there, maybe every Sunday, every end of the month, they have a certain amount of money that each person is supposed to bring and then at the end of the year, they spread the money or they divide the money. Whatever you save, that's what you will get. They call you to say that they don't have money for njangi, at 2 am. For crying out loud, do you people really think about us? Do you really consider when you start asking for money, when you start demanding for all these things? I'm like "Vita, I don't have 50 000, I will send 10 000 frs" you send 10 000, they do not call you. They beep you and you call and say "what is it?" They say "I wanted to tell you thank you for the money."

Aye you people! *Walai* you people! You people are trying wonders. I send you money, you cannot even call me to tell me thank you. You beep me, you flash my phone. I still call you and you just tell me that 'oh I just wanted to tell you that thanks for the money' you do not even... sometimes you even say 'oh, but the money was small, it was not enough'. Lord God have mercy! Do you know how much is my pay cheque? Do you know how much is my phone bill? Phone bill is America is not the same as back home that maybe you recharge your phone and it's enough. Here phone bill comes monthly, if you don't pay it, they disconnect your phone and the credit bureau starts calling you.

Every day you are asking of money. You are asking for money for graduation to make big party. We send you money you say the money is not enough, how many bottles of drinks will it buy? See, we are suffering here, okay. We are suffering here. We don't have that kind of money that you keep asking. Mama you people have exaggerated it. Yes some of you are our parents, you guys have exaggerated it. Soon it has become the one that you people sit in the house and say "oh, since ten years ago that Honorine went, since ten years ago that Michael went to America, all kind of people have come, they have gone back. Oh, Michael has not even come, he does not care about us, he does not do this, he does not give us money. Oh, he has not built us any house. He has not done this.'"

See, you people don't know what we are going through here. It is true that you guys sacrificed for us to come through here. It is true that some parents sold maybe pieces of land and invested in one way or the other for us to come here. But it is not a guarantee for us to live under stress, mama and papa and brothers and sisters. We have brothers in the family, all their life you work your money you give to them, they eat. They do not invest it in doing anything. But when someone wants to complain about you, they are the first person to sit down and write a whole chapter on the things that you are not doing. They forget the fact that you send the money on monthly basis, weekly basis, they do not do anything about it, you are the one suffering.

Let me tell you, you don't have to stress. You are trying your best and God is recording it. Yes, you do your best. When you do your best and those people keep complaining, let them complain. Let them complain. Don't die here. Because I have people that are living under depression in this country. You say 'What is it?' they say 'Man, my family is putting me under pressure. They want me to do this. But man, can you see I just have this kind of job. I don't have that kind of money' See, stop. Don't be under that kind of pressure. Anyone who wants to kill you because you have not done this or you have not done that and heaven knows you don't have that kind fop money, let that person try to kill you, they will die themselves. You don't have to be under stress.

You have people in this country; they cannot even dress up properly. When there are occasions, they cannot even attend because they do not even have common clothes to wear, cheap clothes that they sell for $10. Why? Because every day they have to send money back home.

Please you people back home you got to consider us. You people have to consider us.

It's about time, you people need to stop. All this money that you are sending up and down, (pion, pion, pion) and these people keep putting you under pressure and they think that it's by right for you to send the money every day and night for them to go and play their njangi, for them to put in their chequing and savings account while you have nothing, while you have nothing. It is not fair. You are not obliged to do that. Do it when it is convenient, when God tells you 'oh my child, do this', when you feel in your heart that these people need money. Yes, that's when you can do it. Do it when it is right, when there is a family emergency.

All this money that I am talking about our direct family members they keep asking. Sometimes some of us go back home, the people who are back home they are properly dressed than us. We send you our money; you people take it and buy Timberland, Timberland that I cannot wear here. I send you my money, you use my $600 to buy your Timberland, you use my $100 to buy your shoe. I am here wearing shoes for $5.99. God have mercy on you people. See, before you call us look at your time, that's my first problem. Start looking at your time; know that there is something called time difference. After you call us, know the kind of things that you are calling us. Sometimes you people can call us to say 'hi, I just wanted to check on you, to find out how you are doing. I wanted to encourage you.' Never! All the time that you call it's for money.

I'm just saying, if you have that kind of a family member, tag them with this video. Solve this problem once and for all. However, thank you guys for watching and have an amazing week. God bless.

28   See
www.facebook.com/permalink.php?story_fbid=1650071258554893&id=13
77345199160835&substory_index=0 , accessed 06 May 2015.

29 See www.bbc.com/sport/0/football/30409963, accessed 06 May 2015.

30
www.facebook.com/permalink.php?story_fbid=1656411337920885&id=13
77345199160835&substory_index=0, accessed Friday 22 May 2015.

31
www.facebook.com/permalink.php?story_fbid=1656411337920885&id=13
77345199160835&substory_index=0, accessed Friday 22 May 2015.

32
www.facebook.com/permalink.php?story_fbid=1656411337920885&id=13
77345199160835&substory_index=0, accessed Friday 22 May 2015.

33
www.facebook.com/permalink.php?story_fbid=1651703141725038&id=13
77345199160835&substory_index=0, accessed 12 May 2015.

34 Here is the full Facebook text in French as posted by Emmanuel Adebayor   at   these   links:
www.facebook.com/permalink.php?story_fbid=1650071258554893&id=13
77345199160835&substory_index=0
   www.facebook.com/permalink.php?story_fbid=1651703141725038&i
d=1377345199160835&substory_index=0

J'ai gardé ses histoires pendant un long moment mais aujourd'hui je pense qu'il est bien de partager avec vous. C'est vrai que les affaires de familles doivent être réglées en famille et pas en public, mais je le fais pour que d'autres familles apprennent les leçons. Il faut noter que tout ceci n'est pas à propos d'argent.

À l'âge de 17 ans, avec mes premiers salaires de footballeur, j'ai construit une maison pour ma famille et je me suis assuré qu'ils étaient en sécurité. Comme vous le savez, j'ai été élu "Meilleur Joueur Africain" en 2008. A cette occasion j'ai emmené ma mère sur le podium pour la remercier pour tout. Pendant cette même année, je me suis assuré qu'elle vienne à Londres pour des plusieurs visites médicales. Quand ma fille est née, on a appelé ma mère pour l'informer mais elle a directement raccroché. En lisant vos commentaires, certains proposent que j'aille voir le pasteur T B Joshua pour parler des problèmes familiaux. En fait, en 2013, j'avais donné de l'argent à ma mère pour aller voir ce pasteur au Nigéria. Elle devait rester pour 1 semaine, mais deux jours après on m'a appelé pour dire quelle est partie. En plus de cela, j'ai donné une grande somme à ma mère pour lancer un business de biscuits et autres produits. Naturellement, je l'ai autorisé à mettre mon nom dessus pour vendre beaucoup plus. Quoi d'autre un fils peut faire pour supporter sa famille?

Il y a quelques années, j'ai acheté une maison pour 1,2 million $ au Ghana. J'ai trouvé normal de mettre ma grande sœur Yabo Adebayor dans cette maison, ainsi que mon demi-frère Daniel. Quelques mois après, je retourne de vacances et j'ai remarqué qu'il y avait beaucoup de voitures devant la maison. La vérité est que ma sœur a loué la maison sans me prévenir. Elle a aussi renvoyé Daniel de la maison. Imaginez que cette maison avait environs 15 chambres. Quand je l'ai appelé pour en discuter, elle m'a insulté au téléphone pendant 30 minutes. Ma mère aussi a fait la même chose. Cette même sœur dit que je suis ingrat. Demandez-lui à propos de la voiture qu'elle conduit ou tout ce qu'elle vend aujourd'hui.

Mon frère Kola est en Allemagne depuis 25 ans et n'est rentré au pays que 4 fois, à mes propres frais. Je supporte les frais d'études de ses enfants. Quand j'étais à Monaco, il est venu me demander de l'argent pour commencer un business. Seul Dieu sait combien il a reçu de moi. Où est ce business aujourd'hui?

Quand notre frère Peter était décédé, j'ai envoyé une grande somme à Kola pour qu'il puisse rentrer au pays. On ne l'a pas vu aux funérailles. Et maintenant il annonce que je suis impliqué dans la mort de Peter. Comment?

C'est le même frère qui a empoché de l'argent de "The Sun" pour raconter des histoires peu précises sur notre famille. Ils ont aussi envoyé une lettre à mon Club quand j'étais à Madrid pour me virer.

Quand j'étais à Monaco je pensais qu'il serait bien d'avoir une famille de footballeur donc j'ai trouvé une académie de football pour mon frère Rotimi en France. Quelques mois après il a volé 21 téléphones des ses coéquipiers. Il y avait 27 joueurs dans l'équipe.

Je ne dirais rien à propos de mon frère Peter Adebayor qui est décédé. Que son âme repose en paix.

Ma sœur Lucia Adebayor dis aux gens que mon père m'a dit de l'emmené en Europe mais j'ai refusé. Quel serait le but de l'emmener en Europe? Tout le monde est ici pour une raison.

J'étais au Ghana quand j'ai reçu les nouvelles que mon frère (Peter) était gravement malade. J'ai conduit le plus vite possible au Togo pour proposer mon aide. A mon arrivée, ma mère a dit que je ne peux pas le voir. Elle a dit de lui donner l'argent et elle allait s'en charger de le guérir. Dieu seul sait combien je lui ai donné. Et les gens disent toujours que je n'ai rien fait pour sauver mon frère. Vous pensez que j'ai conduis 2 heure au Togo pour rien?

J'ai organisé une réunion de famille en 2005 pour régler tous les problèmes. Quand j'ai demandé leur opinion, ils ont voulu que je leur offre une maison à chaque membre de la famille et que je leur donne un salaire mensuel. Aujourd'hui je suis vivant mais ils ont déjà partagé tous mes biens. Pour toutes ses raisons, ma fondation a eu du mal à se lancer. A chaque que je veux aider les plus démunis, ils s'y opposent.

Si j'écris ceci, l'objectif principal n'est pas d'exposer ma famille. Je veux juste que d'autres familles Africaines apprennent de ceci. Merci.

Voici une autre partie de l'histoire que j'ai gardée dans mon cœur depuis longtemps. Aujourd'hui je sens l'envie de la faire sortir. Si je partage mon histoire, c'est parce que je pense qu'elle vient avec une leçon ; et cette leçon est pour ceux qui lisent ce message. Ceci est à propos d'un frère qui dit toujours que je ne suis pas un bon support pour notre famille. Il s'appelle Rotimi Adebayor. Quand il avait 13 ans, il a fait quelque chose de très mauvais. Lui et moi savons de quoi je parle. Pour cette raison, nos parents l'ont envoyé dans un village très loin de la ville. Quand j'ai commencé à avoir un peu de succès, je suis retourné en vacances au Togo et une amie de ma mère est venue nous visiter depuis le village. Elle nous a raconté comment Rotimi souffrait dans le village. Quand elle a raconté cette histoire, j'ai immédiatement ordonné de le remmener en ville. Une fois de retour, je me suis assuré de l'inscrire à l'école. Pour moi cela est normal.

En 2002, je suis parti jouer la CAN au Mali et j'ai eu le privilège d'échanger mon maillot avec Marc-Vivien Foé. Que son âme repose en paix. A mon retour au Togo, j'ai mis ce maillot dans un endroit sécurisé. Mon frère a trouvé un moyen de voler et vendre ce maillot.

Quand j'ai déménagé de Metz à Monaco, nous sommes arrivés à un niveau avancé de la Champions League et on a joué contre le Real Madrid. C'était un des plus beaux jours de ma vie parce que j'étais chanceux de recevoir un maillot signé de la légende Zinedine Zidane. Quand j'ai remmené ce maillot au Togo, mon frère a encore trouvé un moyen de voler et vendre ce maillot.

Quand j'étais à Metz, je gagnais environ 15,000€ par mois. Je voulais faire quelque chose d'unique pour ma mère pour la remercier de tout ce qu'elle a fait pour moi. Je voulais la rendre heureuse, Donc j'ai décidé de prendre 3 mois de mon salaire et je lui ai acheté un collier de la marque Cartier d'environ 45,000€. Rotimi, ses amis Akim(@Yam Freedom) et Tao (@Sao Tao Oyawole) ont fait un plan pour voler ce précieux collier. Ils l'ont vendu pour 800€. Quand nous avons découvert ceci avec ma mère, elle m'a dit de ne pas m'inquiéter parce que c'est le petit frère. Malgré cette situation, j'aimerais utiliser cette occasion pour souhaiter une bonne fête des mères à toutes les mamans du monde.

Dans ma maison, j'ai un magasin où je garde to mes effets personnels quand je voyage. Je suis le seul qui a la clé mais mon frère a trouvé un moyen de faire « un master key » qui était capable d'ouvrir toutes les portes de la maison. Il volait souvent des boissons et d'autres effets dans cette chambre.

Apres toutes ses histoires, nous avons continué à dire que "le sang est plus épais que l'eau" et nous avons passé à autres choses. C'est à ce moment que j'ai décidé de l'emmener jouer au foot à l'endroit où j'ai commencé mon football en Europe. Vous connaissez la suite de l'histoire. Il a volé plusieurs téléphones de ses coéquipiers et il a été viré aussitôt. En fait, quand j'ai publié la première partie de l'histoire il m'a appelé pour dire qu'il n'a pas volé exactement 21 téléphones. Il disait que c'était un peu moins. Quand même…Cela est-il acceptable? Il a aussi ajouté que je dois être content qu'il vole mes boissons parce qu'il est mon frère.

Jacques Songo'o qui est maintenant un joueur de football Camerounais retraité avait aussi son fils dans l'académie de mon frère. Ils étaient des amis proches. Permettez-moi d'ajouter que Songo'o faisait partie de mon développement en tant que joueur et il me donnait de bons de conseils. J'étais au Togo quand il m'a appelé. Il avait l'air très fâché. Il m'a donc expliqué comment mon frère a volé la PSP de son fils. J'ai demandé à mon frère et il a dit qu'il avait oublié l'appareil dans son sac. Comment tu peux oublier l'appareil de quelqu'un d'autre dans ton sac et voyager de la France au Togo? Depuis ce jour, ma relation avec Jacques a changé et il est devenu un peu distant de moi et ma famille.

J'étais à Monaco quand j'ai décidé de collectionner les crampons de tous mes coéquipiers et de les emmener en Afrique pour les plus démunis. J'avais un sac plein. J'ai remmené ce gros sac au Togo.

Quelques jours après, quand j'ai décidé de partager ses crampons aux gens, j'ai remarqué que le sac avait disparu. J'ai compris après que mon frère a volé ce sac pour aller vendre les chaussures dans un marché connu dans mon pays nommé Hedzranawoé.

Un jour, ma mère m'a appelé très tôt le matin quand j'étais toujours au lit. Elle m'a dit que Rotimi a reçu un visa pour aller jouer au foot à Dubaï. Il devait quitter ce jour la sinon son visa allait être annulé. Il était dans la même situation qu'un de ses amis, Kodjovi (@Denilsonde Souza). J'ai demandé à un de mes gars à l'époque (@Agui Mozino), d'aller prendre des billets pour eux. On n'a pas pu trouver de billets « economy» pour ce jour. Donc j'ai décidé d'acheter un billet « First Class » pour chacun d'entre eux. Après tout, c'était une opportunité en or pour lui d'aller faire carrière à Dubaï. Seulement 4 jours après il était de retour à Lomé. Il disait que le style de vie à Dubaï n'était pas fait pour lui. Il ne pouvait pas faire ce qu'il voulait (faire la fête, embrasser les filles en public ou boire). Il a continué en disant que c'était strictement musulman.

La troisième partie va bientôt sortir et ce sera à propos de l'homme qui lui-même se nomme « Le père de la famille » @Kola Adebayor A.K.A Lion of Judah. #GodFirst #BringThemOut #GodIsWatching #LearnTheLessons #TalkAboutYourProblems
35

www.facebook.com/permalink.php?story_fbid=1656411337920885&id=13 77345199160835&substory_index=0, accessed Friday 22 May 2015.

Si j'ai décidé de sortir l'épisode 3 aujourd'hui, c'est parce que mon frère Kola Adebayor et les autres membres de ma famille ont choisi de parler de nos histoires de familles sur les réseaux sociaux, à travers des lettres à mes clubs, radios… Je pourrais écrire une autobiographie et la vendre, mais j'ai décidé de tout partager avec vous ici.

Il y a 25 ans, mon grand frère Kola a quitté le pays pour l'Allemagne ; il est donc devenu l'espoir de notre famille. Nous pensions qu'il allait nous sortir de la misère. Plusieurs années plus tard, nous n'avions toujours pas d'électricité ; nous n'avions pas de téléphone. S'il avait besoin de nous parler, il appelait l'hôtel Atlantique qui était situé très proche de notre maison. On devait courir vers la réception de l'hôtel pour recevoir l'appel.

Quand j'ai eu ma première opportunité d'aller jouer en France, nous avions besoin d'argent pour le billet d'avion ainsi que pour d'autres dépenses. Mon frère n'était jamais présent durant ses moments. Seul Dieu sait ce qu'il faisait en Allemagne.

Quand je suis arrivé en France, j'ai signé tous les documents nécessaires avec mon équipe et ils m'ont logé dans l'académie.

Quelques mois plus tard, mon frère voulait venir me visiter. Je n'avais pas d'argent et je vivais toujours à l'académie. J'étais donc oblige d'emprunter de d'argent pour payer son hôtel ainsi que son voyage retour en Allemagne. N'oubliez pas qu'il est mon grand frère.

Quelques années plus tard, les choses commençaient à aller mieux. Dieu merci, j'ai signé un contrat avec Metz. Depuis ce jour, il m'appelait à chaque fois que c'était le moment de payer ces factures. Parfois c'était son fils qui était malade. J'étais oblige de m'habituer à tout ceci.

Encore une fois, j'étais chanceux de signer un nouveau contrat pour Monaco. J'ai donc déménagé de Metz à Monaco. Un jour, Kola et le regretté Peter Adebayor sont venu me voir à Monaco, sans prévenir. Quelqu'un a dit : « Le sang est plus épais que l'eau ». Donc je les ai bien accueillis. Ils sont arrivés très tôt le matin et j'étais en route pour l'entrainement. Dès mon retour à la maison, nous avions eu une discussion et ils m'ont fait comprendre qu'ils voulaient ouvrir un business de vente de voitures. C'est clair, il s'agissait d'une grande somme d'argent. Donc je leur ai promis de régler ca dès que je reçois mon prochain salaire.

En ce même moment, un jeune Camerounais (Thierry Mangwa) vivait avec moi. Il avait des problèmes personnels et il avait besoin d'un endroit où dormir, donc je l'hébergeais chez moi pendant quelques jours. Un jour quand je suis rentré de l'entrainement il pleurait. Il ne m'a jamais dit pourquoi. Mes frères qui étaient en visite, ne pouvaient pas me l'expliquer. Un autre jour, un de mes amis Togolais (Padjoe) est venu me visiter. Quand il quittait, je lui ai offert environ 500€. Mon frère Kola a remarqué cela et était très énervé. Il me demandait pourquoi j'ai donné de l'argent à mon ami aussi vite alors que lui, non. Ma raison est simple : mon frère Kola avait besoin d'une grande somme que je ne gardais pas chez moi à la maison. Cela a fini avec une longue dispute.

Un autre jour après l'entrainement, j'étais très fatigué et je suis allé faire une sieste. Je me suis réveillé et il y avait un couteau sous ma gorge. Quand j'ai ouvert mes yeux, mes deux frères étaient là. Ils criaient et disaient que je perdais leur temps. Peter devenais très furieux et Kola le supportait. Je leur ai dit « Si c'est le seul moyen de régler ce problème… tuez-moi et prenez l'argent ! » C'est à ce moment qu'ils ont posé le couteau sur la table. Apres tout ceci j'ai trouvé un moyen de sortir de mon propre appartement et j'ai appelé mes parents. Ma mère a proposé que j'appelle la police. C'était ma seul option pour retourner chez moi, en sécurité…En plus j'avais entrainement le lendemain. J'ai donc suivi le conseil de ma mère. La police est venue et ils se sont calmés. Encore une fois, « le sang est plus épais que l'eau », donc j'ai laissé tomber. Quelques jours plus tard, Peter est allé à Paris pour visiter un des amis de Kola. Cela veut dire que je reste seul avec Kola à la maison. Pour ma propre sécurité, je me suis débrouillé pour lui trouver de l'argent le plus vite possible. Seul Dieu sait combien je lui ai donné.

Après tout ceci, je suis allé en vacances au Togo et j'étais surpris quand ma mère m'a demandé pourquoi j'ai appelé la police pour mes propres frères. Vous le savez bien que c'est elle-même qui m'a proposé cette option. Elle a continué en disant que je suis la mauvaise personne dans cette famille. C'est une histoire que je laisse pour le moment...

A chaque fois que je visitais le pays, tout le monde demandais pourquoi Kola ne retourne jamais au pays. Immédiatement, j'ai organisé un vol pour lui pour qu'il vienne visiter la famille.

Le 22 avril 2005, nous avons reçu une mauvaise nouvelle. J'ai reçu un appel disant que mon père était décédé. J'étais dévasté. J'ai appelé mon grand frère pour lui dire qu'on devait être tous ensemble au pays. Je me suis assuré qu'un billet d'avion soit prêt pour lui. On est tous rentré et je me suis occupé de tout. Plusieurs mois avant la mort de mon père, j'étais à l'hôpital pour lui passer une visite, il m'a dit de s'assurer que ses funérailles ne seraient pas des moments de tristesses. Il voulait qu'on célèbre sa vie. Je laisse Dieu décidé si j'ai organisé des funérailles dignes à mon père. Le gars qui se surnomme « le grand de la famille » n'a contribué à rien. Mais il a toujours l'audace de dire que je ne fais rien pour la famille.

En 2006, j'ai eu une grande opportunité de jouer pour Arsenal. Depuis ce moment, mon frère à commencer une série de fausses accusations contre moi.

Le 22 Juillet 2013, une autre triste nouvelle a encore frappé notre famille. Mon frère Peter Adebayor a rendu l'âme. Sa mort était vraiment triste et cela m'a affecté. Une chose que je trouve difficile à encaisser aujourd'hui, c'est que Kola m'accuse ouvertement de la mort de Peter. Il dit que la boutique que j'ai aidé Peter à ouvrir n'était pas bonne. Il continue à m'envoyer des messages disant que ma carrière sera détruite. J'ai tout fait pour Peter quand il était vivant, je l'ai emmené à Metz et Monaco avec moi. Qu'est-ce que Kola peut dire qu'il a fait pour Peter ? Rien. Ce gars ne s'est même pas présenté aux funérailles ; alors que je lui ai envoyé de l'argent pour son voyage.

Il dit que j'ai aussi fait souffrir notre mère, mais il oublie que quand il est parti en Allemagne, j'étais la personne aux côtés de la maman. Quand j'ai commencé à réussir dans le foot, j'ai fait tout ce que vous pouvez imaginer pour ma mère. C'est normal. Mais mon frère n'est jamais satisfait. Il dit que j'ai acheté une voiture de merde à la maman. Pourquoi il n'achète pas mieux ? Tout ce que je veux, c'est de le voir prendre ses responsabilités. Comme je ne le fais pas bien, il devrait me montrer l'exemple en tant que « le grand frère ». Il est en Allemagne, ça fait plus de 20 ans mais il n'a jamais invité notre mère. Pour qu'il revienne même au pays, c'est tout un défi.

Tout ce qu'il répète, c'est que mon père avait dit que je devrais construire une maison à chacun d'entre eux. Je ne pense pas que mon père a dit cela. Est-ce que cela est même raisonnable? En tant que grand frère, il est censé faire tout ce que je suis en train de faire. Il devrait arrêter de se cacher et prendre ses responsabilités. A l'époque de son arrivée en Europe, il était assez jeune pour faire carrière dans le football aussi. Bref, il y a des chauffeurs ici qui se débrouillent pour aider leurs familles. Pourquoi n'a-t-il rien fait de pareil, mais il continue à parler ? D'ailleurs, il devrait emmener Rotimi, Bidemi ou même son propre fils Aziz ici avant de parler de « prendre soin de la famille ». Les actions sont plus fortes que les discours.

Beaucoup dissent que je n'ai pas été à l'école, mais ils oublient de dire que c'est parce qu'on n'avait pas les moyens. Mais je n'ai jamais reproché cela à mes parents. Mais Dieu merci, aujourd'hui je parle plus de 3 langues et je peux envoyer ma fille a l'école. Je suis fier de cela. Les gens peuvent m'accusé de ne pas être allé à l'école ; mais au final ce qui compte, c'est celui que tu deviens et ce que tu as appris dans la vie.

Plusieurs fois, je voulais abandonner. Demandez à ma sœur Iyabo Adebayor combien de fois je l'ai appelé et j'étais prêt à commettre le suicide ? J'ai gardé ces choses pendant plus de 11 ans… Mais si je meurs, personne ne connaitra mon histoire, personne ne retiendra la leçon… Certaines personnes disent que je devrais garder ces histoires, mais quelqu'un doit se sacrifier ; quelqu'un doit en parler. Je sais qu'il y a des gens qui vont établir un rapport avec leurs propres histoires et d'autres vont apprendre les leçons. Pour tous ceux qui me connaissent, je ferais tout pour mon pays et mon peuple.

Message final d'un petit frère à un grand frère : arrête de fumer et arrête de boire. Voilà mon histoire.

[36] Antoinette Muller, www.dailymaverick.co.za/article/2015-05-22-stranger-in-a-strange-land-adebayors-silent-struggles/#.VV7gxUYe4TY, accessed 25 May 2015.

7

Conclusion

Ubuntu-ism is neither fixed nor claimed or practiced homogenously across Africa. In some countries such as South Africa it is an ideal to be recuperated, resurrected or rediscovered through conscious acts of creative imagination and practice – for its emancipatory potential to be mobilised as a critique of and complement to Western modernity (van Binsbergen 2001, 2003; McAllister 2009; Metz 2011; Gordon 2014; Biney 2014; Cornell 2014; Praeg & Magadla 2014b: 3) – from a real or imagined past corrupted by colonialism, apartheid and neoliberal individualism. This recuperation of Ubuntu is perceived as particularly urgent, given the surging economic downturns and ever diminishing possibilities for the rights and entitlements promised all and sundry under the post-apartheid constitution (Ramose 1999, 2014; Mbembe 2006; Nkondo 2007; Thomas 2008; Ntlama & Ndima 2009; Ndlovu-Gatsheni 2009; Metz 2011; Cornell 2014; Praeg 2014; Praeg & Magadla 2014a), which constitution, paradoxically, does not give Ubuntu the centrality it deserves (Ramose 2014; Cornell 2014). The South African state and government may be involved in significant and even commendable social protection measures in conjunction with a relentless pursuit of a market economy (Ferguson 2015), but there are reasons to be critical about the Ubuntu welfare state, which finds itself bedevilled by chronic inequality and mass poverty (Terreblanche 2002; Pillay et al. 2013). In West and Central Africa where a strong and resilient tradition of "wealth in people" contests the market reality of "wealth in things" (Guyer & Belinga 1995), *Ubuntu-ism* is as much a contested reality or questionable moral force as it is an aspiration and a discourse on an ethic of inclusivity and balance between individual and collective agency or private and public interests (Geschiere & Nyamnjoh 1998; Nyamnjoh 2002, 2005, 2011).

As a story of opportunism in a world caught in the web of predatory hunter gatherer relationships and zero sum games, *C'est l'homme qui fait l'homme* is an important vehicle for moral lessons that could rekindle nostalgia for more inclusive futures in Africa and globally. *C'est l'homme qui fait l'homme* and related stories – touched upon cursorily in this study – of the opportunities possible with gift or Ubuntu economies are an art form and form of Ubuntu. They are a way of maintaining, remembering, teaching and unfolding Ubuntu in a nimble-footed, rapidly changing world. Their focus on opportunism should not be mistaken as an indication that the opportunities of Ubuntu are thin or non-existent.

As evidenced in *C'est l'homme qui fait l'homme* and in this study, *Ubuntu-ism* as a principle and a practice is increasingly challenged by the ever more pernicious and invidious ways in which the market is able to penetrate and transform the lives of families and other intimacies – primordial and otherwise – with its overly simplified, abstracted and sterile creed of greed and delusions of context-free rights-bearing, free-floating individuals pregnant with choice, prospects and possibilities (Graeber 2001). Given the vicissitudes and uncertainties of and in the market, do Africans fathom the stakes enough to ensure continuity for *Ubuntu-ism* beyond merely as nostalgia for a lost ideal (van Binsbergen 2001, 2003)? It is far from clear the extent to which *Ubuntu-ism*'s emphasis on community is the answer to corruption, graft, fraud, exclusion, resource wars, and other predations engendered by the patronage of the ruling elite and its "politics of back-scratching" (Nyamnjoh 2013a). To what extent would it help for Africans to see and relate to the opportunity and opportunism of *Ubuntu-ism* as bedfellows, as both emerge from the same environment, and what it affords its inhabitants materially?

If opportunity and opportunism are two sides of the same coin (Graeber 2001), or the same individual for that matter,

128

how does one harness opportunities that are inextricably entangled and interconnected with opportunism? Put differently, how does one curb, mitigate or seek to disentangle opportunity from opportunism without throwing the baby out with the bathwater of opportunism? Like Siamese twins, opportunity and opportunism are often so entangled and interconnected that an operation to "free" the one from the other often results in the death of both. Given this delicate situation, and the reality of *Ubuntu-ism* as opportunity and opportunism, how does one think of society or Africa not in terms of absolutely choosing opportunity and doing away with opportunism, but rather in terms of how to reconcile both opportunity and opportunism and live with the recognition of their inextricable entanglement? Put differently and in more concrete terms, how do the Gohous and the Daous or the Nastous and Amélies of Africa forge a common future? And how should they join forces to demand that France – Europe and the West by extension – assume their obligations towards a continent systematically dispossessed throughout histories of unequal encounters and unreciprocated generosity? Still in other words, what role should diasporic Africans – both recent migrants and descendants of slaves – play in the development of Africa, their home countries, home regions or home villages? How much is it imperative for them to dwell on who and what they left behind? Is the diaspora so widespread and ubiquitous in a globalised world that these questions will become less relevant? Put differently, is there a limit to the affirmation that "Migration produces diasporas and diasporas produce migration" (Collier 2013: 40)? Still in other words, can a diaspora ever really become so integrated into the host community that all links and interconnections with communities of origin are lost? Is total integration possible or even desirable? Isn't belonging to any community always going to be gradated with infinite degrees of insiderness?

The interconnections between gift and market economies materialise in the lives of African migrants and the relationships they seek to maintain with their home countries and communities of origin through remittances. Africans in the diaspora, taken individually, remit significant amounts of money to the continent yearly. Estimates point to a tremendous growth in remittances in Africa, ranging from approximately USD4.9 billion in 1990 to roughly USD 50 billion in 2007 (Lartey 2013). Quite significantly, in their study of micro data from over 12,000 African immigrants in 9-OECD countries (Australia, Belgium, France, Italy, Netherlands, Norway, Spain, UK and USA), Bollard et al (2010) conclude that:

> Africans are found to remit twice as much on average as migrants from other developing countries, and those from poorer African countries are more likely to remit than those from richer African countries. Male migrants remit more than female migrants, particularly among those with a spouse remaining in the home country; more-educated migrants remit more than less educated migrants; and although the amount remitted increases with income earned, the gradiant is quite flat over a large range of income. Finally, there is little evidence that the amount remitted decays with time spent abroad, with reductions on the likelihood of remitting offset by increases in the amount remitted conditional on remitting. (Bollard et al 2010: 605-606)

Daou and Amélie, the two immigrants in France and Germany, would find their place among the 12,000 African immigrants whose remitting practices are highlighted by Bollard et al. (2010). According to a report by the UK-based Overseas Development Institute (ODI) released in April 2014[1], the likes of Daou and Amélie would be able to remit even more, were it not for a "remittance supertax" of nearly $2 billion a year that remitting diasporic Africans have to pay, amounting to an average money transfer cost to sub-Saharan Africa of about 12 per cent, compared with a global average of 7.2 per cent. This remittance supertax goes directly to the world's leading remittances companies such as Western Union and MoneyGram which control two-thirds of Africa's remittances market.

Hence, Africans living abroad like Daou and Amélie are super-exploited not only by the opportunism of the families and friends back home in the likes of Gohou and Nastou, but also by companies such as Western Union and MoneyGram, which thrive on weak competition, concentration of market power and financial regulation to charge exorbitantly for remitting to Africa. Supertaxes are over and above what, for professional and well educated African immigrants, their host high-income countries in Europe or elsewhere are receiving in taxes on their income: "a flow of revenue that is a return on education that the host society has not itself financed" and thus to be rightly regarded as "an inadvertent aid program to host countries" from the countries of origin of the migrants in question (Collier 2013: 226).

While it is tempting to argue as well that migrant remittances – supertaxes notwithstanding – could be considered partly as indirect aid by host countries to countries where migrants remit, it is worth noting that remittances by migrants usually flow directly to families, village and other local community development initiatives that seek to bypass the state or compensate for its failings and irrelevance. Multi- and bilateral aid on the other hand is usually directed at and managed by the state and its bureaucracies (some of whom employ their own citizens and import their own technologies even where local and cheaper alternatives exist), with little or no evidence of trickle down to those in need.

The situation is further compounded by illicit financial outflows from Africa, which according to Thabo Mbeki, "drain hard currency reserves, heighten inflation, reduce tax collection, cancel investment, undermine trade, worsen poverty, and widen income gaps." In a report prepared for the African Union, Mbeki draws on the conclusions of a study by Global Financial Integrity (GFI) on illicit financial flows from Africa that give a conservative estimate of approximately $854 billion of illicit financial outflows from Africa during the period 1970 to 2008. The report indicates that the total could be as high as $1.8 trillion, with the bulk of such outflows coming from sub-Saharan, and especially West and Central African, regions. Significantly, the GFI study remarks that illicit financial outflows from the entire region of sub-Saharan Africa "outpaced official development assistance going into the region at a ratio of at least 2 to 1," and that "Illicit financial outflows from Africa grew at an average rate of 11.9 percent per year."[2] Comments about corrupt, incompetent and undemocratic Africans aside, such blatant opportunism by corporate investors and international capital in general means African states often lack what it takes to create industries and jobs as an incentive to their citizens and nationals to stay at home instead of pursuing what is largely an illusion of greener pastures on foreign shores.

Writing in connection with South Africa, which incidentally is among the top five victims of illicit financial outflows in Africa[3], Drucilla Cornell calls for a "revolutionary Ubuntu" to unchain the humanity of a large majority of black Africans super-exploited by corporate greed with "a thoroughgoing economic transformation" (Cornell 2014: 170). If movement in goods, capital, and ideas are to serve as alternatives to moving people, as Collier (2013: 11) suggests, then ways must be explored to tame corporate greed which only further compounds the predicament of "the bottom billion" trapped in mass poverty (Collier 2013: 11) in so-called underdeveloped societies.

This study of *C'est l'homme qui fait l'homme* has attempted a discussion of the predicaments and perils that those in African diasporas confront as they attempt to develop back home. It tackles in considerable detail a theme often captured in fiction, but rarely discussed in anthropological and sociological discourses. The intent is to unpack, explain, and perhaps account for the lagging behind of the continent of Africa in terms of economic development using conventional Western indicators that foreground the autonomous individual as a unit of analysis of opportunities, prospects and choices. *C'est l'homme qui fait l'homme* has coherence in its fiction, and the fact of its deep foundation in reality makes it even more powerful than many an ethnography of real life encounters of a similar nature. Further sociological research could explore Ivorians glean from watching *C'est l'homme qui fait l'homme*. With whom do people watching the show identify? Is the show perceived by viewers as some type of moral lesson – making the case for Ubuntu as does the popular *Zouglou* song by Meleke[4] with the same title of *C'est l'homme qui fait l'homme*? To what extent is the choice of a popular musical form and a popular song both informed by endogenous values of inclusivity, to address topical concerns in urban Côte d'Ivoire, a statement on the imperative to reconcile autochthonous cosmopolitanism with the cosmopolitanism resultant from histories of encounters with France, Europe and the rest of the West?

The experiences underscored in this study of *C'est l'homme qui fait l'homme* partly justify the reason why many an Ivorian (or any other African) diaspora may choose not to develop back home or do so only most grudgingly. Yet, at a continental level, the experiences explain why Africa remains poor, regardless of its status as probably the biggest provider of labour globally from the époque of slavery through colonialism to neoliberal globalisation – one continent with perhaps the largest number of migrant workers abroad. With the ever-rising brain drain from Africa to Europe, the Americas and elsewhere and in view of the fact that not every brain drain is a brain down the drain but 'brain gain' for both the place of origin and destination (Davies 2007; Ratha & Shaw 2007; Collier 2013: 195-206)[5], one would wonder why the continent remains poor, despite a noted increase in remittances, notwithstanding "remittance supertax" and other forms of exploitation. For those diasporic Africans who choose to develop back home, how should they ensure that their hard earned money is put

133

into good use by those whom they trust on the basis of *Ubuntuism* or the philosophy of collective and inclusive success?

Some answers to these questions are provided in the experiences of mismanagement and misappropriation of remittances channelled home by two migrants in Europe – Daou and Amélie – to Gohou (a kin) and Nastou (a friend). The study of their predicaments suggests that relationships, be they based on blood or choice or both, are as capable of opportunity as they are of opportunism. It is important, however, to note that not every relationship is characterised by opportunism. There are many examples of friends and kin who are honest and trustful, and who execute whatever projects with which they are charged with absolute integrity and respect for the diasporans and themselves and their hard-earned remittances.

The comparison of Nastou and Gohou is interesting to explore further. How is opportunism extended through opportunity afforded by relationships based on friendship and on blood? Nastou starts off being reluctant to help her friend Amélie because she did not want to get involved with money, to avoid conflicts that have the potential to destroy relationships. Gohou had already mastered the game using his cousin Daou's hard earned remittances to enrich him. After learning to play the game Nastou excels in the game even managing to build a house and own properties. Yet, Gohou uses most of the money received from Daou to entertain girls and enjoy himself in parties at clubs and bars. Gohou comes across as someone living in the moment and heavily reliant on Daou for remittances. In addition, Gohou does not seem to invest in property; we only get to experience some of the tricks he uses to sell the same plot of land to different people. But these plots of land seemed to be what was remaining from the six plots of land Daou had left in his charge. When Daou announces his arrival, Gohou is stressed and worried about being discovered by Daou. When Daou finds him at the club, it is Gohou's own bodyguard that prevents him from making an escape. What does this tell us about opportunity and opportunism? Gohou's bodyguard may not be happy with the way he has squandered Daou's money in the clubs and wants him to face Daou. Alternatively, their relationship may have been marred by exploitation and the bodyguard seizes the opportunity to exact vengeance on Gohou. After showing Daou the house that Gohou had sold to someone else, Gohou makes an escape and his future is not so certain, given that the only source of money from Daou would immediately come to an end.

Nastou, on the other hand, seems to have outperformed and potentially had a more secure future than Gohou. Having subscribed to the game, we meet Nastou at a construction site of her new house. Unlike Gohou who had to be the one calling Daou, Nastou answers the phone impatiently after it rings and then realises that she was speaking to Amélie. At this point, she tells her to send more money and that she was at the construction site. This is similar to the way Gohou would demand and use construction of the house to extort money from Daou. Nastou spends her time buying expensive furniture for the house. Arriving unannounced, Amélie is amazed at how beautiful the house was and even how radiant Nastou looked herself. But Nastou did not seem too surprised and in fact pretends rather impressively, maintaining not knowing anything about Amélie's accusations. When Amélie continues pushing with the accusations, Nastou calls the guard to escort her guest out of the property. Without hesitation the guard escorts Amélie by physically holding her out the gate. It is interesting to note that shortly after getting the guard to escort her friend out, Nastou then answers the phone and we learn that she is speaking to another friend, also in Europe. Just like Amélie, on the phone we learn the friend is about to get into the same dupe of sending money with the hope that it would build her a house. Nastou even makes reference about how the friend has seen how beautiful her own house was, and that the friend was going to get something similar.

Unlike Gohou, Nastou's ability to dupe others has become business. It is through opportunity enabled by friendship that Nastou would continue to sustain and potentially grow her business of opportunism. Such a future for Gohou is not necessarily that clear. But this is not to say that Gohou could not recover and learn to play the game better when another close relative happens to go abroad. The point of the comparison is to highlight the extent that in making money at all cost necessarily depends on relationships to generate and grow profits. In other words, the philosophy of *Ubuntu-ism* helps us understand endeavours to grow opportunity as not just the other side of the coin but in this case reliant on relationships of opportunism to maximise monetary returns.[6]

While many an African are clearly very careful with how and to whom they remit and follow up on their investments judiciously, many as well have fallen prey to the sort of opportunism that this study captures. Increasingly, however, Africans abroad and in general, are wising up to the tricks of family and friends and no longer indulging in such blind trust as witnessed with Daou and Amélie.[7] Incidents and rumours of misappropriation of funds have increased migrants' awareness and alertness to the extent that some of them purposely go home regularly either to supervise their projects or at least ensure that work is effectively progressing.[8] Notwithstanding the importance of such alertness on the part of migrants, it is hardly entirely correct to blame the opportunism of relations and friends back home entirely on the waywardness and unethical behaviour of the individuals involved. Structural factors informing global poverty, inequality and the tendency to privilege the market over all other forms of economy play an important role in determining relationships of opportunity and opportunism at global and local levels, by individuals, states and corporations, among other actors. And so does history as a technology of domination and control.

Daou and Amélie's negative experiences explain in part why remittances by African migrants abroad have a noted "significant positive impact on income inequalities in African countries" (Anyangwu 2011), even when the fact of remitting does not necessarily achieve the envisaged outcome for those doing the remitting (Collier 2013: 206-213). Remittances, it has been noted, also contribute significantly to economic growth in Africa (Lartey 2013), with Singh et al (2010: 312) suggesting that "countries with well-functioning domestic institutions" appear to "be better at unlocking the potential for remittances to contribute to faster economic growth."

It is perhaps this recognition of the importance of institutional capacity to maximise the opportunities and minimise the opportunism of *Ubuntu-ism* that has led to calls for diasporic Africans not only to increase and sustain their remittances to the continent, but also for greater coordination and channelling of remittances through development banks and related institutions that in turn could lend the remittances to national residents for various enterprises. This is a call for diasporas to consider remitting over and above the small amounts which usually target individuals, families and friends, and which at best venture as far as but hardly ever beyond village or regional development associations of the type some scholars have documented ethnographically (Barkan et al. 1991; Nyamnjoh & Rowlands 1998; Platteau 2004; Fonchingong & Ngwa 2005; Mercer et al. 2009; Nyamnjoh 2014). It remains to be established the extent to which diasporic Africans would be willing to place funds into an abstract state and business structure over which they have little control and would not necessarily help their own kin directly. In view of the vicissitudes, precarity and precariousness of interested humans strung together by hierarchical relationships of opportunity and opportunism, to what extent should one willingly put one's eggs in one basket, instead of distributing them strategically across institutions or one's kin?

As long as the market economy is not reconciled with gift economies of mutual obligations and reciprocity such as represented by Ubuntu, the implicit tension and contradiction

137

in the logics underpinning the two systems of economy would not abate in the relationships that characterise Africans caught between and betwixt them. Diasporans committed to continue with development projects mediated by those left behind in their home countries and villages need to remain resolute and supportive to the logic and philosophy of Ubuntu while vigilant on how their remittances are being used by those entrusted with projects.

The focus of *C'est l'homme qui fait l'homme*, the basis of the current study, is less about a documentation of the opportunities of Ubuntu. It is more of a moral lens through which to glean the opportunism of Ubuntu when individuals caught between and betwixt are forced to choose between two otherwise complementary economies and ways of being human – the market and gift economies. Such surging opportunism and the corruption of Ubuntu that comes with it are a clarion call to rediscover, reinvent and reinvest in the interconnections and interdependencies between market and gift economies, obligation and reciprocity, autonomy and sociality. Put differently, it is a clarion call to reunite the hunter and the hunted, each with the capacity to tell the story of the hunt, ever conscious as they both should be of the prospect that the hunter can be hunted and the hunted the hunter. It is in this sense that we might understand why, to quote Barack Obama once more, it took a man like Nelson Mandela "to free not just the prisoner, but the jailor as well; to show that you must trust others so that they may trust you; to teach that reconciliation is not a matter of ignoring a cruel past, but a means of confronting it with inclusion, generosity and truth."[9]

Trust – a word repeatedly used in the dialogue of *C'est l'homme qui fait l'homme* – and intimacy are central in the relationships between Africans abroad and the relations and friends to whom they remit back home. Collier has argued that trust is essential for sustained cooperation, adding that "High-trust societies are better able to cooperate and also face lower costs of transactions because they are less dependent upon processes of formal enforcement" (Collier 2013: 32). Trust, he adds, "must be underpinned by a reasonable presumption that it will be reciprocated" (Collier 2013: 62). Given that cases of lack and betrayal of trust and of opportunism as evidenced in this study are quite common in and among Africans caught in the predatory web of global capitalism and neoliberal globalisation (Collier 2013: 63-67; Geschiere 2013), it is only appropriate to question why incidences of repeated attempts to repair relationships recur.

As Jimu (2012) demonstrates in peri-urban land transactions in Malawi, trust is a delicate issue. The context is important. In the case of land transactions, the context includes principles for determining descent and inheritance, both of material and non-material possessions, including positions of power and influence. Trust is a taken-for-granted asset, though it is not so to date as land cannot be sold and security of tenure guaranteed under the current arrangements. Currently, land buyers require documented "written" agreements and some seek registration of title with the state through "leasing". These practices provide new forms of evidence upon which trust is constructed and negotiated. They suggest that past arrangements cannot be trusted any longer. The absence of documented evidence is not in any case a cause of land disputes common to peri-urban land transactions, just as the availability of a document would not stop disputes from occurring. As a common socio-cultural currency central to Ubuntu, trust is a non-economic asset that enables actors to interact with each other.

With trust, even when the main actors follow economic agendas, the process is "at the intersection of cultural and social reproduction" (Förster 2009: 345). Trust is informed by the assumption and predictability that others will act in a particular and predictably cooperative rather than competitive manner. Like intimacy, trust is never self-evident; it is a leap of faith inspired by the suspension of doubt (Geschiere 2013: 32). As Johnson and Johnson (2005) observe in relation to market exchange, trust rests on the credibility of institutions governing the exchange relations, perfect competition, supply and demand trends, predictability and impersonal self-regulation. However, when the exchange environment is not highly institutionalised, or when information is monopolised by certain groups, trust is constructed on personalised relationships, at least through knowledge of other's personality, family, history, and so on (Narotzky 1997; Shipton 2007). Long (2001) stresses the need to understand how specific actors and networks of actors engage with and thus co-produce intersubjectively their own (inter)personal and also collective social worlds. If "trust is conducive to the social cooperation that is valuable for prosperity" (Collier 2013: 67), Africans caught between and betwixt the lure and allure of global consumer capitalism and the moral economy of *Ubuntu-ism* must explore ways of distilling and institutionalising trust from the vantage point of their reality as frontier beings compelled to reconcile the centrifugal and centripetal forces in their lives (Nyamnjoh 2015).

Against this background and in view of the imperative to reconcile gift and market economies in the interest of more just and more decent societies politically and economically (Graeber 2001, 2011), perhaps envisaged institutions should seek to build on endogenous rotating credit philosophies and practices that rely on trust and intimacy without necessarily being exclusive (Ardener 1964; Delancey 1978; Ardener & Burman 1995; Niger-Thomas 1995; Biggart 2001; Nyamnjoh 2013a). These philosophies are common throughout Africa and well beyond into places like Japan and China, through South East Asia and India, to the Caribbean and the South of the USA (Geertz 1962; Anderson 1966), as well as among diasporas from these regions in Europe, North America and elsewhere (Ardener & Burman 1995; Mercer et al. 2009; Nyamnjoh 2014). This, of course, does not preclude seeking to enhance such widespread endogenously informed institutional prospects and practices with legal, market-driven frameworks that have proven themselves within corporate bodies, detached or not from any familial relationship. If trust is central to transactions of various kinds – from the economic to the political, through the social and the cultural – as has been argued (Lewis & Weigert 1985; Doney et al. 1998; Dasgupta 2000; Uslaner 2000-2001; Newton 2001; Möllering 2001; Jiménez 2011; Geschiere 2013), then it is important to research further into what else neoliberalism and *Ubuntu-ism* as apparently different logics of accumulation just might have in common – something that both Mauss (1990[1950]) and Graeber (2001, 2011) have broached.

With the ever-increasing global integration of markets and interpenetration of culture, the concepts of humanity, human rights and democracy can no longer be considered apart from the resultant economics, culture and politics of inequality. They are intimately linked and, in many cases, sharply juxtaposed. What practical prospects and possibilities are there for *Ubuntu-ism* in the twenty-first century – an age of the crudest paradoxes: unbelievable wealth amidst implausible penury; record levels of food amidst spiralling levels of hunger; and the paradox of rising economic growth and the concentration of wealth in too few hands alongside rising levels of poverty (Piketty 2014)? Theoretically *Ubuntu-ism* would and should triumph in a context like our current world where there is more than enough wealth to go around, enough food being produced to feed everyone sufficiently, and enough resources for everyone to enjoy at least a minimal standard of living. The problem in its simplest form is one of equity and distribution of the resources that make human rights and human dignity a real possibility: we do not use the world's resources wisely, and we do not share the world's resources with those who need them most. This existential situation is absurd.

As *C'est l'homme qui fait l'homme* demonstrates, victims of a continent victimised by unequal encounters and their iniquities are caught up in a vicious cycle of the illusion of greener pastures in the heart of marginality and opportunism. Africa might be poor economically but not necessarily materially, and as Guyer and Belinga (1995) suggest, and indeed, as the accounts in this study demonstrate, economic wealth, as Bourdieu (1990) would argue, is not the only form of capital available, nor is it necessarily always more important than social, cultural, symbolic and other forms of capital. Marketisation, monetisation, commodification and rationalisation are not the only, nor necessarily the most important system of value for social life (Sandel 2012).

Indeed, as Michael Sandel argues with regard to Americans – who are said to be massively wasteful and inefficient in their celebration of the holidays by buying and presenting gifts to one another instead of just giving cash –, to understand gift-giving simply in terms of maximizing the welfare or utility of the recipient, and to see value purely in monetary terms is to corrupt relationships by suffusing them with utilitarian norms (Sandel 2012: 98-107). As behaviourist economist Richard Thaler argues, apparently irrational behaviour remains the normal way of life even in the most marketised, monetised, commodified and rationalised economies (Thaler 2015). In this regard, it is worth reiterating Graeber's argument that because money is too generic to accumulate history, it cannot add to the holder's identity in the same manner that other things – however wasteful or valueless they might appear in the utilitarian eyes of an economist – are able to, and thus "its identity does not cling to the former owner" the way things more historically entangled with their owners intermingle or are mangled up with these owners (Graeber 2001: 213-214). Thus, the tendency to focus overly on economic wealth, monetary and commodity value of sociality is delusory as it creates an illusion of the omnipotence of economics – and a particular form of economics: that of the market economy. Wealth in things and a fixation with economic capital and a logic of rational choice seem rather reductive when placed alongside philosophies and practices of inclusiveness, African or otherwise. Economic gain might be a primary human motive, but it is hardly the only motive or the most important in every circumstance, as "human motives change over time, responding to experience and the surprises of history" (Simon 1993: 160). One has to partake of a cosmological epistemology of infinite possibilities of forms and transformations of being to see things in people and people in things.

Because history and human behaviour are continually unfolding, understanding and providing for *Ubuntu-ism* is unfinished business in Africa and beyond. Ubuntu provides a framework where poverty and wealth are constantly on the move, changing hands and changing places, ensuring that everyone shall have their fair share of opportunity and possibility – of sunshine, rainfall, windfall, pitfall and downfall – in life. Ubuntu's subscription to interconnection and interdependence is a refusal to confine some from birth to a fate worse than death when too many things are in too few hands and mutual obligations downplayed. Ubuntu invites all and sundry to dream and aspire for an inclusive world of flexible mobility and flexible citizenship.

This study has broached the context of globalisation and the histories of unequal encounters that have shaped relations in Africa and beyond under global capitalism. The study has used the intricate relationships of opportunity and opportunism captured in *C'est l'homme qui fait l'homme* to argue that mobility and identities in Africa should be understood not as investments in the elusive and illusive quest of purity and authenticity. In the spirit of Ubuntu, Africans, their identities and mobilities are part and parcel of the experience of being human. To recognise and provide for a world enriched by African experiences is to recognise the creativity and innovativeness that come with the entanglements and messiness provoked by social encounters and ambitions of dominance.

143

Notes

[1] see www.ft.com/cms/s/0/2c1451ce-c4b9-11e3-9aeb-00144feabdc0.html#axzz2z1Maon1S, see also www.theguardian.com/global-development/2014/apr/16/uk-western-union-moneygram-overseas-development-institute-odi-remittances-africa, accessed 16 April 2014

[2] www.thabombekifoundation.org.za/Pages/Tackling-Illicit-Capital-Flows-for-Economic-Transformation.aspx, accessed 25 May 2015.

[3] According to the GFI report cited by Thabo Mbeki, the top five countries with the highest outflow measured from 1970 to 2008 "were: Nigeria ($89.5 billion) Egypt ($70.5 billion), Algeria ($25.7 billion), Morocco ($25 billion), and South Africa ($24.9 billion)" www.thabombekifoundation.org.za/Pages/Tackling-Illicit-Capital-Flows-for-Economic-Transformation.aspx, accessed 25 May 2015.

[4] www.youtube.com/watch?v=9Kiq0Gv_Rr8, accessed 26 July 2015.

[5] See 'From brain drain to brain gain', in *Education Today* (the newsletter of UNESCO's Education Sector), No. 18, October 2006 – January 2007, pp. 4 – 7; see also 'Drain or gain? Poor countries can end up benefiting when their brightest citizens emigrate', in *The Economist*, available from: www.economist.com/node/18741763, accessed 17 July 2012.

[6] I am particularly grateful to an extended discussion of this and related issues with Ayanda Manqoyi, at a writing workshop that took place from 3-5 July 2015 at Mont Fleur, Stellenbosch. I also acknowledge his subsequent written comments.

[7] See for example, Honorine Express, a US-based Cameroonian bushfaller, renowned for her critical YouTube video postings castigating opportunistic relationships among bushfallers and between bushfallers and their family relations and friends back in Cameroon, provides excellent illustrations of these tendencies in two of her postings: "Demanding and ungrateful family members," www.youtube.com/watch?v=OJ3wZ97Ab0w and "Feel free to go home," www.youtube.com/watch?v=cBK-yqs9ETI, both accessed 07 August 2015. In "Feel free to go home," Honorine urges bushfallers defy family members and their incessant demands by going home once in a while, especially at Christmas, and doing as they please without feeling guilty. This particular posting is in Pidgin English. I provide a full transcript below:

I hope say all man be get a good week. Anyway na weekend this, I say make I come throwe small story we finish am for this week. I know say people they dey wey they don be for this country for 16 years, 20 sef, 25. Each time they member say they want go home, they just check na the problem wey they di go back go meet up am form all kind na people wey you no even know some of them sef for on top table wey e di wait you. They want make you come solve that their problem them. You talk say "No, I no go better go. I go just shidon send my Mamie some 100 000, make e just hold e skin there, chop that Christmas"

You know something, you no fit deprive yourself from that desire. If you get that's desire for go back home go see your loved ones them, your Mamie, your sister, whosoever you miss am, you know what, you get fro go. If you want go sef na say you want go see Cameroon, taste that mimbo for Cameroon, chop that fish for beach noh, you get for go. Even if you get na just your 100 000 wey e go correct for you, just go. Because that problem I di tell you and I di tell wuna again, no matter how wey you go reach back home, you solve that problem them, no man no go tell you thank you. No man no go tell you say "You don do am". You go sef you give na mimbo for quarter, for quarter people they go only want drink. You hear me! Today they drink, tomorrow you want pass, they drink. Another tomorrow, as you want pass, some different man go still dey there e say "Weh grand frère, you be come so, you no be give me mimbo." As you say "Okay, take one bottle," e say "No, grand free you no go shidon down sef with man massa" as you take chair so you shidon for down, you want see table don dark, that friend don call all kind man make e come drink mimbo wey na you work am.

When you reach, when you go back home eh, you no need for give mimbo for no man. That money, na your money. You no owe no man no mimbo. No man no send you for side wey you dey. You dey for side wey you dey, no man no ever cut dry eru send am for you say "Take this dry eru begin di chop am first so, di work that money" So when you go back eh, you no be indebted to any man for give any man here.

I di tell wuna this thing because some people they go there for go make big talk, boucant, they carry big name. They come back for here come back come suffer, they hear their kanda for inside. Some one they say they di go go struggle, they no know how for talk say "No". When you go eh, they ask that beer, tell them say "No, I no fit give wuna beer." Because we get some this fine grand frères them for corner road wey eh, they don dey there year in year out, they di only wait na bush faller them make they come make they drink beer. Then when you no give am, they di telly you say you conto. Or if you give am they drink they no flop, they still tell you say you conto.

You know something, you get for take a step, bold step, struggle go you back home. Juts make your own style wey you fit make am with your family, just be happy. Chop your burning corn wey you want chop am, chop your eru. Go for that Mamic Pou wey e di cook puff-puff and beans eh, you buy that puff-puff and beans you chop am. No way

145

no dey wey you fit solve people their problems them, they tell you say eh "You don do am. They go still talk say "This bushfaller eh, this bush faller aye massa, e no even farotey sef fine. Man drink man no flop" Family members them wey you no know am since time wey you start go school, no one never ever buy you pencil sef. Form the day wey they hear say you don come, they di come with you all kind na problem them, no matter say you try way for solve am, na your Mamie e name go pass go for front that time. They go say "This Mamie e pikin don come with e money, take chair shidon for on top."

You know something, you go Africa or you go back home, if na emergency solve am, if no be emergency make any man take e problem wey e don bring am for your front, go back with am because for this place so noh, na you self sef di hear your kanda. Na you know how wey you di dig am for inside snow, na you know how many hours you di stand up, na you know how many hours wey you shidon down because say you di hustle. The money no easy, e strong, you get your bills them, you get your debts them. But people their demands them no fit deprive you from spending quality time with family, form giving your own very self quality time.

I get people wey they don work all their life, invest am for family, invest am for some extended people wey you no even know am sef. All time they di call beg na money with craze friend them. At the end of the day they ask them say eh "Massa you sef sef you go that your own Etats sef or that your own Europe you di do na how noh massa? People they don come open big big business " yes, people they open big big business but the people they be get for reach for some stage too noh, turn turn tie heart on top their money, conto with am small so that they fit get small capital. I di tell you say if you do am for that style so wey you di go satisfy people their trouble them with your money. I mean, I no know how wey e go dey eh, e go surely worry for you and you go run out of cash.

I di talk am, any man wey e want call me conto, you talk am. No e you sef send me for place wey I dey. If I get am, I give you, if God say give you, I give you. If I no want give you, I stay, especially my money, no be for take am buy beer. I no di buy no man no beer with my money. I don talk am, na so e get for dey for me. I no know about wuna, wuna share wuna views. This one na terrible palava.

[8] On reading this paragraph, Kathryn Toure narrated to me the story of a Ugandan taxi driver in Washington DC. This driver has a company in Kampala – that he monitors from his taxi, via video camera. He rents out TV cameras and music equipment to folk. He knows what leaves his place at what time and when it comes back! "The first thing I do in the morning and the last thing I do before I go to bed is check in on the office in

Kampala." When staff painted the lobby the wrong colour, he got on their case. "I had to show who's boss, even though I am supervising from a distance."

[9] See The White House Office of the Press Secretary, "Remarks of President Barack Obama – As Prepared for Delivery Remembering Nelson Mandela, Johannesburg, South Africa December 10, 2013," www.whitehouse.gov/the-press-office/2013/12/10/remarks-president-barack-obama-prepared-delivery, accessed 24 July 2015; see also www.youtube.com/watch?v=4vUB363cRqE&spfreload=10, accessed 24 July 2015.

Epilogue

Crossroads

This book's readers will recognize how acutely it projects the very contemporary experience of "being African" and its predicaments. Predation and altruism, monopolization and circulation of resources, unequal exchanges and *Ubuntu*-like generosity, who "belongs" and who doesn't to shifting constellations of wealth, power and community, market and gift economies: the worlds of Milton Friedman (with not at all subtle touches of Ayn Rand) and Desmond Tutu, converge and mingle. So, also, the text is informed by the fluid, transactional character of human lives not defined by such binary constraints.

Since Francis Nyamnjoh's first two books, *Mind Searching* (1991) and *The Disillusioned African* (1995), made him known in his native Cameroon and subsequent scholarly and creative writings expanded his range and audience, he has tracked these landscapes, interrogating the colonial experience and scrutinizing African peoples' subsequent condition. Now, in my reading, elaborated below to conclude this book, both *C'est l'homme qui fait l'homme...* and his own life register Nyamnjoh's innovative role, as observer and participant, in Africa's current scholarship and "whither Africa?" debates.

Consider the benchmarks for 20th century African study. Field ethnographies like Schapera's on the Tswana and Griaule's on the Dogon were foundational. Sometimes attached to the colonial enterprise, usually based on multiple site visits over time, they illuminated modes of production, community structure, governance, knowledge about the terrestrial and belief about the cosmological domains. "Thick" profiles of peoples across original and adaptive features

149

emerged, further complicated and enriched as the claims of colonialism and then nation-states entered the reckoning.

A century into the genre, additional, quite different forms of enquiry and sources of knowledge contribute to the continent's study. Nyamnjoh's life and his writings leading to and including *C'est l'homme...* mark changes in the production and transmission of what can be understood as a new form of collective African ethnography, which covers Africans previously less (or un-) known, brought to life, and light, by circumstances not previously experienced, especially since the digital age began.

***

Born in 1961, Nyamnjoh's childhood in Cameroon's North West Province, recounted in his preface to Jean-Pierre Warnier, *Cameroon Grassfields Civilization* (2012), placed his first decade in a remote valley precinct ("I was hardly aware of the world beyond the hills") of a deeply rural village, Bum, seat of a significant rural polity but without a paved (or in local parlance "tarred") road to this day. His next ten years brought him to the palace of the kingdom of Mankon and to Sacred Heart College between the palace and the provincial capital, Bamenda. These were three quite different terrains. Bum's customary life remained largely intact. Educational, commercial and political transitions substantially altered periurban Mankon's (where, as the same preface makes clear, Nyamnjoh witnessed Warnier's classic style of ethnographic research). Bamenda significantly incorporated Cameroon's secular national experience. This early rural-periurban-urban tapestry framed Nyamnjoh's familiarity with, and flexible approach to, experiences and values in a local version of life across the African spectrum.

Did these teen years' periurban life, sorting out "bush" and "town" features and their intersections, make a special impact, and translate into Nyamnjoh's mature interests and academic

150

career, which explore the myriad terrains where contemporary lives on the continent and the diaspora play out? Consider his 1980s profile, as he reached adulthood, began university in the anthropology and sociology faculties at Yaounde, and matured as Cameroon went through economic stasis and decline, a serious military coup attempt in 1984 and subsequent episodes of political and constitutional unrest. He spent the latter 1980s in Great Britain, crossing disciplines to complete doctoral studies in media and communication studies at Leicester in 1990. Early writings published in Cameroon took the measure of that decade's surroundings. *Mind Searching* (1990, dedicated "To The Wretched Of The Earth") was dystopic on Cameroon. *The Disillusioned African* (1995) incorporated Cameroon's political crisis of the early 1990s, invented a Voltaire-like exchange of letters between Cameroonians at home and in Britain, and fired substantive and satirical volleys domestically and at the British "Queendom" people's reception of Africans.

Much of Nyamnjoh's writing since 1990 has appeared in the formal scholarship of his academic career path. But not all, since novels, poems and drama continue to build a notably versatile canon. And so I venture to invoke in what follows, and place Nyamnjoh within, a more spacious authorial landscape than the conventional professoriate creates in Africa or elsewhere, and to suggest how his cumulative experience, his critical and imaginative intelligence, and his soundings on the African world at large bring his work to the point reached with *C'est l'homme...*

***

Wole Soyinka, among Africa's touchstone writers, locates a liminal "crossroads." The deity Esu, who doubles as a "trickster," commands this terrain where fateful challenges and decisions await the Yoruba in their commingled realms of the human and divine: unpredictable, Esu can both confound and

151

illuminate. In related ways, the ethereal meets the ephemeral and *Ubuntu*'s aura frames quite worldly Ivorians' disputes in *C'est l'homme…* as it cultivates the theme of African identities framed, negotiated, dissolved and framed anew as fluid circumstances require. This, his latest excursion into the worlds of "belonging" (written on his own and collaboratively for two decades, partly via short vignette documentaries that would work well as films) imparts both substance and edge to Nyamnjoh's revision of the ethnographic genre.

He writes of "my quest for the interconnection between ethnography and fiction" (p. 19 above; one could add "history" to this mix, as Nyamnjoh does elsewhere) and he directly links it to Stephen Clingman's observation (2009) that "With regard to the current theme of mobility of Africans, transnational fiction can tell us a lot about the nature of boundaries and the grammar of identities." Continuing (as already noted) to mingle scholarship, novels, poems and drama in his own writing, Nyamnjoh moves (and moves us as readers) along new paths of enquiry, using new materials, in a fresh grammar or epistemology the digital world captures and drives forward. Its networks compress the time and expand the space in which significantly more, and more varied, human transactions take place than older ethnographies addressed. Raw materials newly introduced from this informal ethnographic repertoire include vernacular expressions and unconventional idioms drawn from indigenous experience. Soyinka himself has applauded his late compatriot Amos Tutuola as his own mid-20th century precursor who brought similar materials to African writing, made choices whether or not to be prompted by centuries-old influences from abroad, and found a British publisher who took a chance on him, to their own and the larger world's advantage.

Nyamnjoh's methods mine the new producers and consumers of goods, services and ideas that drive new genres' micro-narratives. The current text measures *Ubuntu* as a philosophical and ethical proposition and shifts its shape through the internet, cell phones, smart phones, social and popular culture media (especially through music): excerpts from the intercontinental dialogues Nyamnjoh gleans from conversations between the Ivorians Daou and Gohou, Amélie and Nastou, almost make protagonists of their multiple cell phones as one's conversation gives way to another's and the speakers' deceptions play out at one of this generation's crossroads. Combining the sacred in *Ubuntu* and the profane from what were once largely unknown and unsung, indeed silent Africans, Nyamnjoh now provides the latter agency, mapping the continent's and its diaspora's moral economy with nuanced commentary. Seeming ephemera become material in (his term, p. 133 above) "an ethnography of real life" that I would (to repeat) rephrase: it is "a new form of collective African ethnography" with a global reach shaped by Nyamnjoh's life experience, his acquired command of both the contemporary social science and communications literatures, and his use of the digital world, all of which provide him crossroads vantage points turned to productive use.

***

All these developments should be viewed in the light of indigenous knowledge promotion worldwide from ca. 1970, identified abroad by David Brokensha and his scholarly associates, but also through very much African projects like yesterday's African socialism and *négritude* and today's *Ubuntu-ism*. Africans feel, write and act more autonomously as they scan the worlds they are creating at home. And they evaluate what they find both there and abroad (like *Mind Searching* and *The Disillusioned African* for Nyamnjoh).

One more parallel experience from my perspective frames Nyamnjoh's. The late David Kimble, founding editor of an early major African periodical, *The Journal of Modern African Studies*, was (like *JMAS* remains) a paragon of versatility, and professional itinerancy. He may still, and always, be the one person who—crossing the fields of history, political science and public administration, from colonial to post-colonial times—by his mid-fifties served in high academic and administrative posts in all five African regions: West in Accra, East in Dar-es-Salaam, North in Tangier, Southern in Roma, Central in Zomba. Not a typical "Queendom"-ite, a careerist in colonies while they lasted but an advocate and partner for nation-states as they emerged, modern and contemporary concerns drove Kimble, harnessing the impetus of his British homeland's Workingmens' Institutes and leading to opportunities for adults as well as cadets in Africa's higher education. Another pioneer in cognate fields transplanted to Africa, Lalage Bown, concluded Kimble's obituary in *The Guardian* (19 June 2009) by noting how he "relished the opportunities for developing African agencies for African needs."

Returning, again and finally, to Nyamnjoh: since 1990, now approaching fifty-five, no longer a cadet, not yet a true elder but moving along that path, he is Kimble's African parallel for the late 20th-early 21st centuries (with his current service on the *JMAS* editorial board a symbolic link to Kimble). The previously mentioned doctoral study at Leicester as the digital world arrived, "Broadcasting for Nation-Building in Cameroon: Development and Constraints" (1990) led to work in Dakar, 2003-2009, directing CODESRIA's publications and communications bureau, in an interlude between previous academic postings in Yaounde, Buea, Gaborone and (since Dakar) Cape Town. His apprenticeship and career to this point, marked by the multiple crossroads this epilogue traces, constitute Nyamnjoh's own versatile and signal contribution to contemporary African knowledge, and its potential trajectories forward in space and time. There is now also, alongside the institutional ventures, Langaa Press, his independent creation, with a base of operations in Buea and Bamenda and an increasingly Pan-African compass for multi-genre productions: certainly a digital-world African agency for African needs, and opportunities, with Tutuola among Nyamnjoh's muses (and perhaps voices like Tutuola's on Langaa's publications roster?). Academic travels with related research and publications over twenty-five years (Stanford, Uppsala, Prague, Mauritius, Kyoto…) keep Nyamnjoh continually engaged with Africans and their experiences abroad.

Francis Nyamnjoh's odyssey, from Bum and Mankon to Cape Town on African soil, and so many places abroad? A continuer, with *C'est l'homme…* as a current marker, and with the full kaleidoscope of Africa's people—their links to objects and possessions, informal dealings with each other, formal dealings with institutional structures, however complicated and mediated by crossroads circumstances he's so familiar with—surely in the forefront.

Milton Krieger
Emeritus Professor
Western Washington University

References

Krieger, M., (July, 1996), Conversations with David Kimble, Chagford (Devon)

Nyamnjoh, F. B., (1991), *Mind Searching*, Awka, Kucena Damian Nigeria Limited

_____, (1995), *The Disillusioned African*, Limbe, Nooremac Press.

_____ and Rowlands, M., (1998), "Elite Associations and the Politics of Belonging in Cameroon," *Africa* 68(3): 320-337

_____, (2011), "Cameroon Bushfalling: Negotiation of Identity and Belonging in Fiction and Ethnography," *American Ethnologist* 38(4): 701-713

_____, (unpubl. ms.), "Amos Tutuola and the Elusiveness of Completeness"

Warnier, J-P, (2012), *Cameroon Grassfields Civilization*, Bamenda, Langaa RPCIG

References

Adam, H. and Moodley, K. (2015), *Imagined Liberation: Xenophobia, Citizenship, and Identity in South Africa, Germany, and Canada*, Philadelphia, Pennsylvania: Temple University Press.

Adey, P. (2010), *Mobility*, London: Routledge.

Agamben, G. (2013), *The Highest Poverty: Monastic Rules and Form-Of-Life*, Stanford: Stanford University Press.

Agbohou, N. (2000), *Le Franc CFA et L'Euro Contre L'Afrique*, Coignieres: Solidarité Mondiale.

Aker, J. C. and Mbiti, I. M. (2010), *Mobile Phones and Economic Development in Africa (June 1, 2010)*. Center for Global Development Working Paper No. 211. Available at SSRN: http://ssrn.com/abstract=1693963 or http://dx.doi.org/10.2139/ssrn.1693963.

Alhaji, J.J., (As told to FB Nyamnjoh) (2015), *Sweet Footed African: James Jibraeel Alhaji*, Bamenda; Langaa.

Alpes, M.J. (2011), *Bushfalling: How Young Cameroonians Dare to Migrate*, PhD dissertation, Department of Anthropology, University of Amsterdam, the Netherlands.

Amadiume, I. (1997), *Reinventing Africa: Matriarchy, Religion &Culture*, London: Zed.

Anderson, R.T., (1966), "Rotating Credit Associations in India," *Economic Development and Cultural Change*, 14(3): 334-339.

Anyangwu, J.C. (2011), *International Remittances and Income Inequality in Africa*, African Development Bank Group, Working Paper Series, No.135. August 2011.

Appadurai, A. (2000), "Grassroots, Globalization and the Research Imagination," *Public Culture*, 12(1):1–19.

Apter, A. (1999), "IBB=419: Nigerian Democracy and the Politics of Illusion," in John L. and Jean Comaroff, (eds).

Civil Society and the Political Imagination in Africa: critical perspectives. Chicago IL: University of Chicago Press.

Ardener, E. (1996 [1970]), "Witchcraft, Economics and the Continuity of Belief," in: S. Ardener (ed.) *Kingdom on Mount Cameroon: Studies in the History of the Cameroon Coast, 1500–1970,* Oxford: Berghahn Books pp. 243–266.

Ardener, S. (1964), "The Comparative Study of Rotating Credit Associations," *Journal of the Royal Anthropological Institute,* 94: 201-229.

Ardener, S., and Burman, S. (eds.) (1995), *Money-Go-Rounds: The Importance of Rotating Savings and Credit Associations for Women.* Oxford: Berg.

Bahi, A. (2010), "Jeunes et Imaginaire de la Modernité à Abidjan," *Cadernos de estudos africanos,* n°18/19, p.47-61

Bahi, A. and Dakouri, G. (2009), "Football et Politique dans la Côte d'Ivoire en Crise: Une Lecture des Appels de Drogba à la Réconciliation Nationale,» *Revue Africaine de Sociologie,* 13(2): 2-15.

Barkan, J.D., McNulty, M.L., and Ayeni, M.A.O. (1991), "'Hometown' Voluntary Associations, Local Development, and the Emergence of Civil Society in Western Nigeria," *The Journal of Modern African Studies,* 29(3): 457-480.

Battle, M. (2002), "A Theology of Community: The Ubuntu Theology of Desmond Tutu," *Interpretation* 54(2): 173-182.

Bell, R.H. (2002), *Understanding African Philosophy: A Cross-Cultural Approach to Classical and Contemporary Issues,* New York: Routledge.

Benzon, P. (2011), "Digital Media, 419, and the Politics of the Global Network." *CLCWeb: Comparative Literature and Culture* 13.3: <http: //dx.doi.org/10.7771/1481-4374.1805>

Bergson, A. and Ngnemzué, L. (2008), "French Policy on Immigration and Co-development in Light of the Dakar Speech," *CODESRIA Bulletin,* Nos. 1&2, Dakar: CODESRIA. Pp. 62-67.

Bessis, S. (2003), *Western Supremacy: The Triumph of an Idea?*, London: Zed Books.

Beti, M. (2010 [1972]), *Main Basse sur le Cameroun: Autopsie d'une Decolonisation*, Paris: Editions La Découverte.

Bidwell, N. (2010), "Ubuntu in the Network: Humanness in Social Capital in Rural Africa," *Interactions* pp. 68-71 (Under Development) doi: 10.1145/1699775.1699791.

Biel, R. (2000), *The New Imperialism: Crisis and Contradictions in North/South Relations*, London: Zed Books.

Biggart, N.W. (2001), "Banking on Each Other: The Situational Logic of Rotating Savings and Credit Associations," *Advances in Qualitative Organization Research*, 3: 129-153.

Biney, A. (2014), "The Historical Discourse on African Humanism: Interrogating the Paradoxes," in: Leonhard Praeg and Siphokazi Magadla (eds), *Ubuntu: Curating the Archive*, Pietermaritzburg: University of KwaZulu-Natal Press.pp.27-53.

Blixen, K. (1999 [1937]), *Out of Africa*, London: Penguin.

Bodomo, A. (2012), *Africans in China: A Socio-Cultural Study and its Implications on Africa-China Relations*, Amherst: Cambria Press.

Bollard, A., Mckenzie, D. and Morten, M. (2010), "The Remitting Pattern of African Migrants in the OECD," *Journal of African Economies*, 19(5): 605-634.

Boron, A.A. (ed) (2004), *New Worldwide Hegemony: Alternatives for Change and Social Movements*, Buenos Aires: Clacso.

Boshoff, A. (2007), "Ethics and the Problem of Evil: S v Makwanyane," *Law, Democracy & Development* 11(2): 47-56.

Bourdieu, P. (1990), *The Logic of Practice*. Stanford: Stanford University Press.

Bourdieu, P. (1996), *The State Nobility*. Cambridge: Polity.

Branch, A. and Mampilly, Z. (2015), *Africa Uprising: Popular Protest and Political Change*, London: Zed.

Brinkerhoff, J.M. (2009), *Digital Diasporas: Identity and Transnational Engagement*, Cambridge: Cambridge University Press.

Broodryk, J. (2002), *Ubuntu: Life Lessons from Africa* Pretoria: Ubuntu School of Philosophy.

Broodryk, J. (2007), *Understanding South Africa: The Ubuntu Way of Living*, Pretoria: Ubuntu School of Philosophy.

Brudvig, I. (2014), *Conviviality in Bellville: An Ethnography of Space, Place, Mobility and Being in Urban South Africa*, Bamenda: Langaa.

Burrows, M. (1986), "'*Mission Civilisatrice*': French Cultural Policy in the Middle East, 1860-1914," *The Historical Journal*, 29(1): 109-135.

Bwemba-Bong, R. (2005), *Quand l'Africain Était L'Or Noir de l'Europe: L'Afrique: Actrice ou Victime de la "Traite Des Noirs"?*, Paris: Edition Menaibuc.

Calhoun, C. (2000), "Pierre Bourdieu," in: George Ritzer, (ed.) *Blackwell Companion to the Major Social Theorists*. Cambridge, MA: Blackwell, 274–309.

Castles, S. (2002), "Migration and Community Formation under Conditions of Globalization," *International Migration Review*, 36(4): 1143–1168.

Chabal, P. (2009), *Africa: The Politics of Suffering and Smiling*, London: Zed Books.

Chafer, T. (1992), "France's Mission Civilisatrice in Africa: French Culture not for Export?," in: Chapman, R. and Hewitt, N., (eds) *Popular Culture and Mass Communication in Twentieth Century France:*. Ontario: Edwin Mellen Press, 142-164.

Chinweizu, (1975), *The West and the Rest of Us: White Predators, Black Slavers and the African Elite*, New York: Random House.

Christians, C. G. (2004), "Ubuntu and Communitarianism in Media Ethics," *Ecquid Novi*, 25(2): 235-256.

Clifford, J. (1988), *The Predicament of Culture: Twentieth-Century Ethnography, Literature, and Art*, Cambridge, MA: Harvard University Press.

Clingman, S. (2009), *The Grammar of Identity: Transnational Fiction and the Nature of the Boundary*, Oxford: Oxford University Press.

Coetzee, J.M. (1999), *Disgrace*, London: Vintage.

Collier, P. (2013), *Exodus: Immigration and Multiculturalism in the 21st Century*, London: Penguin Books.

Comaroff, J.L. and Comaroff, J. (2009), *Ethnicity, Inc.* Durban: University of KwaZulu Natal Press.

Cornel, D. (2014), "Ubuntu and Subaltern Legality," in: Leonhard Praeg and Siphokazi Magadla (eds), *Ubuntu: Curating the Archive*, Pietermaritzburg: University of KwaZulu-Natal Press.pp.167-175.

Crais, C., and Pamela, S. (2009), *Sara Baartman and the Hottentot Venus: A Ghost Story and a Biography*, Johannesburg: Wits University Press.

Dasgupta, P. (2000), "Trust as a Commodity," in Gambetta, Diego, (ed.), *Trust: Making and Breaking Cooperative Relations*, electronic edition, Department of Sociology, University of Oxford, Chapter 4, pp.49-72, www.sociology.ox.ac.uk/papers/dasgupta49-72.pdf

Davies, R. (2007), "Reconceptualising the Migration-Development Nexus: Diasporas, Globalisation and the Politics of Exclusion," *Third world quarterly*, 28 (1), 59 – 76.

De Bruijn, M., Nyamnjoh, F.B. & Brinkman, I. (eds) (2009), *Mobile Phones: The New Talking Drums of Everyday Africa*, Bamenda: Langaa.

De Bruijn, M., van Dijk, R. and Foeken, D., (eds) (2001a), *Mobile Africa: Changing Patterns of Movement in Africa and Beyond*. Leiden: Brill.

De Bruijn, M., van Dijk, H. and van Dijk, R., (2001b), "Cultures of Travel: Fulbe Pastoralists in Central, Mali and Pentecostalism in Ghana," in: M. de Bruijn, R. van Dijk and D. Foeken, (eds) *Mobile Africa: Changing Patterns of Movement in Africa and Beyond*. Leiden: Brill, 63–88.

DeLancey, M.W. (1978), "Institutions for the Accumulation and Redistribution of Savings among Migrants," *Journal of Developing Areas*, 2: 209-224.

Demirgüç-Kunt, A. and Klapper, L.F., (2012), "Financial Inclusion in Africa: An Overview," World Bank Policy Research Working Paper No. 6088. Available at SSRN: http://ssrn.com/abstract=2084599.

Depelchin, J. (2005), *Silences in African History: Between the Syndromes of Discovery and Abolition*, Dar Es Salaam: Mkuki Na Nyota.

Depelchin, J. (2011), *Reclaiming African History*, Nairobi: Pambazuka.

Diop, C.A. (1991), *Civilization or Barbarism: An Authentic Anthropology*, New York: Lawrence Hill Books.

Dolamo, R. (2013), "Botho/Ubuntu: The Heart of African Ethics," *Scriptura* 112, pp. 1-10.

Doney, P.M., Cannon, J.P. and Mullen, M.R. (1998), "Understanding the Influence of National Culture on the Development of Trust," *The Academy of Management Review*, 23(3): 601-620.

Duffield, M. and Hewitt, V. (eds) (2013), *Empire, Development & Colonialism: The Past in the Present*, Cape Town: HSRC Press.

Elias, N. (2000), *The Civilizing Process*. Oxford: Blackwell.

Eltis, D. (2000), *The Rise of African Slavery in the Americas*, Cambridge: Cambridge University Press.

Eltis, D. and Richardson, D. (2008), *Extending the Frontiers: Essays on the New Transatlantic Slave Trade Database*, New Haven: Yale University Press.

Enslin, P. and Horsthemke, K. (2012), "Can Ubuntu Provide a Model for Citizenship Education in African Democracies?" *Comparative Education* 40(4): 545-558. doi: 10.1080/0305006042000284538.

Etzo, S. and Collender, G. (2010), "The Mobile Phone 'Revolution' in Africa: Rhetoric or Reality?," *African Affairs*, 109(437): 659-668.

Feibleman, J.K. (1975), *Understanding Civilizations: The Shape of History*, New York: Horizon Press.

Ferguson, J. (1990), *The Anti-politics Machine: 'Development', Depoliticization and Bureaucratic Power in Lesotho*. Cambridge: Cambridge University Press.

Ferguson, J. (1999), *Expectations of Modernity: Myths and Meanings of Urban Life on the Zambian Copperbelt*. Berkeley: University of California Press.

Ferguson, J. (2006), *Global Shadows: Africa in the Neoliberal World Order*, Durham: Duke University Press.

Ferguson, J. (2015), *Give a Man a Fish: Reflections on the New Politics of Distribution*, Durham: Duke University Press.

Ferguson, N. (2011), *Civilization: The West and the Rest*, London: Penguin Books.

Foé, N. (2008), "Negritude and Postcolonialism: The Dakar Satire, or the Ideological Revenge of the West," *CODESRIA Bulletin*, Nos. 1&2, Dakar: CODESRIA. Pp. 68-73.

Fonchingong, C. and Ngwa, C. (2005), "Grassroots Participation for Infrastructure Provisioning in Northwest Cameroon: Are Village Development Associations the Panacea?," *Canadian Journal of Development Studies / Revue canadienne d'études du développement*, 26(3): 443-460

Förster, T. (2009), "Limiting Violence-Culture and the Constitution of Public Norms: with a Case Study from a Stateless Area," in: A. Peters, L. Koechlin, T. Förster and G.F. Zinkernagel (eds) *Non-state Actors as Standard Setters*, Cambridge: Cambridge University Press, pp. 324-347.

Foucault, M. (1975), *Surveiller et Punir: Naissance de la Prison*, Paris: Gallimard.

Foucault, M. (1988), "Technologies of the Self," in: Martin, L.H., Gutman, H. and Hutton, P.H. (eds), *Technologies of the Self: A Seminar with Michel Foucault*, Amherst: University of Massachusetts Press, pp.16-49.

Foucault, M. (1995), *Discipline and Punish: The Birth of the Prison*, New York: Vintage Books.
163

Frei, B.A. (2013), *Sociality Revisited? The Use of the Internet and Mobile Phones in Urban Cameroon*, Bamenda: Langaa.

Friedman, J. (1994), *Cultural Identity & Global Processes*, London: Sage.

Gandoulou, J.D. (1989), *Dandies a Bacongo: Le Culte de l'Elégance dans la Société Congolaise Contemporaine*, Paris: L'Harmattan.

Geertz, C. (1962), "The Rotating Credit Association: A 'Middle Rung' in Development," *Economic Development and Cultural Change*, 10(3): 241-263.

Geschiere, P. (1997), *The Modernity of Witchcraft: Politics and the Occult in Postcolonial Africa*, Charlottesville: University Press of Virginia.

Geschiere, P. (2009), *The Perils of Belonging: Autochthony, Citizenship, and Exclusion in Africa and Europe*, Chicago, IL: University of Chicago Press.

Geschiere, P. (2013), *Witchcraft, Intimacy, and Trust: Africa in Comparison*. Chicago: University of Chicago Press.

Geschiere, P. and Nyamnjoh, F.B. (1998), "Witchcraft as an Issue in the 'Politics of Belonging': Democratization and Urban Migrants' Involvement with the Home Village," *African Studies Review*. 41 (3): 69-91.

Geschiere, P. and Rowlands, M. (1996), "The Domestication of Modernity: Different Trajectories," *Africa*, 66(4): 552-554.

George, S. (1990), *A Fate Worse than Debt: The World Financial Crisis and the Poor*, New York: Grove Press.

Gibbon, P. and Olukoshi, A. (eds) (1996), *Structural Adjustment and Socio-Economic Change in Sub-Saharan Africa: Some Conceptual, Methodological and Research Issues (Research Report)*, Uppsala: Nordiska Afrikainstitutet.

Gondola, (2010), "La Sape Exposed! High Fashion among Lower-Class Congolese Youth: From Colonial Modernity to Global Cosmopolitanism," in: Suzanne Gott and Kristyne Loughran (eds), *Contemporary African Fashion*, Bloomington: University of Indiana, pp.157-173.

Gordon, L.R. (2014), "Justice Otherwise," in: Leonhard Praeg and Siphokazi Magadla (eds), *Ubuntu: Curating the Archive*,

Pietermaritzburg: University of KwaZulu-Natal Press.pp.10-26.

Gott, S and Loughran, K. (eds) (2010), *Contemporary African Fashion*, Bloomington: University of Indiana.

Graeber, D. (2001), *Towards an Anthropological Theory of Value: The False Coin of Our Own Dreams*, New York: Palgrave.

Graeber, D. (2011), *Debt: The First 5,000 Years*, New York: Melville House.

Greenblatt, S., Zupanov, I., Meyer-Kalkus, R., Paul, H., Nyiri, P. and Pannewick, F. (2010), *Cultural Mobility: a Manifesto*, Cambridge: Cambridge University Press.

Gupta, A. and Ferguson, J. (1992), "Beyond 'Culture': Space, Identity, and the Politics of Difference," *Cultural Anthropology*, 7(1): 6–23.

Gupta, A. and Ferguson, J. (eds) (1997). *Culture, Power, Place: Explorations in Critical Anthropology*, Durham: Duke University Press.

Guyer, J. and Belinga, S.M. E. (1995), Wealth in People as Wealth in Knowledge: Accumulation and Composition in Equatorial Africa, *Journal of African History*, 26 (1): 91-120.

Hailey, J. (2008), "Ubuntu: A Literature Review," A Paper Prepared for the Tutu Foundation, November 2008, pp. 1-26.

Hancock, G. (1989), *Lords of Poverty: The Freewheeling Lifestyles, Power, Prestige and Corruption of the Multi-billion Dollar Aid Business*, London: Macmillan.

Hart, K. (2007), "Marcel Mauss: In Pursuit of the Whole. A Review," *Comparative Studies in Society and History*, 49(2): 473–485.

Hay, P.L. (2014), *Negotiating Conviviality: The Use of Information and Communication Technologies by Migrant Members of the Bay Community Church in Cape Town,* Bamenda: Langaa.

Hollaway, J. (2000), *All Poor Together: The African Tragedy and Beyond,* Johannesburg: Capricorn Books.

Hudson, H.E. (2013), *From Rural Village to Global Village: Telecommunication for Development in the Information Age*, London: Routledge.

Jiménez, A.C. (2011), "Trust in Anthropology," *Anthropological Theory*, 11(2): 177-196.

Jimu, I.M. (2012), *Peri-urban Land Transactions. Everyday Practices and Relations in Peri-urban Blantyre, Malawi*, Bamenda: Langaa.

Johnson, D.W. and Johnson, R.T. (2005), "New directions in social interdependency theory," *Genetic, Social and General Psychology Monographs* 131(4): 285 – 358.

Koulibaly, M. (2005), *Les Servitudes du Pacte Colonial*, Abidjan: NEI/CEDA.

Krings, M. and Okome, O. (eds) (2013), *Global Nollywood: The Transnational Dimensions of an African Video Film Industry*, Bloomington: Indiana University Press.

Landau, L.B. (ed.) (2011), *Exorcising the Demons Within: Xenophobia, Violence and Statecraft in Contemporary South Africa.* Johannesburg: Wits University Press.

Lartey, E.K.K. (2013), "Remittances, Investment and Growth in Sub-Saharan Africa," *The Journal of International Trade and Economic Development: An International and Comparative Review*, 22(7): 1038-1058.

Lentz, C. (2013), *Land, Mobility, and Belonging in West Africa*, Bloomington: Indiana University Press.

Letseka, M. (2012), "In Defense of Ubuntu," *Studio Philos Educ* 31: 47-60. doi: 10.1007/s11217-011-9267-2.

Lewis, D. (2014), *Non-Governmental Organizations, Management and Development*, London: Routledge.

Lewis, J.D. and Weigert, A. (1985), "Trust as Social Reality," *Social Forces*, 63(4): 967-985.

Li, Z., Ma, L.J.C. and Xue, D. (2009), "An African Enclave in China: The Making of a New Transnational Urban Space," *Eurasian Geography and Economics*, 50(6): 699-719.

Long, N. (2001), *Development Sociology: Actor Perspectives.* London and New York: Routledge.

Lonkog, T. (2013), *The Black Man and His Visa*, Bamenda: Langaa.

Lovejoy, P.E. (2011), *Transformations in Slavery: A History of Slavery in Africa (African Studies)*, Cambridge: Cambridge University Press.

Lucht, H. (2012), *Darkness Before Daybreak: African Migrants Living on the Margins in Southern Italy Today*, Berkeley: University of California Press.

Mabovula, N. C. (2011), "The erosion of African communal values: a reappraisal of the African Ubuntu Philosophy Inkanyiso," *Jnl Hum & Soc Sci* 3(1): 38-47.

Magubane, Z. (2004), *Bringing the Empire Home: Race, Class, and Gender in Britain and Colonial South Africa*, Chicago, IL: University of Chicago Press.

Magubane, Z. (2007), "Brand the Beloved Country: African in American Celebrity Culture Post 9/11," *CODESRIA Bulletin*, 1&2, 4–8.

Malaquais, D. (2001), "Anatomie d'une Anarque: Feymen et Feymania au Cameroun," *Les Etudes du CERI* No.77. pp.1-46.

Malaquais, D. (2002), "Blood Money: A Douala Chronicle," *Chimuringa* No.3.

Mangezvo, P.L. (2014), *Xenophobic Exclusion and Masculinities among Zimbabwean Male Migrants: The Case of Cape Town and Stellenbosch*, Thesis [PhD], Department of Sociology and Anthropology, Stellenbosch University, Stellenbosch, South Africa.

Martin, L.H., Gutman, H. and Hutton, P.H. (eds) (1988), *Technologies of the Self: A Seminar with Michel Foucault*, Amherst: University of Massachusetts Press.

Mauss, M. (1990[1950]), *The Gift: The Form and Reason for Exchange in Archaic Societies*, New York: W.W. Norton.

Mawere, M. (2014), *Environmental Conservation through Ubuntu and Other Emerging Perspectives*, Bamenda: Langaa.

Mbembe, A. (2006), 'South Africa's Second Coming: the Nongqawuse Syndrome', *Open Democracy*, 15 June, www.opendemocracy.net/content/articles/PDF/3649.pdf

McAllister, P. (2009), "Ubuntu – Beyond Belief in Southern Africa," *Sites: New Series* 6(1): 1-10.

Mercer, C., Page, B. and Evans, M. (2009), *Development and the African Diaspora: Place and the Politics of Home.* London: Zed.

Mentan, T. (2010a), *The New World Order Ideology and Africa. Understanding and Appreciating Ambiguity, Deceit and Recapture of Decolonized Spaces,* Bamenda: Langaa.

Mentan, T. (2010b), *The State in Africa. An Analysis of Impacts of Historical Trajectories of Global Capitalist Expansion and Domination in the Continent,* Bamenda: Langaa.

Mentan, T. (2013), *Democracy for Breakfast. Unveiling Mirage Democracy in Contemporary Africa,* Bamenda: Langaa.

Messina, A.M. and Lahav, G. (eds) (2006), *The Migration Reader: Exploring Politics and Policies,* Boulder: Lynne Rienner Publishers.

Metz, T. (2011), "Ubuntu as a Moral Theory and Human Rights in South Africa," *African Human Rights Law Journal,* 11(2): 532-559.

Metz, T. (2014), "What Do We Mean When We Speak of Ubuntu?" mg.co.za/article/2014-11-14-what-do-we-mean-when-we-speak-of-ubuntu.

Miller, D. (2015), "The Tragic Denouement of English Sociality," *Current Anthropology*, 30(2): 336-357.

Möllering, G. (2001), "The Nature of Trust: From Georg Simmel to a Theory of Expectation, Interpretation and Suspension," *Sociology*, 35(2): 403-420.

Muller, M. (2008), "Good Governance and Ubuntu as Prerequisites for Poverty Alleviation in Northern KwaZulu-Natal," *Idilinga – African Journal of Indigenous Knowledge Systems* 7(2): 198-210.

Murove, M. F. (2014), "Ubuntu," *Diogenes* 59(3-4): 36-47 doi: 10.1177/0392192113493737.

Murphy, D. (1989), *Cameroon with Egbert*. London: Arrow Books.

Nabudere, D.W. (2011), *Afrikology, Philosophy and Wholeness: An Epistemology*, Pretoria: Africa Institute of South Africa.

Nabudere, D.W. (2012), *Afrikology and Transdisciplinarity: A Restorative Epistemology*, Pretoria: Africa Institute of South Africa.

Narotzky, S. (1997), *New Directions in Economic Anthropology*. London: Pluto Press.

Ndjio, B. (2005), "Carrefour de la joie: Popular Deconstruction of the African Postcolonial Public Sphere," *Africa*, 75(3): 265-294.

Ndjio, B. (2006), *Feymania: New Wealth, Magic Money and Power in Contemporary Cameroon*, Amsterdam: University of Amsterdam (PhD dissertation).

Ndjio, B. (2008), *Cameroonian Feymen and Nigerian '419'Scammers: Two Examples of Africa's 'Reinvention' of the Global Capitalism*, Leiden: African Studies Centre, ASC working paper 81.

Ndjio, B. (2012), "'Sagacity Spirit' and 'ghetto ethic': Feymania and New African Entrepreneurship," in: Jon Abbink, *Fractures and Reconnections: Civic Action and the Redefinition of African Political and Economic Spaces: Studies in Honor of Piet J.J. Konings*, Berlin: LIT Verlag. (pp.151-178).

Ndlovu-Gatsheni, S.J. (2009), 'Africa for Africans or Africa for "Natives" Only? "New Nationalism" and Nativism in Zimbabwe and South Africa', *Africa Spectrum* 44(1): 61-78.

Neocosmos, M. (2010), *From 'Foreign Natives' to 'Native Foreigners': Explaining Xenophobia in Post-Apartheid South Africa: Citizenship and Nationalism, Identity and Politics*, Dakar: CODESRIA.

Newell, S. (2005), "Migratory Modernity and the Cosmology of Consumption in Côte d'Ivoire," in: Lillian Trager (ed.), *Migration and Economy: Global and Local Dynamics*, Oxford: Altamira Press, pp.163-192.

Newell, S. (2006), "Estranged Belongings: A Moral Economy of Theft in Abidjan, Côte d'Ivoire," *Anthropological Theory*, 6(2): 179-203.

Newell, S. (2009a), "Enregistering Modernity, Bluffing Criminality: How Nouchi Speech Reinvented (and Fractured) the Nation," *Journal of Linguistic Anthropology*, 19(2): 157–184.

Newell, S. (2009b), "Godrap Girls, Draou Boys, and the Sexual Economy of the Bluff in Abidjan, Côte d'Ivoire," *Ethnos: Journal of Anthropology*, 74(3): 379-402.

Newell, S. (2012a), "Le Goût des Autres: Ivoirian Fashion and Alterity," *Etnofoor*, 24(2): 41-56.

Newell, S. (2012b), *The Modernity Bluff: Crime, Consumption, and Citizenship in Côte d'Ivoire*, Chicago: Chicago University Press.

Newell, S. (2013), "Brands as Masks: Public Secrecy and the Counterfeit in Côte d'Ivoire," *Journal of the Royal Anthropological Institute*, 19(1): 138-154.

Newton, K. (2001), "Trust, Social Capital, Civil Society, and Democracy," *International Political Science Review*, 22(2): 201-214.

Nfon, C. (2013), *Greener from a Distance*, Bamenda: Langaa.

Niger-Thomas, M. (1995), "Women's Access to and Control of Credit in Cameroon: The Mamfe Case," in: S. Ardener, & S. Burman (eds), *Money-Go-Rounds: The Importance of Rotating Savings and Credit Associations for Women* (pp. 95-110). Oxford: Berg.

Nkondo, G.M. (2007), 'Ubuntu as National Policy in South Africa: A Conceptual Framework,' *International Journal of African Renaissance Studies* 2(1): 88-100.

Nkwi, W.G. (2014), "Men Stay at Home While Women Move Out: New Trends of Mobility to China amongst Bamenda Grassfields Women (Cameroon)" *Modern Africa: Politics, History and Society*, 2(1): 95-113.

Nkwi, W.G. (2015), *African Modernities and Mobilities. An Historical Ethnography of Kom, Cameroon, C. 1800-2008*, Bamenda: Langaa.

Nnaemeka, O. (2005), "Bringing African Women into the Classroom: Rethinking Pedagogy and Epistemology," in: O. Oyewumi, (ed.) *African Gender Studies: A Reader.* New York: Palgrave Macmillan, 51–65.

Ntlama, N. and Ndima, D.D. (2009), 'The Significance of South Africa's Traditional Courts Bill to the Challenge of Promoting African Traditional Justice Systems,' *International Journal of African Renaissance Studies* 4(1): 6-30.

Nubukpo, K. (2011), *L'Improvisation Économique en Afrique de l'Ouest: Du Coton au Franc CFA*, Paris: Karthala.

Nyamnjoh, F.B. (1999), "Cameroon: A Country United by Ethnic Ambition and Difference," *African Affairs*, 98(390): 101-118.

Nyamnjoh, F.B. (2001), "Delusions of Development and the Enrichment of Witchcraft Discourses in Cameroon" in: Henrietta L. Moore and Todd Sanders (eds.), *Magical Interpretations, Material Realities: Modernity, Witchcraft and the Occult in Postcolonial Africa.* Routledge: London. (pp. 28-49).

Nyamnjoh, F.B. (2002), "'A Child Is One Person's only in the Womb': Domestication, Agency and Subjectivity in the Cameroonian Grassfields," in: R. Werbner (ed.), *Postcolonial Subjectivities in Africa.* London: Zed. (pp.111-138).

Nyamnjoh, F.B. (2005a), "Images of Nyongo amongst Bamenda Grassfielders in Whiteman Kontri," *Citizenship Studies*, 9(3): 241-269.

Nyamnjoh, F.B. (2005b), "Fishing in Troubled Waters: Disquettes and Thiofs in Dakar," *Africa*, 75(3): 295-324.

Nyamnjoh, F.B. (2006), *Insiders and outsiders: citizenship and xenophobia in contemporary Southern Africa.* London: Zed/CODESRIA.

Nyamnjoh, F.B. (2010a), *Souls Forgotten*, Bamenda: Langaa.

Nyamnjoh, F.B. (2010b), *Intimate Strangers*, Bamenda: Langaa.

Nyamnjoh, F.B. (2011), "Cameroonian Bushfalling: Negotiation of Identity and Belonging in Fiction and Ethnography," *American Ethnologist* 38(4): 701-713.

Nyamnjoh, F.B. (2013a), "Politics of Back-Scratching in Cameroon and Beyond," in: Petr Drulák and Šárka Moravcová, (eds), *Non-Western Reflection on Politics,* Frankfurt am Main: Peter Lang. (pp.35-53).

Nyamnjoh, F.B. (2013b), "Fiction and Reality of Mobility in Africa," *Citizenship Studies,* 17(6-7): 653-680

Nyamnjoh, F.B. (2013c), "The Nimbleness of Being Fulani," *Africa Today,* 59(3): 105-134

Nyamnjoh, F.B. (2015), "Incompleteness: Frontier Africa and the Currency of Conviviality," *Journal of Asian and African Studies,* DOI: 10.1177/0021909615580867, pp. 1-18.

Nyamnjoh, F.B., and Fokwang, J. (2005), "Entertaining Repression: Music and Politics in Postcolonial Cameroon," *African Affairs,* 104(415): 251-274.

Nyamnjoh, F.B. and Page, B., (2002), "Whiteman Kontri and the Enduring Allure of Modernity Among Cameroonian Youth" *African Affairs.* 101(405): 607-634.

Nyamnjoh, F.B. and Rowlands, M. (1998), "Elite Associations and the Politics of Belonging in Cameroon" *Africa.* 68(3): 320-337.

Nyamnjoh, F.B. and Shoro, K. (2011), "Language, Mobility, African Writers and Pan-Africanism," *African Communication Research,* 4(1):35-62.

Nyamnjoh, F.B. and Shoro, K. (2014), "Testing the Waters of African Renaissance in Post-Apartheid South Africa," in: Thenjiwe Meyiwa, Muxe Nkondo, Margaret Chitiga-Mabugu, Moses Sithole and Francis Nyamnjoh, (eds), *State of the Nation 2014: South Africa 1994-2014: A Twenty-year Review,* Cape Town: HSRC. (pp. 477-495)

Nyamnjoh, H.M. (2010), *"We Get Nothing from Fishing" Fishing for Boat Opportunities Amongst Senegalese Fisher Migrants,* Bamenda/Leiden: Langaa.

Nyamnjoh, H.M. (2014), *Bridging Mobilities: ICTs Appropriation by Cameroonians in South Africa and The Netherlands*, Bamenda/Leiden: Langaa.

Obenga, T. (2004), *African Philosophy: The Pharaonic Period: 2780-330 BC*, Popenguine: Per Ankh.

Obijiofor, L. (2015), *New Technologies in Developing Societies: From Theory to Practice*, Basingstoke: Palgrave Macmillan.

Olukoshi, A. (ed.) (1998), *The Politics of Opposition in Contemporary Africa*, Uppsala: Nordiska Afrikainstitutet.

Omwansa, T. and Sullivan, N.P. (2012), *Money, Real Quick: Kenya's Disruptive Mobile Money Innovation*, Croydon: Ballonview.

Onoma, A.K. (2009), *The Politics of Property Rights Institutions in Africa*, Cambridge: Cambridge University Press.

Owen, N.J. (2011), *'On se Débrouille': Congolese migrants' search for survival and success in Muizenburg, Cape Town.* Thesis [PhD], Department of Social Anthropology, Rhodes University, Grahamstown, South Africa.

Parsons, N. (2002), "One Body Playing ManyParts-Ie Betjouana, el Negro, and il Bosquimano," *Pula: Botswana Journal of African Studies*, 16(1): 19-29.

Peet, R. (2003), *Unholy Trinity: The IMF, World Bank and WTO*, London: Zed Books.

Pelican, M. (2013), "International Migration: Virtue or Vice? Perspectives from Cameroon," *Journal of Ethnic and Migration Studies*, 39(2): 237-257.

Pelican, M. and Şaul, M. (eds) (2014), Special Issue: Global African Entrepreneurs, *Urban Anthropology™ and Studies of Cultural Systems and World Economic Development*, Volume 43; Numbers 1, 2, 3.

Pelican, M. and Tatah, P. (2009), "Migration to the Gulf States and China: Local Perspectives from Cameroon," *African Diaspora* 2(2): 229-244.

Petras, J. and Veltmeyer, H. (2005), *Empire with Imperialism: The globalizing Dynamics of Neo-liberal Capitalism*, London: Zed Books.

Picarelli, E. (2015), "Elegance and Retrospective Sartorialism among Young African Males," *Clothing Culture*, 2(2): 209-223.

Piketty, T. (2014), *Capital in the Twenty-First Century*, Cambridge, Massachusetts: The Belknap Press of Harvard University Press.

Pillay, U., Hagg, G., Nyamnjoh F. with Jansen, J. (eds) (2013), *State of the Nation: South Africa 2012-2013: Addressing Inequality and Poverty*, Cape Town: HSRC Press.

Piot, C. (2010), *Nostalgia for the Future: West Africa after the Cold War*. Chicago, IL: University of Chicago Press.

Platteau, J.-P. (2004), "Monitoring Elite Capture in Community-Driven Development," *Development and Change* 35(2): 223–246.

Plumelle-Uribe, R.A. (2001), *La Férocité Blanche: Des Non-Blancs aux Non-Aryens, ces Génocides Occultés de 1492 à nos Jours*, Paris: Albin Michel.

Powell, C. (2012), *Me and My Cell Phone: And Other Essays on Technology in Everyday Life*, Bamenda: Langaa.

Powell, C. (2014), *ICTs and the Reconfiguration of Marginality in Langa Township: A Study of Migration and Belonging*, Bamenda: Langaa.

Praeg, L. (2014), *A Report on Ubuntu*, Pietermaritzburg: University of KwaZulu-Natal Press.

Praeg, L. and Magadla, S. (eds) (2014a), *Ubuntu: Curating the Archive*, Pietermaritzburg: University of KwaZulu-Natal Press.

Praeg, L. and Magadla, S. (2014b), "Introduction," in: Leonhard Praeg and Siphokazi Magadla (eds), *Ubuntu: Curating the Archive*, Pietermaritzburg: University of KwaZulu-Natal Press.pp.1-9.

Ramose, M.B. (1999), *African Philosophy Through Ubuntu*, Harare: Mond Books.

Ramose, M.B. (2014), "Ubuntu: Affirming a Right and Seeking Remedies in South Africa," in: Leonhard Praeg and Siphokazi Magadla (eds), *Ubuntu: Curating the Archive*,

Pietermaritzburg: University of KwaZulu-Natal Press. pp.121-136.

Ramsès, B.T. (2010), *La Sorcellerie n'Existe Pas*, Abidjan: Les Éditions du CERAP.

Ratha, D. and Shaw, W. (2007), *South-South migration and remittances*. World Bank Working Paper no. 102. Washington, DC: The World Bank.

Ricard, M. (2015), *Altruism: The Power of Compassion to Change Yourself and the World*, New York: Little, Brown and Company.

Rodney, W. (2012[1972]), *How Europe Underdeveloped Africa*, Dakar: CODESRIA& Pambazuka Press.

Rowlands, M. (1996), "The Consumption of an African Modernity", in: M. J. Arnoldi et al. (eds) *African Material Culture*. Bloomington and Indianapolis: Indiana University Press, pp. 188-212.

Rowlands, M. (2007), "The Elderly as 'Curators' in North London," in: Elizabeth Pye, (ed.), *The Power Of Touch: Handling Objects in Museums and Heritage Contexts*, Walnut Creek, Ca: Left Coast Press.

Sachs, J. (2005), *The End of Poverty: How We Can Make it Happen in Our Lifetime*, London: Penguin Books.

Sandel, M.J. (2012), *What Money Can't Buy: The Moral Limits of Markets*, New York: Farrar, Straus and Giroux.

Shipton, P. (2007), *The Nature of Entrustment: Intimacy, Exchange and the Sacred in Africa*. New Haven & London: Yale University.

Shoichiro, T. (2015), "Economic Development of the 'Medieval' West African Societies: Revising African History," Paper presented at the National Museum of Ethnology, Osaka, Japan, 13 July 2015.

Sichone, O. (2008), "Xenophobia and Xenophilia in South Africa: African migrants in Cape Town," in: P. Werbner, (ed.) *Anthropology and the new cosmopolitanism: rooted, feminist and vernacular perspectives*. Oxford: Berg, 309 – 332.

Simon, H.A. (1993), "Altruism and Economics," *The American Economic Review*, 83(2): 156-161.

Simmel, G. and Jacobson, C. (1965), "The Poor," *Social Problems*, 13(2): 118-140.

Singh, R.J., Haacker, M., Lee, K. and Le Goff, M. (2010), "Determinants and Macroeconomic Impact of Remittances in Sub-Saharan Africa," *Journal of African Economies*, 20(2): 312-340.

Steinberg, J. (2015), *A Man of Good Hope*, London: Jonathan Cape.

Stolcke, V. (1995), "Talking Culture: New Boundaries, New Rhetorics of Exclusion in Europe," *Current Anthropology*, 36(1): 1–24.

Tazanu, P.M. (2012), *Being Available and Reachable. New Media and Cameroonian Transnational Sociality*, Bamenda: Langaa.

Terreblanche, S. (2002), *A History of Inequality in South Africa 1652-2002*, Scottsville: University of Kwazulu-Natal Press.

Thaler, R.H. (2015), *Misbehaving: The Making of Behavioral Economics*, New York: W. W. Norton & Company.

Thomas, C.G. (2008), "*Ubuntu*. The Missing Link in the Rights Discourse in Post-apartheid Transformation in South Africa," *International Journal of African Renaissance Studies* 3(2): 39-62.

Triulzi, A. and Mckenzie, R. (2013), *Long Journeys: African Migrants on the Road*, Leiden: Brill.

Trivers, R.L. (1971), "The Evolution of Reciprocal Altruism," *The Quarterly Review of Biology*, 46(1): 35-57.

Tutu, D. (1999), *No Future Without Forgiveness* Johannesburg: London: Random House.

Tutu, D. (2004), *God Has a Dream: A Vision of Hope for Our Times*, Cape Town: Double Day publishers.

Ugor, P. (2013), "Nollywood and Postcolonial Predicaments: Transnationalism, Gender and the Commoditization of Desire in *Glamour Girls*," in: Krings, M. and Okome, O. (eds), *Global Nollywood: The Transnational Dimensions of an*

African Video Film Industry, Bloomington: Indiana University Press, pp. 158-177.

Urry, J. (2007), *Mobilities*, Cambridge: Polity.

Uslaner, E.M. (2000-2001), "Producing and Consuming Trust," *Political Science Quarterly*, 115(4): 569-590.

Van Binsbergen, W. (2001), "Ubuntu and the globalisation of Southern African Thought and Society," in: P. Boele van Hensbroek (ed.) African Renaissance and Ubuntu Philosophy, special issue of: *Quest: An African Journal of Philosophy*, 15(1-2): 53-89.

Van Binsbergen, W. (2003), *Intercultural Encounters: African and Anthropological Lessons Towards a Philosophy of Interculturality*, Munster: Lit Verlag.

Varoufakis, Y. Halevi, J. and Theocarakis, N. (2011), *Modern Political Economics: Making Sense of the Post-2008 World*, New York: Routledge.

Veblen, T. (1979 [1899]), *The Theory of the Leisure Class*, London: Penguin Books.

Verschave, F.-X. (1998), *La Françafrique: Le Plus Long Scandale de la République*, Paris: Stock.

Verschave, F.-X. (2005), *De la Françafrique à la Mafiafrique*, Paris: Tribord.

Wacquant, L.J.D. (1996), "Foreword," in: P. Bourdieu, (ed.) *The State Nobility*, Cambridge: Polity, ix–xxii.

Warnier, J.-P. (1993a), "The King as a Container in the Cameroon Grassfields," *Paideuma*, 39: 303-319.

Warnier, J.-P. (1993b), *L'Esprit d'Entreprise au Cameroun*, Paris: Karthala.

Warnier, J.-P. (2012), *Cameroon Grassfields Civilization*, Bamenda: Langaa.

Warnier, J.-P. (2013), "Quelle Sociologie du Politique? À l'École de Weber et Foucault en Afrique," *Socio 01*, 95-108.

Weber, M. (2005[1930]), *The Protestant Ethic and the Spirit of Capitalism*, London: Routledge.

Whitworth, A. and Wilkinson, K. (2013), "Tackling Child Poverty in South Africa: Implications of Ubuntu for the

System of Social Grants," *Development Southern Africa*, 30(1): 121-134 doi: 10.1080/0376835X.2013.756219.

Xulu, M. (2010), "Ubuntu and Being Umuntu: Towards Ubuntu Pedagogy through Cultural Expressions, Symbolism and Performance," *Skills@work, Theory and Practice* 3: 81-87.